# IN ADAM'S FALL

# Challenges in Contemporary Theology

Series Editors: Gareth Jones and Lewis Ayres
Canterbury Christ Church University College, UK and Emory University, US

Challenges in Contemporary Theology is a series aimed at producing clear orientations in, and research on, areas of "challenge" in contemporary theology. These carefully coordinated books engage traditional theological concerns with mainstreams in modern thought and culture that challenge those concerns. The "challenges" implied are to be understood in two senses: those presented by society to contemporary theology, and those posed by theology to society.

*Published*

*These Three Are One: The Practice of Trinitarian Theology*
David S. Cunningham

*After Writing: On the Liturgical Consummation of Philosophy*
Catherine Pickstock

*Mystical Theology: The Integrity of Spirituality and Theology*
Mark A. McIntosh

*Engaging Scripture: A Model for Theological Interpretation*
Stephen E. Fowl

*Torture and Eucharist: Theology, Politics, and the Body of Christ*
William T. Cavanaugh

*Sexuality and the Christian Body: Their Way into the Triune God*
Eugene F. Rogers, Jr

*On Christian Theology*
Rowan Williams

*The Promised End: Eschatology in Theology and Literature*
Paul S. Fiddes

*Powers and Submissions: Spirituality, Philosophy, and Gender*
Sarah Coakley

*A Theology of Engagement*
Ian S. Markham

*Alien Sex: The Body and Desire in Cinema and Theology*
Gerard Loughlin

*Scripture and Metaphysics: Aquinas and the Renewal of Trinitarian Theology*
Matthew Levering

*Faith and Freedom: An Interfaith Perspective*
David Burrell

*Keeping God's Silence*
Rachel Muers

*Christ and Culture*
Graham Ward

*Theology in the Public Square: Church, Academy and Nation*
Gavin D'Costa

*Rewritten Theology: Aquinas After His Readers*
Mark D. Jordan

*God's Companions: Reimagining Christian Ethics*
Samuel Wells

*The Trial of the Witnesses: The Rise and Decline of Postliberal Theology*
Paul J. DeHart

*Theology and Families*
Adrian Thatcher

*The Shape of Theology*
David F. Ford

*The Vietnam War and Theologies of Memory*
Jonathan Tran

*In Adam's Fall: A Meditation on the Christian Doctrine of Original Sin*
Ian A. McFarland

# IN ADAM'S FALL

## A Meditation on the Christian Doctrine of Original Sin

Ian A. McFarland

**WILEY-BLACKWELL**

A John Wiley & Sons, Ltd., Publication

This edition first published 2010
© 2010 Ian A. McFarland

Blackwell Publishing was acquired by John Wiley & Sons in February 2007. Blackwell's publishing program has been merged with Wiley's global Scientific, Technical, and Medical business to form Wiley-Blackwell.

*Registered Office*
John Wiley & Sons Ltd, The Atrium, Southern Gate, Chichester, West Sussex, PO19 8SQ, United Kingdom

*Editorial Offices*
350 Main Street, Malden, MA 02148-5020, USA
9600 Garsington Road, Oxford, OX4 2DQ, UK
The Atrium, Southern Gate, Chichester, West Sussex, PO19 8SQ, UK

For details of our global editorial offices, for customer services, and for information about how to apply for permission to reuse the copyright material in this book please see our website at www.wiley.com/wiley-blackwell.

The right of Ian A. McFarland to be identified as the author of this work has been asserted in accordance with the UK Copyright, Designs and Patents Act 1988.

All rights reserved. No part of this publication may be reproduced, stored in a retrieval system, or transmitted, in any form or by any means, electronic, mechanical, photocopying, recording or otherwise, except as permitted by the UK Copyright, Designs and Patents Act 1988, without the prior permission of the publisher.

Wiley also publishes its books in a variety of electronic formats. Some content that appears in print may not be available in electronic books.

Designations used by companies to distinguish their products are often claimed as trademarks. All brand names and product names used in this book are trade names, service marks, trademarks or registered trademarks of their respective owners. The publisher is not associated with any product or vendor mentioned in this book. This publication is designed to provide accurate and authoritative information in regard to the subject matter covered. It is sold on the understanding that the publisher is not engaged in rendering professional services. If professional advice or other expert assistance is required, the services of a competent professional should be sought.

*Library of Congress Cataloging-in-Publication Data*

McFarland, Ian A. (Ian Alexander), 1963–
  In Adam's fall : a meditation on the Christian doctrine of original sin / Ian A. McFarland.
    p. cm. – (Challenges in contemporary theology)
  Includes bibliographical references and index.
  ISBN 978-1-4051-8365-9 (hardcover: alk. paper)
  1. Sin, Original – History of doctrines.  I. Title.
  BT720.M38 2010
  233'.14–dc22
                                               2010010189

A catalogue record for this book is available from the British Library.

Set in 10.5/12.5 Bembo by Toppan Best-set Premedia Limited
Printed and bound in Malaysia by Vivar Printing Sdn Bhd

01   2010

For my teachers

# Contents

| | |
|---|---|
| Preface | ix |
| Acknowledgments | xv |

**Part I Setting the Stage: The Problem of Original Sin**     1

| | |
|---|---|
| 1 Creation Gone Wrong: Thinking about Sin | 3 |
|    *A Doctrine Grown Strange* | 3 |
|    *Biblical Configurations of Sin* | 5 |
|    *Contemporary Attempts to Reclaim Sin-Talk* | 11 |
|    *Original Sin and Actual Sin* | 18 |
| 2 Original Sin as Christian Doctrine: Origins, Permutations, Problems | 29 |
|    *The Emergence of the Doctrine* | 29 |
|    *The Augustinian Turn* | 32 |
|    *Augustinian Revisions* | 35 |
|    *Assessment* | 45 |

**Part II Reconfiguring the Debate: Sin, Nature, and the Will**     59

| | |
|---|---|
| 3 Augustine of Hippo: Willing and the Ambiguity of Desire | 61 |
|    *Augustine's Views in Outline* | 62 |
|    *Concupiscence: Humanity Internally Divided* | 66 |
|    *The Fall: Humanity Temporally Divided* | 71 |
|    *Assessing Augustine's Doctrine of the Will* | 75 |

| | |
|---|---|
| 4 Maximus the Confessor: Willing Is Not Choosing | 88 |
| *Maximus' Christology in Context* | 90 |
| *Dyothelite Christology in Outline* | 92 |
| *Maximus' Analysis of the Will* | 94 |
| *Maximus' Interpretation of Christ's Willing* | 97 |
| *Anthropological Implications* | 100 |
| *Conclusion* | 104 |
| | |
| 5 The Status of Christ's Will: Fallen or Unfallen? | 117 |
| *The Question in the Tradition* | 119 |
| *Preliminary Assessment* | 122 |
| *The Problem of Christ's Will* | 125 |
| *Theological Implications* | 128 |

**Part III Reconstructing the Doctrine: Original Sin in Christian Practice** — 141

| | |
|---|---|
| 6 Original Sin and Human Nature: Solidarity in Sin | 143 |
| *Original Sin and the Damaged Will* | 144 |
| *The Problem of the Origin of Original Sin* | 148 |
| *Reconceiving the Ontology of Original Sin* | 154 |
| | |
| 7 Original Sin and the Individual: Being a Sinner | 170 |
| *The Scope of Sin* | 172 |
| *Sin and Agency* | 176 |
| *From Actual Sin to Original Sin* | 182 |
| | |
| 8 Original Sin and the Christian Life: Confronting Sin | 193 |
| *From Original Sin to Actual Sin* | 195 |
| *Original Sin as Unbelief* | 200 |
| *Vocation and the Defeat of Sin* | 205 |
| *Conclusion* | 212 |
| | |
| References | 220 |
| Index | 230 |

# Preface

First published in Boston in around 1690, the *New England Primer* shaped the education of generations of children throughout North America, with total sales over the nearly two hundred years it remained in print estimated in the millions. Its most famous feature was its alphabet pages: a series of rhyming couplets, accompanied by woodcut illustrations, used to teach the letters. The first of these (and the only one never changed in any of the *Primer*'s many editions) gave a concise summary of the Western Christian doctrine of original sin: "In Adam's Fall / We Sinned all." Because once upon a time Adam sinned, all of us in the present are sinners.

In contemporary North America, this doctrine has none of the resonance with popular culture that once made it a natural reference point for teaching basic literacy. Its key terms are little used outside of churches and often little valued even within them. At the same time, few doctrines continue to excite as much passion among believers and non-believers alike. While traditional beliefs about the Trinity or justification are easily passed over as bits of theological esoterica, talk of original sin invariably elicits a strong – and overwhelmingly negative – response even among those who identify themselves as Christian. The idea that we are all guilty because of an ancestor's misdeed is viewed as morally outrageous and historically incredible, summing up for many everything that is wrong with Christianity.

It is the aim of this book to challenge that perception. In my previous work on the doctrine of the human person ("theological anthropology" in the technical jargon of systematic theology), one of my central aims was to overcome what appears to me a Hobson's choice latent in the tradition. On the one hand, Christians have tried to defend human equality before God by identifying some feature common to all human beings (e.g., reason, freedom, self-consciousness) as the ground of God's regard for us – of our "personhood." One consequence of this strategy is to render the differences between human beings theologically unimportant, notwithstanding the fact that in human relationships it is precisely that which is distinctive about others that catalyzes our love for them. On the other hand, where human difference is taken seriously, it is all too readily taken as evidence that all human beings are not equal. I have argued that the horns of this dilemma can be avoided by rooting anthropology in Christology: if the basis of our "personhood" is not any quality we possess (whether in equal or different measure), but simply the fact that God in Christ addresses us *as* persons – speaking to us in time the same Word spoken eternally within the Trinity – then acknowledgment of human difference and human equality no longer stand in tension with one another. As members of Christ's body, we all are equal as recipients of Christ's call, but utterly distinct in that to which we are called.[1]

But if life "in Christ" is a matter of God's incorporating us into the divine life by making us equal but mutually unsubstitutable members of Christ's body, what of life "in Adam" – our state apart from or prior to redemption? Here, too, the Christian tradition has wanted to affirm a kind of equality, but one based on a defect – sin – rather than any positive feature of human nature. In the Western churches this defect has traditionally been further qualified as *original* sin – a congenital resistance to and alienation from God that, while not intrinsic to human nature as such, is now characteristic of all human beings by virtue of the fact that the first human beings disobeyed God's command: "In Adam's fall / we sinned all."

The chapters that follow are my attempt to examine this dimension of human equality before God, in the conviction that the doctrine of original sin, though one of the most unsettling aspects of Christian teaching, is also stimulating and productive for the life of faith. In reaction to a wide range of criticisms leveled against the idea of original sin, a number of Christian theologians in the modern period have attempted to develop a doctrine of sin in which the idea of original sin is heavily qualified or even rejected. Against these perspectives, I will argue that it is not only theologically defensible, but inseparable from the confession of Jesus Christ as Savior and Lord. Indeed, I will defend the doctrine in what is arguably its most extreme form, as developed by Augustine and later defended in the Reformed theological tradition under the designation of "total depravity" – the claim that no aspect of our humanity is untouched by sin. Yet what follows is not simply a restatement of earlier positions, because modern critics raise questions that cannot be ignored about how the doctrine has been defended and deployed in the past, even if (as I shall try to show) these questions can be answered in ways that confirm the place of original sin within the logic of Christian faith.

The course I will follow in making this argument falls into three parts. The first is primarily diagnostic: in Chapter 1 I will lay out some of the issues connected with sin-talk in general, after which I will proceed in Chapter 2 both to discuss the development of the doctrine of original sin and to review some of the ways it has been defended, criticized, and modified over the centuries. In the process, I isolate three particularly trenchant objections to the idea that human beings are congenital sinners: first, that it cannot be squared with the best current science regarding the origin and development either of the human species (phylogeny) or of the individual human being (ontogeny); second, that it undermines basic Christian convictions regarding human freedom and thus promotes either moral indifference or despair; and third, that it vitiates the pursuit of justice in society by excusing systemic sins as inevitable and accusing those who resist them of sinful presumption.

Though it is in many respects the heart of my argument, the book's second part does not deal directly with the doctrine of original sin at all. Instead, it serves as something of a ground-clearing operation, in which I elaborate some basic principles of theological anthropology that provide the conceptual basis for my reconstruction of the doctrine of original sin in Part III. Specifically, I seek to counter the idea that the will is the source of human identity and freedom by developing an alternative anthropology, in which the will does not have this determinative role. Drawing on the thought of Augustine in Chapter 3 and Maximus the Confessor in Chapter 4, I argue that Christians have both good reasons and effective theological resources for making just this move. Though developing their respective positions in response to significantly different theological concerns, both figures challenge the equation of free will with the power of self-determination in favor of an anthropology in which the will's freedom lies in its being so drawn to the proper end of human nature as to draw human nature as a whole to its proper end. Within this framework God rather than the will is the source of individual identity, since it is God whose call defines the good for a person; nevertheless, it remains the case that individual identity is only realized through the will, as I claim – or fail to claim – God's will for my life as my own. This idea is developed in Chapter 5, where I undertake an analysis of seemingly esoteric debates in the tradition over whether the human nature assumed by Christ was fallen or unfallen in order to bring into relief the ontological oddity of the will as that aspect of human nature by virtue of which individual identity, though not a matter of libertarian self-determination, remains ineluctably our own.

Building on this understanding of the will, I proceed in the third part of the book to answer the principal objections to the doctrine of original sin outlined at the end of Part I. Chapter 6 addresses the question of the coherence of the doctrines of the fall and original sin with natural history, arguing that the doctrine does not depend either on the literal truth of Genesis 1–3 or on a biological theory of inherited sin. In Chapter 7 I turn to the question of the compatibility of Augustinian doctrine with fundamental Christian convictions regarding human freedom and responsibility. Using the anthropology developed in Part II, I argue that it is possible to affirm a complicity in sin shared by all human beings as personal agents who cannot disown their actions, without reducing this complicity to a matter of choice for which the agent is appropriately blamed. Finally, Chapter 8 counters the charge that the doctrine of original sin promotes social conservatism by arguing that appreciating the depths of human sinfulness actually serves as a prod to disrupt complacency in the face of the status quo. Because sin is recognized only as it is overcome, we can know our sin only as we attend to those whose suffering discloses to us both how we sin and how we must change if we are genuinely to repent of it. In short, the argument moves from the question of how it is that we are all sinners *ontologically* (Chapter 6), to an analysis of what it means for us all to be sinners *existentially* (Chapter 7), to reflection on how to acknowledge and address our sinfulness *vocationally* (Chapter 8).

The anthropology in terms of which this defense of original sin is constructed cuts against some of the most deeply held convictions of post-industrial consumer culture, which all too often equates humanity with what philosophers call "freedom of indifference," but which is more immediately comprehensible in market terms as "freedom of choice." A refusal to define human being in these terms is fundamental to the argument that follows. This refusal is rooted in the conviction that to succumb to the market's vision of humanity is to betray the good news of Jesus Christ, which is that we have been chosen and not that we have done the choosing. This is not to deny that we quite obviously do choose all manner of things, still less to suggest that our relationship to God in Christ is anything other than free; but it is to insist that while we love God – and thereby are most truly and properly human – freely, that love, like all love, is, in its joy and freedom, beyond our capacity to choose.

## Note

1 See Ian A. McFarland, *Difference and Identity: A Theological Anthropology* (Cleveland, OH: Pilgrim Press, 2001) and *The Divine Image: Envisioning the Invisible God* (Minneapolis, MN: Fortress Press, 2005).

# Acknowledgments

As with any writing project, this one has depended on the help of many to see it through to print. First in the rank of those to whom thanks are due is Lewis Ayres, who not only extended to me the invitation to write this volume for the Challenges in Contemporary Theology series, but was always ready to discuss Augustine over coffee. I am also profoundly grateful to John Webster, Kathryn Tanner, and Iain Torrance, whose invitation to contribute the chapter on "The Fall and Sin" to the *Oxford Handbook of Systematic Theology* provided the occasion for me to begin to put my ideas in order. As I have worked, I have benefited from the insights of many, but from none more than Al McFadyen and Stephen Ray, whose own careful and compelling reflections on sin have proved a constant stimulus and reference point for me. I would also like to express my deepest appreciation to Caroline Richards and all the other people at Wiley-Blackwell who have shepherded this project through to print. Finally, I am thankful for seminar conversations with colleagues and students in Emory's Graduate Division of Religion, especially Noel Erskine, Wendy Farley, Pam Hall, Mark Jordan, Joy McDougall, and Andrea White, whose comments were always wise and have helped me to repair some of the most egregious faults in the text. The many that doubtless remain lie on my own head.

## Author's Note

At points throughout the book, text from the New Revised Standard Version (NRSV) of the Bible has been used. New Revised Standard Version Bible, copyright 1989, Division of Christian Education of the National Council of the Churches of Christ in the United States of America. Used by permission. All rights reserved.

# Part I

# Setting the Stage: The Problem of Original Sin

# 1

# Creation Gone Wrong: Thinking about Sin

At bottom, talk about sin (or, in the technical jargon of Christian dogmatics, hamartiology) is rooted in the twin convictions that things are not right in the world, and that human beings are deeply implicated in what has gone wrong. Stated in these terms, sin-talk may not seem especially controversial. It is hard to imagine many who live in the modern world, marked as it is by the realities of extreme and chronic poverty, environmental degradation, terrorism, torture, and war, who would not be willing to affirm as much. Christians, however (especially those whose roots lie in the Latin or Western tradition of the church), have tended to go considerably farther. They talk about *original* sin, claiming on the one hand that human beings' implication in sin is both congenital and irresistible, and on the other that every human being nevertheless remains accountable for her sin. That set of claims tends to meet considerable resistance, and it is the aim of this book to explore and respond to it.

## A Doctrine Grown Strange

For centuries few beliefs were more widely and deeply held in Western society than the doctrine of original sin. There was, of course, plenty of disagreement with respect to detail. Catholics and Protestants differed over the character and effects of original sin after baptism. And many groups tracing their lineage back to the radicals of the Reformation era attacked the idea that persons could be damned on the basis of original sin alone, leading them to reject the practice of baptizing infants. But very few would have seen no truth whatever in the opening couplet of the *New*

---

*In Adam's Fall: A Meditation on the Christian Doctrine of Original Sin*, by Ian A. McFarland.
© 2010 Ian A. McFarland.

*England Primer*, "In Adam's Fall / We Sinned all."[1] Even Immanuel Kant, champion of Enlightenment and relentless critic of traditional forms of Christian teaching, retained a place in his *Religion within the Limits of Reason Alone* for a doctrine of radical evil that bears a notable resemblance to original sin.

By contrast, one is hard pressed to find much interest in – let alone enthusiasm for – the doctrine of original sin in present-day Western culture. This changed situation is, of course, bound up with the weakening of the power and influence of the churches in Europe and the Americas over the last two centuries, but even among committed Christians original sin has lost much of its hold on the imagination.[2] Although in one form or another it remains the official teaching of many denominations, it has ceased practically to be a central tenet of Christian belief even in those churches that are formally committed to it. And though (especially in the United States) Christians of all persuasions continue to be very active in seeking to influence public policy, their language is shaped by images of personal autonomy and individual freedom worlds removed from the idea of universal solidarity in sin.

Interestingly, however, this shift away from original sin has not in any sense been accompanied by a diminished sense of the power of evil in the world. On the contrary, the language of Christians, from liberation theologians on the left to premillennial dispensationalists on the right, is marked by a profound sense of the many ways evil impinges on human existence. And while it may be the case that such movements pay particular attention to evil's supra-personal (i.e., social or cosmic) dimensions, it is far from clear that this has in any way displaced the call for individual transformation. Christians remain committed to the message, "Repent and believe" (Mark 1:15), but they are not typically inclined to develop it in terms of a doctrine of original sin. Why not?

One obvious answer is that the doctrine of original sin is simply not gospel, or good news. It is tempting to dismiss this consideration as nothing more than a sign of the church's collective failure of nerve – a market-driven desire to avoid some of the more depressing elements of the Christian tradition. But there is more at stake here than mere salesmanship. It is true that the doctrine of original sin is not the gospel; and because it is not, there *is* something problematic about making it a defining feature of the church's proclamation. In his prison letters, Dietrich Bonhoeffer was highly critical of those styles of evangelistic preaching that seek first to persuade people how wretched and miserable they are and only then introduce Jesus Christ as the cure for their condition. He called it "religious blackmail" and thought it both ignoble and completely inconsistent with Jesus' own preaching.[3] In line with what will be an important claim of this book, Bonhoeffer objected that such preaching confused sin with personal weakness or guilt.[4] This confusion, Bonhoeffer argued, failed to reckon with the fact that Jesus' own preaching was not predicated on searching out his hearers' flaws but rather addressed them in their entirety.

Yet if it is wrong to place original sin at the center of the gospel message, I will argue that it remains an important feature of the Christian understanding of the human condition and thus a crucial part of that message. Before addressing the topic of original sin in particular, however, it is necessary to clarify what it means to speak of sin in general – and that task presents significant challenges of its own. After all, in contemporary Western culture the word "sin" is used seriously (i.e., to name something genuinely fatal to human existence rather than a penchant for rich desserts) only within the church – and even there its use is not uncontested. Again, this reluctance to talk about sin cannot simply be attributed to the fact that people inside or outside the church lack a strong sense of right and wrong or are indifferent to the power of evil. Instead, it reflects profound uneasiness with the connotations of the word "sin" that is arguably a problem of the churches' own making. The fact that Christians often have focused their sin-talk on issues of marginal moral significance (e.g., smoking, dancing, playing cards) – so that the churches most vehement in their denunciations of "sin" have often seemed unconcerned about war, poverty, or racism – has contributed to the sense that the concept of sin, far from contributing to the identification of and resistance to evil, only serves to distract attention from "the weightier matters of the law" (Matt. 23:23).[5] In light of this situation, recovery of the doctrine of original sin needs to begin with an appreciation of some of the ways in which the way the idea of sin is used in Christian Scripture challenges popular understanding of the concept.

## Biblical Configurations of Sin

The consumerist anthropology that shapes so much of contemporary Western culture is predicated on a model of freedom in which choice is determined exclusively by the will of the chooser. To be sure, possible objects of choice are constrained by material circumstances (e.g., a person with neither money nor credit cannot buy a hat), and the choices one makes may entail consequences that are not themselves desired by the chooser (e.g., someone who steals a hat is subject to arrest); but the act of choosing itself is conceived as radically private and autonomous: the individual is finally responsible only to herself for what she chooses. Within the consumerist paradigm, a person's choices will certainly affect other people and will themselves be affected by other people's advice and opinions; but however much such relationships may impact the calculus of choice, they remain external to the act of choosing, which can always be abstracted from them as a decision that is essentially by and for the self.[6] The moral character of an individual's acts is, correspondingly, determined by assessment of her capacities and intentions.[7]

## *Unintentional sin*

Christian language of sin challenges the private character of choice, because it locates human deeds within a context of a relationship with God that is prior to and independent of any human choosing. This is not to suggest that the theological concept of sin is univocal. The Old Testament speaks of sin in various ways, distinguishing, for example, between active rebellion (*pāša*) against God (e.g., Amos 4:4) and a more passive failure to attain some good (*hātā'*) through error or ignorance (e.g., Gen. 20:6).[8] In no case, however, is sin reducible to a purely private decision about personal behavior. Indeed, the Old Testament also includes what to modern ears sounds like a contradiction in terms: unintentional sin (*š$^e$gāgāh*). Though the fact that such sin is unintentional means that it falls outside the power of choice, it nevertheless renders the individual who committed it culpable in a way that requires ritual expiation (see Lev. 4:1–5; 19; Num. 15:22–30; cf. Ezek. 45:20).

In order to appreciate how radically this differs from modern sensibilities, it is important to recognize that the Old Testament category of unintentional sin is not reducible to culpable ignorance, as though the offending party's fault could be attributed to her having failed to take account of a particular moral or legal principle that she ought to have known. If that were the case, the sin could still be interpreted in terms of autonomous choice – something that could have been avoided had the person's moral calculations been more thorough.[9] Instead, in terms of content, unintentional sin refers to "any one of the things which the Lord has commanded not to be done" (Lev. 4:2, 13, 22, 27). In this way, the category of unintentional sin suggests that the model of moral calculus is inadequate precisely because it conflates human responsibility *for* sin with the conscious choosing *of* sin. Some sins may well be deliberately chosen (Num. 15:30 contrasts unintentional sins with sins committed "with a high hand"), but the range of terms employed for sin in the Old Testament suggests that sin cannot simply be equated with conscious choice. Instead, it seems better understood as any human action that deviates from God's will, whatever the particular combination of factors that may have contributed to it. In this way, the Old Testament suggests that sin be identified in terms of the character and quality of one's relationships with God and neighbor. One can, correspondingly, be convicted of sin when one's action damages those relationships, even where that damage was not freely chosen.

Though the vocabulary for sin in New Testament Greek is more limited than that of Old Testament Hebrew,[10] it, too, bears witness to a refusal to limit sin to conscious choices. In one of his more anguished reflections on the human situation, Paul writes:

> I do not understand my own actions. For I do not do what I want, but I do the very thing that I hate. Now if I do what I do not want, I agree that the law is good. But in fact it is not longer I that do it, but sin that dwells within me. For I know that nothing good dwells within me, that is, in my flesh. I can will what is right, but I cannot do it. For I do not do the good I want, but the evil I do not want is what I do. (Rom. 7:14–19)

While the interpretation of this passage remains disputed,[11] it is clear at least that Paul distinguishes between the good that he wants and the evil that he commits. It does not seem appropriate to interpret this disparity as a simple collapse of Paul's powers of choice, as though he found himself physically unable to keep his limbs from committing murder or adultery in a particular instance.[12] Aside from the fact that such a scenario flatly contradicts Paul's claim elsewhere that he was personally blameless with respect to God's law (Phil. 3:6), it implies a mind–body dualism that is inconsistent with Paul's overall anthropology. A better option seems to view the situation he describes as one in which the material consequences of his willing escape his control, so that the results of his actions go wrong in a way that bears little or no relation to his intentions.[13] In this respect, his sin, too, is unintentional – though not for that reason any less catastrophic.

In both the Levitical and Pauline contexts, unintentional sin opens up a perspective in which the sinfulness of an action is assessed primarily by reference to its external effects on one's relationships to God and neighbor. Insofar as the law is understood as the framework regulating those relationships, this conclusion appears consistent with the biblical definition of sin as "lawlessness" (*anomia*, 1 John 3:4). Crucially, this objective mode of assessment decouples the fact of sin from the sinner's internal dispositions. To be sure, sin is regarded differently depending on whether or not it is committed with "a high hand," but the fact that sin was unintended does not eliminate the sinner's responsibility. Though sin may not be within one's direct control, the fact that it is a matter of damaged or distorted relationship means that the sinner cannot dissociate herself from the situation as a purely passive victim of circumstances. On the contrary, moving to the context of relationship in analyzing sin subverts any simple binarism according to which responsibility is assessed solely in terms of whether or not the sin was intentional. A person's responsibility is not dependent on the ability to exercise conscious control over her thoughts and actions, but rather derives from that fact that her agency cannot be abstracted from the network of interpersonal relationships in which she participates. Indeed, Jesus' insistence that the two great commandments are love of God and neighbor (Matt. 22:37 and pars.) suggests that this impossibility of abstracting oneself from one's relationships is central to his vision of what it means to be a moral agent. Quite contrary to the consumerist perspective, complicity in sin is a function of one's ineluctable participation in a web of relationships and is thus not simply reducible to the choices one makes.

## Sin as external power

Though the idea of unintentional sin breaks the link between responsibility and conscious control, it nevertheless continues to operate with the model of sin as a particular act performed by an identifiable agent. Yet biblical language about sin goes considerably further in rubbing against modern sensibilities when it challenges even the apparently self-evident idea that sin is something a person does. In this context, it is worth noting that though the transgression of Adam and Eve is easily the most well-known sin in the Bible, it is not named as a sin in Genesis. The first explicit reference to sin in Scripture comes only after humanity is expelled from Eden, in the story of Cain and Abel. When Cain grows angry because of the favor shown to Abel's offering, God warns him: "if you do not do well, sin [*hattā't*] is lurking at the door; its desire is for you, but you must master it" (Gen. 4:7).[14] The implication is that while a person may avoid committing sin in any given instance, at no point can she avoid reckoning with sin as a force at large in the world. In short, sin is not simply a kind of act people commit; it is a power that hovers around all human acting.

This way of characterizing sin is not limited to the primordial world of Genesis. In the verse that follows immediately on the passage quoted in the previous section, Paul makes the extraordinary claim that "if I do what I do not want, it is no longer I that do it, but sin that dwells within me" (Rom. 7:20). As the subsequent verses of the letter make clear, Paul does not say this as a means of absolving himself from responsibility for his actions. His point is rather that his identity is inextricably bound up with the power of sin, so that he can describe his state as that of a person "sold under sin" and "a slave to the law of sin" (Rom. 7:20, 25). For Paul in these verses, sin does not merely threaten him in a way that he might (in line with the language of Gen. 4:7) in principle overcome, but presses on his agency with such force as to render him seemingly helpless to resist it.

In short, Paul's language in Romans 7 furthers the decoupling of sin from intentionality, with the imagery of sin as an external power that impinges on human action deepening appreciation for the ways in which human action is bound up with sin. Far from guaranteeing the kind of untrammeled control over themselves that allows them to be masters of their fate, human beings' status as agents actually renders them vulnerable to the power of sin, which (following the personification of sin found in places like Genesis 4 and Romans 7) seeks to appropriate their agency for its own ends. Taking this language seriously means recognizing that an understanding of sin informed by the full range of the biblical witness is not reducible to a list of prohibited acts. On the contrary, human beings' commission of particular *sins* conceived along these lines is bound up with the power of *sin* as a reality antecedent to any particular deed a person might do.

### Sin as universal condition

The third way in which biblical language about sin challenges contemporary sensibilities regarding the link between culpability and conscious choice is by suggesting that sin is not only a *power* that impinges on human action from without, but a universal existential *condition* out of which we act. From this perspective sin is not just something human beings more or less culpably produce, or even a force with which they find themselves engaged in struggle. Both those perspectives still distinguish sin from human agency, even if they imply that it is something over which human agents have some control. By contrast, to characterize sin as a universal condition is to locate it within agency itself: human beings are not sinners because of the *ways* that they act (or fail to act), but by virtue of the mere *fact* of their acting.

In the Old Testament this understanding of sin is closely connected with the claim that sin is universal, as found in texts like Pss. 14, 143; 1 Kings 8:46; 2 Chron. 6:36; Prov. 20:6, 9; Eccl. 7:20. Perhaps most famous of all is the opening of Psalm 51:

> Have mercy on me, O God, according to your steadfast love;
>   according to your abundant mercy blot out my transgressions.
> Wash me thoroughly from my iniquity,
>   and cleanse me from my sin!
> For I know my transgressions, and my sin is ever before me.
> Against you only have I sinned, and done what is evil in your sight,
>   so that you are justified in your sentence
>   and blameless in your judgment.
> Behold, I was brought forth in iniquity,
>   and in sin did my mother conceive me. (vv. 1–5)

Sin is here certainly conceived in terms of particular actions ("transgressions"), but it is also conceived as a more general state ("iniquity" or "sin") that characterizes the sinner as such.[15] And lest the reader should think that this state is to be understood as merely the consequence of the psalmist's actions, he (following the traditional attribution of this psalm to David) adds that it has characterized him from birth. To be sure, he is a sinner because he sins – but it is also apparently the case that he sins because he is a sinner.

Once again, in the New Testament this perspective finds articulation in the letters of Paul (though the idea is arguably also implicit in passages like Luke 13:1–5; John 8:7). In his letter to the church at Rome, Paul affirms sinfulness as a universal state of humankind, quoting Psalm 14 and arguing that the law convicts all persons of sin (Rom. 3:10–19). And just as the psalmist connected his sinfulness to his very humanity, so Paul invokes the primordial transgression of Adam as a means of emphasizing universal human sinfulness in the present (Rom. 5:19).

It is important to note that I am not claiming that these passages from Paul (or, for that matter, the Psalms) teach that human beings acquire sin either through biological transmission across the generations or by means of some forensic ascription of Adam's guilt to his descendants. Their function is simply to establish sin's universality – to affirm all human beings' status as sinners in need of forgiveness or redemption – without providing an account of its ultimate cause or essential character.[16] In so doing, however, they illustrate a further respect in which biblical ways of characterizing sin are at odds with the individualism of popular moral discourse, since the universal reach of sin runs afoul of the market's model of the self-determining consumer who makes choices from a position of unconditioned freedom.

Together, these three ways in which various biblical writers push reflection on hamartiology beyond the framework of consciously chosen action bring into relief three distinct dimensions of what it means to be a sinner. At first glance, the category of unintentional sin appears to be based on a crudely objective construal of sin as transgression (by whatever means) of established legal norms, but this kind of objective understanding of sin suggests an anthropology in which a person is not separable from her relationships with other persons (whether human or divine), so that one is a sinner whenever and for whatever reason one's actions adversely affect those relationships. The depiction of sin as a malevolent power further destabilizes the consumerist self by portraying sin as a force capable of overwhelming even one's own intentionality, bending human agency to evil in a way that nevertheless implicates the agent as (to use Paul's words) a slave to sin. Finally, the depiction of sin as a universal condition undermines the possibility of claiming any dimension of human agency that is untouched by sin: the individual does not more or less deliberately acquire the status of sinner through her acts, but finds herself always already a sinner when confronted by the reality of her relationships with God and neighbor – relationships for the character of which she is unable to deny her responsibility as agent because life in these relationships is precisely what identifies her as an agent in the first place.[17] Through this multi-layered depiction of sin as both essentially interpersonal in its manifestation and mysteriously supra-personal in its origins, biblical patterns of sin-talk destabilize the model of the agent who is free to construct and deconstruct her identity from an internally secure position of radical self-determination.

## Contemporary Attempts to Reclaim Sin-Talk

Though these three biblical ways of talking about sin are all arguably quite counterintuitive to the sensibilities of contemporary Western societies, it is possible to see their influence in the persistent, if culturally somewhat marginal, voices defending the value of sin-talk in the public sphere. Reflecting a serious appropriation of the tongue-in-cheek claim that original sin is "the only empirically verifiable doctrine of the Christian faith,"[18] most such defenses are grounded in the conviction that the language of sin constitutes an important and possibly irreplaceable resource for a proper appreciation of the human experience of evil. In line with this basic orientation – and notwithstanding significant divergences with respect to their ancillary theological commitments – contemporary advocates for a recovery of sin-talk take a pragmatic approach to hamartiology, arguing in different ways that the language of sin helps both to interpret and to resist the concrete evils that otherwise threaten to overwhelm human beings.

## The responsibility model

Contemporary efforts to reclaim the category of sin within public discourse include three trajectories, each of which highlights a different dimension of the traditional Christian characterization of sin.[19] One, corresponding to what Stephen G. Ray has termed the "responsibility model," focuses on the objectivity of sin as a class of acts or attitudes that damages or disrupts the relationships necessary for human well-being. Representatives of this position argue that a strong doctrine of sin produces a more decent and humane society by stressing individuals' role in maintaining the quality of the many relationships that shape common life and, correspondingly, deepening their sense of responsibility for the general welfare.[20] In line with the approach taken by Cornelius Plantinga in his book *Not the Way It's Supposed to Be*, this stress on individual responsibility is often developed rhetorically by contrasting the contemporary indifference to the idea of sin with the greater moral rigor characteristic of earlier times, when the idea of sin was much more to the fore of public discourse and private sensibility alike.[21] Thus, although Plantinga recognizes that past generations were also beset by sin, he views them in a far more favorable light than contemporary North American culture, whose population is portrayed as captive to shallow, narcissistic selfishness.[22] Yet however successful his account is in identifying the ways in which specific behaviors both directly harm individuals and damage the network of relationships necessary for their collective flourishing, his focus on human responsibility for identifying and correcting one's own moral shortcomings effectively recapitulates the ideal of individual autonomy and self-control that is one of the defining elements of the consumer culture he wants to critique.

This focus on individual action characteristic of the responsibility model goes along with a comparative lack of attention to the supra-personal dimensions of sin. For example, Plantinga has little to say about the ways in which deeply (though not necessarily consciously or willfully) held presuppositions regarding nation, class, sex, and race distort the perceptions and actions of individuals in ways that are not reducible to individual selfishness or indifference. Indeed, his emphasis on sin as the product of the bad decisions of individual moral agents has the effect of placing the burden of guilt for the fact that things are not the way they're supposed to be on socially marginalized persons whose own capacity for flourishing has been most severely circumscribed by supra-personal forms of sin that restrict their access to social goods.[23] In this way, the responsibility model is prone to overlook the variety of ways in which the interactions of individual agents are shaped by factors that block the kind of shared reading of a given situation upon which agents' capacities to negotiate the terms of their mutual well-being depend.

The problems with the responsibility model are not limited to the risk of cultural and generational myopia.[24] Most obviously, the fact that individuals with no commitment to the language of sin regularly show themselves capable of responsible behavior, even as people deeply committed to sin-talk acquiesce to and even participate in horrific acts of violence and cruelty, raises serious questions about the power of the concept of sin by itself to improve the caliber of human resistance to evil. Indeed, the responsibility model may actually work against this end insofar as its focus is strengthening the conscience by appealing to human beings' own sense of sinfulness. The problem here is that from a Christian perspective the supposition that one's own sense of right and wrong, as determined by the conscience, corresponds to God's will is highly problematic. Bonhoeffer put the matter as follows:

> Conscience claims to be the voice of God and the norm for relating to other people. By relating properly to themselves, human beings think to regain the proper relationship to God and to others ... Human beings have [in this way] become the origin of good and evil. They do not deny their own evil. But in the voice of their conscience those who have become evil call themselves back to their authentic self, their better self, to the good. It is [identified with] God's good ... Bearing the knowledge of good and evil within themselves, human beings have now become the judge of God and others, just as they are their own judge.[25]

In other words, from a specifically theological perspective the kind of appeal to conscience on which the responsibility model is based is not a credible solution to the problem of sin. On the contrary, it is itself a manifestation of the problem, since it presupposes just the kind of autonomous human ability to discern what counts as sinful in a given situation that attention to the full range of biblical accounts of sin calls into question. In so doing, the responsibility model opens human beings to just the kind of blindness regarding the range and depth of their own complicity in sin that haunts Plantinga's analysis, in which the accusing finger he directs at the wider culture never quite seems to include himself. Therefore, while the responsibility model does highlight the objectivity of sin as a disruption of creaturely well-being, it is ultimately inadequate because it equates sin's objectivity with its transparency to the human agent's moral gaze.

## The participation model

A second stream of contemporary attempts to recover the language of sin for the public sphere highlights the supra-personal dimension of sin as a power that undermines creaturely well-being. This perspective takes the form of what might be called a "participation model" of sin, which is conceived in terms of a series of structures within and between individuals in which all unavoidably participate, but which all are also called to transcend through transformative practices that identify and resist them. Within a participatory framework individual responsibility remains an important theme, but it is understood primarily as subsequent to rather than the cause of the experience of sin in the world. As a result, attempts to resist sin are understood as fundamentally ameliorative (i.e., addressing an already existing situation of sin) rather than preventative (i.e., keeping sin from occurring in the first place).

One of the most important examples of the participatory model is Marjorie Hewitt Suchocki's *The Fall to Violence*.[26] Though she, like Plantinga, roots her analysis of sin in the experience of that which "ought not to be the case,"[27] she differs sharply from him in criticizing traditional doctrines of sin precisely on the grounds that their tendency to equate sin with willful rebellion against God overestimates individual responsibility for sin. Noting that in the vast majority of cases sin takes the form of acquiescence to evil rather than Promethean defiance of the good, she argues that the power of sin (manifest especially in the dynamics of violence) is ontologically prior to the sinful act.[28] Much of her argument is, correspondingly, devoted to showing the various ways in which violence structures human experience: biologically in aggressive behaviors inherited from our evolutionary past, existentially through the relationships of interdependence that communicate the effects of violence across space, and sociologically by way of cultural transmission of patterns of violence through time. The result is a situation in which "[t]o be human is to be embroiled in sin before one even has the means to assent."[29]

Yet if this emphasis on sin as the unavoidable context of all human action renders Suchocki's analysis less naive than Plantinga's, close examination of her argument suggests that her understanding of sin is no less deeply invested in the modern idea of individual freedom. Quite simply, "if there is no freedom, then neither is there sin;"[30] and freedom for Suchocki remains fundamentally "the ability to choose."[31] Thus, as much as she recognizes that the structures that predispose human beings to sin are not subject to individual decision (viz., the biological, existential, and cultural mediations of violence mentioned in the previous paragraph) and locates freedom within the context of relationships (so that its exercise is inevitably constrained by the range of options available to an agent at any given time), the index of sin remains the conscious choice of the sinner.[32]

In developing these ideas, Suchocki argues that all ineluctably participate in sin by virtue of their being enmeshed in the structures of violence that permeate human life; nevertheless, not all are guilty. For while the structures of violence that implicate us in sin are beyond our control, guilt is a function of decision; it arises "when freedom to transcend these structures is present, and one does not transcend those structures."[33] Thus, even though a person's guilt will vary with her intellectual and emotional maturity and is in no case limited to the individual (since even a mature adult cannot be isolated from the social forces that shaped him or her), guilt is ultimately a matter of personal failure. One is guilty because one *ought to* and *could have* acted differently in engaging the power of sin. Thus, while she argues that the dynamics of violence render sin unavoidable, her anthropology leads her to affirm that for the mature adult sin nevertheless remains controllable.

The central role of choice in Suchocki's understanding of sin becomes still more apparent in the context of her reflection on forgiveness, which, she insists, is "fundamentally a matter of intellect rather than of emotions,"[34] and, more specifically, an "act of will" rather than a matter of "loving feelings" toward the one forgiven.[35] This claim is motivated by a desire to avoid any understanding of forgiveness that might suggest an obligation on the part of the victim to embrace the violator. Such an expectation, she argues, would place an intolerable burden on victims that could actually facilitate further sin.[36] Instead, she defines forgiveness as "willing the well-being of victim(s) and violator(s) in the context of the fullest possible knowledge of the nature of the violation."[37] She thereby seeks to avoid any understanding of forgiveness that fails to reckon with the damage wrought by sin by confusing forgiveness with simply overlooking sin. As a willing of well-being in response to acts that damage well-being, forgiveness is a means of transforming the structures of violence that produce sin – and this requires facing up to the material realities that serve as the conditions of the possibility of sin in any given instance.[38]

Yet as much as Suchocki demonstrates both a profound understanding of the insidious ways in which sin implicates human beings in violence and an equally profound appreciation for the damage suffered by sin's victims, the terms of her analysis ultimately subvert her desire to check the focus on the individual that she sees as a weakness of traditional theologies of sin. Like Plantinga, she sees the (mature) individual as able to position herself over against even the most deeply engrained patterns of violence in a way that lends itself to just the kind of moralistic understanding of sin she wants to resist. Thus participants in sin stand under an obligation to transcend the conditions of their sinning by challenging the social structures that promote it. Similarly, victims of sin stand under an equally firm obligation to forgive, inasmuch as to fail to do so – to do other than will the well-being of all those involved in violation – corresponds precisely to Suchocki's definition of sin as "rebellion against creation's well-being."[39]

This is not to suggest that the ideas that sinners should repent (and thus, by implication, work to transform the internal and external bases for their sinning) and that victims of sin should forgive are in themselves problematic; on the contrary, both are among the most basic of Christian convictions.[40] The problem with Suchocki's suggested responses to sin lies not in their content, but rather in her claim that they are rooted in an implicit human capacity to transcend sin. Repentance and forgiveness are thereby understood as autonomous activities of the will that are, correspondingly, measurable in terms of a describable set of practices. To be sure, Suchocki's insistence on the importance of context dictates that the form these practices take will vary from situation to situation, but – and however much an informed understanding of the pervasiveness of violence will challenge any Pollyannaish dreams of perfection – the solution to the problem of sin remains essentially a matter of human moral reform. In this way, both the responsibility and participatory models, for all their significant differences, are one in viewing sin within the context of a distinctly modern vision of human responsibility.

## The tragic model

A further model that needs to be mentioned here may be described as the "tragic model." It can be characterized as an attempt to recover sin-talk only in a somewhat modified sense, since Wendy Farley and other proponents of this position actually appeal to the tragic as an *alternative* to traditional Christian ways of talking about the human experience of evil.[41] Thus, according to Farley it is suffering (understood as an inevitable outcome of human passion for justice exercised under conditions of creaturely finitude) rather than sin (understood as the product of some primordial transgression) that is the key to the human condition.[42] Nevertheless, I include it here as a mode of contemporary sin-talk because of its parallels with the third biblical configuration of sin discussed above: the model of sin as an inescapable, universal condition.

Farley herself is by no means dismissive of the category of sin. But the fact that she accepts the conventional characterization of sin as fundamentally a matter of self-conscious human choice leads her to view it as insufficient to provide an adequate account of human suffering.[43] Like Suchocki, Farley recognizes the ways in which evolutionary and cultural history impinge negatively on the choices human beings make, but she argues that the roots of suffering are not reducible to human choosing in a way that would justify making sin the fundamental category for analyzing human experience, and that the very conditions of finite existence give the world a tragic structure in which various created goods (e.g., the well-being of predator and prey) are inevitably in conflict. While this structure is not evil in itself, it "makes suffering both possible and inevitable prior to any human action."[44] In short, human action results in suffering because of conditions that constrain the possibilities of creaturely agency for a virtuous actor no less than a vicious one.

This framework does not in any way represent a weakening of the distinction between virtue and vice. Although she recognizes that the corrupting effects of the environment within which human beings act means that even instances of genuine sin cannot simply be identified with pure viciousness,[45] Farley holds that it is both possible and necessary to differentiate certain human acts as sin insofar as they include "a tacit or explicit acceptance of evil."[46] It is precisely for this reason, however, that Farley is so critical of traditional theology, since its tendency to make sin the sole basis of (rather than an aggravating factor in) human suffering subverts efforts to resist evil by suggesting that all suffering is ultimately deserved: because all are sinners, all are guilty and thus worthy of punishment.[47] By contrast, acknowledging the inherently tragic character of human existence means recognizing that "susceptibility to radical evil [is] built into the human condition prior to any individual's act or choice, prior to any possibility of guilt."[48]

Even here, however, there is room for further clarification. It is not Farley's intention to use her analysis of suffering to draw a sharp distinction between "guilty" perpetrators and "innocent" victims of sin.[49] In addition to the rather obvious point that persons who are sin's victims on one level may be its perpetrators on another (e.g., the oppressed farm laborer who beats his wife), Farley cites the ways in which the dynamic of sin co-opts even the agency of the victims in their victimization, citing Simone Weil's observation that "In anyone who has suffered affliction for a long enough time there is a complicity with regard to his own affliction."[50] Nevertheless, she goes on to insist that this *complicity* cannot be equated with the *guilt* that comes with sin and concludes that those who "who are so badly hurt that they become accomplices in their own destruction, far from sharing responsibility for their defeat, are persons already broken by pain."[51]

The contrasts that Farley develops between tragedy and sin, complicity and guilt, responsibility and fault are at once the great strength and the difficulty of her analysis. On the one hand, they allow her to approximate more closely than either of the other two models the ways in which the very conditions of human action are corrupted in ways that make the choice of the good impossible.[52] At the same time, her refusal to designate this situation as one of sin invariably undermines what was more to the fore in the responsibility and participatory models: the ineluctable sense of human responsibility in and for this situation. While she seeks to avoid any facile opposition of perpetrator and victim in her analysis of suffering, the contrastive character of her analytical framework makes it difficult for such qualifications to stick. Quite simply, it is hard to know what it means to affirm that the inalienable agency of victims of sin renders them "accomplices in their own destruction" while at the same time denying that they share any responsibility for it. This contradiction is driven by the best of motives (namely, the refusal to accept that such people might be blamed for their suffering), but it effectively reintroduces the perpetrator–victim dichotomy and thereby also reflects – albeit in a different mode – the strong modern correlation of sin-talk with a capacity for choice also characteristic of the other two models.

## Original Sin and Actual Sin

What I have termed the "responsibility," "participation," and "tragic" models for the contemporary reappropriation of sin-talk are all grounded in the human experience of evil.[53] None of them, however, succeeds in bringing together the notions of humanity's *radical responsibility for sin* and *radical powerlessness in the face of sin* that characterize the full range of biblical sin-talk. Indeed, proponents of each of these models seem predisposed to reject any such synthesis in order to ensure that their use of the category of sin can speak effectively to contemporary human experience of evil. Thus, both the responsibility and participation models presuppose (albeit in quite distinctive ways) human capacities to limit and control sinful behavior that conflicts with the idea of radical human powerlessness before sin. By contrast, the tragic model, while certainly no less concerned with cultivating human resistance to sin, finds traditional emphasis on radical human responsibility for evil misplaced: given the degree to which humans – especially those who suffer most grievously from evil's effects – are not masters in their own house, the value of sin-talk for Christian theology is severely circumscribed.[54]

By contrast, the doctrine of original sin is marked precisely by the attempt to do equal justice to biblical language suggesting both human responsibility for and human powerlessness with respect to sin. This is not to claim that the doctrine can be read directly off Scripture. Like most of the classical doctrines of Christianity (e.g., the Trinity, creation from nothing), it cannot be derived so straightforwardly. Nor is the doctrine an obvious deduction from experience; indeed, though many down through the centuries have sought to defend the doctrine of original sin on empirical grounds, the particular claims of the doctrine render all such efforts problematic. To be sure, Christians attribute the fact that they and their neighbors sin in and through particular, identifiable deeds to the fact that all are burdened by original sin, but it is a mistake to suppose that the latter can be inferred from the former. On the contrary, both the theological significance and plausibility of the Christian doctrine of *original sin* require that it be kept conceptually quite distinct from analyses of the *actual sins* human beings commit. The difficulty of maintaining the proper tension between these two categories is visible in the three contemporary models of sin-talk examined above: the responsibility and participation models' emphasis on human responsibility tends to accentuate the emphasis on actual sin at the expense of a doctrine of original sin; the tragic model's stress on the distorted conditions of human action does a much better job of highlighting the tradition's emphasis on human powerlessness before sin, but precisely for that reason its advocates are reluctant to speak of the problem as essentially one of sin, insofar as the term connotes precisely the kind of responsibility for one's actions that is being called into question.

As a further index of the difficulty involved in holding the categories of actual and original sin together, consider one theologian's claim that "human beings sin if they can, and as much as they can."[55] Empirically speaking, this proposition is manifestly false; indeed, if it were true, human coexistence in society would be impossible. It is certainly true that human beings enact all manner of evil at a variety of levels; but it is equally evident that people also abstain from particular acts of sin, sometimes in heroic fashion and at considerable cost to themselves, but more often quite unspectacularly and as a matter of course. For example, though I am quite happy to describe myself as a sinner, I do not routinely subject those around me to a continual stream of verbal and physical abuse, even though I have uncounted opportunities to do so. Nor do I find that I am in any way exceptional in this regard. Thus, to the extent that those who reject the doctrine of original sin understand it to mean that people sin "if they can, and as much as they can" – that is, that the doctrine is to be justified by a (quantitative) appraisal of actual sin – their incredulity is fully justified.

In fact, however, this definition reflects a false understanding of the Christian doctrine of sin in general and of original sin in particular. Nor is the problem that it offers too pessimistic or harsh a picture of human beings. On the contrary, from the perspective of the classical doctrine of original sin, the idea that people sin "if they can" implies far too *optimistic* an understanding of human agency, since the doctrine of original sin teaches that there is no conditionality whatsoever to human sinfulness. Sin is not properly conceived as a possibility that human beings choose to enact as the opportunity presents itself. Rather, it describes *every* human action without qualification; indeed, to affirm original sin is to claim that human beings are sinners even before and apart from their acting. It is not that human beings sin "if they can, and as much as they can," but that they sin always and everywhere, whether they do much, little, or nothing at all. Moreover, they sin because they are born sinners; and this means, in turn, that they are all equally sinners. In short, the doctrine claims that to be a sinner, and thus to sin in one's every act, is simply coterminous with what it means to be a human being under present circumstances.[56]

Whatever one makes of this claim, it is not the sort of belief that can be established empirically. We have empirical access to human actions and (more indirectly and to a more limited degree) human thoughts, and, based on such data, it is hard to see how one might conclude, for example, that Gandhi and Stalin are equally sinners. Yet the doctrine of original sin claims just that. Clearly, however, the credibility of such a claim will not be established by attempts to measure the quantity or quality of the actual sin committed by human beings, whether considered individually or collectively – and this is the case precisely because of the radical nature of human sinfulness under a doctrine of original sin. Because sin is something of which everyone is guilty all the time, the very capacity to know it and name it is vitiated by human beings' status as sinners. It follows that human beings can know the depth of their sin only as it is forgiven – and thus only as it is made known to us by the one who forgives. Otherwise, we may well affirm that we are sinners as a matter of principle, but identifying all the manifold, concrete ways in which we are sinners will always elude us. Indeed, some of the most insidious examples of sin may be of a piece with those aspects of human life that seem the most natural and the least problematic (e.g., the systematic subordination of women to men); and even those examples of cruelty that seem most obviously sinful to outside observers – not to mention victims – are rarely viewed in the same light by the perpetrators (e.g., instances of genocide).

In short, this book will operate from the perspective that if it is pointless to harangue people over their sinfulness in the way that Bonhoeffer found so objectionable, that is because the concept only has meaning from *within* the context of Christian belief. In other words, because sin is knowable in its depths – precisely as *original* sin – only as it has been forgiven, and thus only *after* the Christian gospel of forgiveness has been proclaimed and believed, it is a concept internal to the logic of the faith and not an apologetic lever that can be used to render that faith somehow more relevant or credible. In this way, the approach to the doctrine taken here reflects Pascal's affirmation that sin is at once "the mystery which is furthest removed from our knowledge" and yet that without which "we can have no knowledge of ourselves."[57]

As the latter half of the quotation from Pascal implies, however, eschewing all attempts to show that original sin helps to demonstrate the credibility of Christian belief does not mean weakening the conviction that the doctrine is itself credible. It means only that the defense of original sin attempted here will take the form of a careful exegesis of the doctrine: exploring how it relates to other elements of the Christian faith (especially beliefs about creation and human freedom on the one hand, and redemption and divine grace on the other), and on that basis assessing the degree to which it can meet objections raised against it both inside and outside the church. In order to achieve this aim, a lot of space will be devoted to clarifying the relationship between original sin and actual sin. For if, as argued above, the two must be kept distinct, their distinction reveals a tension between the two concepts that demands, in turn, an account of how they are to be related to one another. This tension lies in the fact that while original sin is necessary to do justice to

Christian convictions regarding sin's universality, for this very reason it seems less suited to making sense of the differences between concrete manifestations of sin in the world (e.g., explaining how one might justify a preference for Gandhi's politics over Stalin's, in spite of the fact that both men are equally sinners). By contrast, while the category of actual sin gives much more space for just this kind of comparative evaluation of concrete instances of sin, for that very reason it appears to weaken any claims regarding sin's universality (since it is hard to see how one might both acknowledge the fact of rape and go on to describe both the rapist and his victim as equally sinners). As the first step in this process, the next chapter will explore in detail the development of the doctrine of original sin and the particular sorts of objections that have been raised against it.

## Notes

1 Among those few were the Socinians and the Quakers, as well as Latitudinarian Anglicans.
2 I do not mean to suggest that the popularity of original sin underwent a gradual and steady process of erosion only recently completed, or that it can be viewed merely as a function of secularization. On the contrary, amid the enthusiasm with which the nineteenth century embraced an ideology of progress, the doctrine's collapse was precipitous and arguably no less characteristic of evangelical Christians than free-thinking radicals. By contrast, the horrors of the twentieth century arguably allowed for a modest renaissance of the idea in the work of influential public figures like Reinhold Niebuhr and others. See the largely anecdotal but nevertheless perceptive reflections of Alan Jacobs in *Original Sin: A Cultural History* (New York: HarperOne, 2008), especially chs. 9–10.
3 Dietrich Bonhoeffer, Letters of 8 July and 30 June 1944, in *Letters and Papers from Prison*, ed. Eberhard Bethge (New York: Macmillan, 1972), pp. 327, 344; cf. p. 341.
4 "... it is thought that a man can be addressed as a sinner only after his weakness and meanness have been spied out. ... On th[is] first point it is to be said that man is certainly a sinner, but is far from being weak or mean on that account." Bonhoeffer, Letter of 8 July 1944, p. 345.
5 Needless to say, such popular perceptions are not always entirely fair or accurate. For example, while the Women's Christian Temperance Union is often viewed as a particularly glaring example of Christian moral priggishness, in its early years it stood foursquare in the progressive vanguard, promoting women's suffrage, workers' rights, and pacifism; it was also one of the few

nationally prominent organizations in the late nineteenth century to actively recruit African-American members.
6   Alistair McFadyen gives a nice characterization of this quintessentially modern perspective on the self: "the freedom understood to characterize human being and action is supposed to be not only inalienable but unqualified by anything external to the person." Alistair McFadyen, *Bound to Sin: Abuse, Holocaust and the Christian Doctrine of Sin* (Cambridge: Cambridge University Press, 2000), p. 32.
7   Though I have argued that this position is typical of the modern West, it is not limited to that context. For example, Peter Abelard's definition of sin as that which is done against conscience (see his *Ethics or the Book Called "Know Thyself,"* chs. XIII–XIV) reflects the same principle, though developed in a feudal rather than a capitalist context. Note, too, that because this principle has to do exclusively with the conditions for assigning *responsibility* to a moral agent in any given case rather than with the proper *rationale* to be offered for a virtuous action, it can be combined with an aretological, deontological, or utilitarian ethic.
8   The difference in nuance between these two terms should not be pressed too far: in many particular cases they function more or less synonymously (e.g., Isa.1:28); nevertheless, they reflect a recognition of the breadth of ways in which human beings can go wrong that is absent from much contemporary moral reflection, where moral responsibility is typically reduced to intentionality.
9   Admittedly, some of the situations described in Lev. 5 (e.g., failure to testify in court, the taking of a rash oath) do seem amenable to correction by means of making better choices (viz., through more deliberate ethical reflection, greater self-control). Nevertheless, it appears that they were categorized among the unintentional sins because the choosing involved does not constitute a clear-cut violation of a commandment. For though the Torah prohibits false witness and breaking oaths, it does not specify the conditions under which testimony is to be given or vows made; therefore, appeal to established precepts will not itself provide a basis for avoiding these sorts of sin. Indeed, it may not be possible to establish the sinfulness of such acts until *after* the choice has been made (e.g., the judgment that a particular oath is rash can arguably be made only a posteriori). See the discussion in Mark E. Biddle, *Missing the Mark: Sin and Its Consequences in Biblical Theology* (Nashville, TN: Abingdon Press, 2005), pp. 98–104.
10   While it is possible draw etymological parallels between and the Hebrew *pāša* and *hātā'* on the one hand and the Greek *paraptōma* and *hamartia* on the other, the latter term and its cognates (*hamartēma, hamartanō, hamartōlos*) predominates in the New Testament over the various *para-* compounds (including, in addition to *paraptōma, parabasis, parakoē,* and *paranomia*) for the designation of sin.

11  See Chapter 3 for a detailed discussion of Augustine's attempts to make sense of Paul's situation here.

12  In this context, it is important not to conflate Paul's argument in vv. 14–20 with his discussion of covetousness in vv. 7–11, where he does seem to describe a disrupting of his powers of choice. Without getting into the (again, disputed) details of Paul's understanding of the law, it seems that in the earlier verses it is precisely Paul's will that is the problem (insofar as covetousness is an inner disposition), whereas in the later he insists that he wills what is right but that his external actions somehow go wrong.

13  As Ernst Käsemann puts it, "What a person wants is salvation. What he creates is disaster. This is also true, and especially so, of the pious who are faithful to the law." *Commentary on Romans* (Grand Rapids, MI: William B. Eerdmans, 1980), p. 203.

14  The hypostatization of sin in this passage resonates with the description of the devil in 1 Pet. 5:8 as a "roaring lion" who "prowls around, looking for someone to devour." Similarly, Paul can attribute the same kind of nefarious agency to sin that he elsewhere attributes to Satan (cf. Rom. 7:11, 13 and 2 Cor. 2:11).

15  In this Psalm the NRSV uses "transgressions" to translate *pāša*; "iniquity" translates *awōn*, and "sin" is used for both *hātā'* and *ra*.

16  Don B. Garlington echoes contemporary exegetical consensus when he avers that the discussion of Adam in Romans 5 "concerns man's immediate involvement in Adam's sin and death, not moral corruption as such." *Faith, Obedience, and Perseverance: Aspects of Paul's Letter to the Romans* (Tübingen: Mohr-Siebeck, 1994), p. 86. Cf. G. C. Berkouwer *Sin* (Grand Rapids, MI: William B. Eerdmans, 1971), p. 488.

17  It should be noted that this formulation is not intended to promote a relational understanding of personhood, as though human beings were constituted as persons by their relationships. As I have argued elsewhere, such a position raises the specter of a hierarchy according to which the quantity and quality of relationships might be taken to imply that some individuals are more "personal" than others. All I am claiming in the present instance is that biblically (1) to be an agent is to be in relationship with God (always) and (in varying numbers and degree) other human beings, and (2) therefore one cannot at any point abstract one's agency from the quality or character of those relationships. Thus, where the relationship is damaged, I am always implicated somehow, though – as will be discussed in greater detail in the third part of this book – in different ways depending on the particular place I occupy within the damaged relationship.

18  Reinhold Niebuhr, to whom this remark is often attributed, claimed to have found it in the *Times Literary Supplement*. See his *Man's Nature and His Communities: Essays on the Dynamics and Enigmas of Man's Personal and Social Existence* (New York: Charles Scribner's Sons, 1965), p. 24. Alan Jacobs attributes it to G. K. Chesterton (*Original Sin*, p. x).

19  These three are not the only approaches to be found in recent literature. For example, Christof Gestrich in his book *The Return of Splendor to the World: The Christian Doctrine of Sin and Forgiveness* (Grand Rapids, MI: William B. Eerdmans, 1997 [1989]) proposes an aesthetic approach to hamartiology, according to which sin is understood as a loss of creaturely glory. On this model (which is conceived as a corrective to what Gestrich regards as the pessimistic view of creation that he sees as having infected Christian attitudes to the world as a whole and humanity in particular), sin is essentially a noetic problem, such that its forgiveness "is not an event of cleansing, but the return of an awareness of God in my person and the return of splendor in my world" (p. 246).

20  Stephen G. Ray, Jr., *Do No Harm: Social Sin and Christian Responsibility* (Minneapolis, MN: Fortress Press, 2003), p. 26; see p. 27: "A goal of this method is therefore to lobby for an approach to sin-talk that not only recognizes the social results of sin but focuses attention on the behavior of culpable agents."

21  Cornelius Plantinga, Jr., *Not the Way It's Supposed to Be: A Breviary of Sin* (Grand Rapids, MI: William B. Eerdmans, 1995).

22  A noteworthy characteristic of Plantinga's analysis is its similarity to purely secular accounts of the sort found in, e.g., Alan Bloom, *The Closing of the American Mind: Education and the Crisis of Reason* (New York: Simon & Schuster, 1987), or William J. Bennett, *The Broken Hearth: Reversing the Moral Collapse of the American Family* (New York: Broadway, 2003). Although Plantinga emphasizes that sin is properly defined in reference to God, the rhetorical force of his argument draws more on what he presumes is a shared dissatisfaction with the current state of Western society than on specific claims to divine revelation. He argues that sin offends God because it spoils shalom, which (in line with the book's title) is correlated primarily with the autonomous individual's own sense of how things are supposed to be. As a result, the upshot of his book is more that our experience of sin gives us a reason to believe in God (since it is our sense of dissatisfaction that points to an objective notion of shalom) than the converse.

23  Thus, the example of sin with which Plantinga opens (and sets the tone for) his argument is a vignette from the film *Grand Canyon* (1991), in which an affluent white man whose car breaks down in inner-city Los Angeles is threatened by a group of young black men (*Not the Way It's Supposed to Be*, pp. 7–8). For a brilliant counter-reading of this episode from the perspective of the youths indicted by Plantinga, see Ray, *Do No Harm*, pp. 25–33.

24  In an earlier version of the same genre, Karl Menninger was careful to avoid the kind of dualistic opposition between past and present characteristic of Plantinga's book. He conceded, for example, that the disappearance of sin as a moral category in Western society was at least partly due to "a softening not of moral fiber but of human compassion." Karl Menninger, *Whatever Became of Sin?* (London: Hodder & Stoughton, 1973), p. 29.

25 See Bonhoeffer, *Ethics*, vol. 6 of *Dietrich Bonhoeffer Works*, ed. Clifford J. Green (Minneapolis, MN: Fortress Press, 2005), p. 308. Bonhoeffer's analysis here shows a certain consistency with his rejection of evangelical attempts to promote the gospel by first convicting human beings of their sinfulness (see pp. 4–5 above). In both cases he is resisting the idea that a person's own sense of her weakness or fallibility is a reliable index or measure of sin.

26 Marjorie Hewitt Suchocki, *The Fall to Violence: Original Sin in Relational Theology* (New York: Continuum, 1994). Though she works from within a process theism, Suchocki's analysis of sin shares many crucial features with other works not committed to Whiteheadian metaphysical categories. Cf., e.g., Ted Peters, *Sin: Radical Evil in Soul and Society* (Grand Rapids, MI: William B. Eerdmans, 1994).

27 Suchocki, *Fall to Violence*, pp. 130, 141. This parallel points to an even stronger point of convergence between the two authors that is characteristic of much contemporary theological reflection on sin: a preference for defining sin primarily in terms of harm inflicted against creatures (what Suchocki describes as "violation of creaturely well-being" and Plantinga as the "breaking of shalom") rather than resistance to God. To be sure, neither author either advocates or practices a thorough secularization of sin (and Suchocki's commitment to process metaphysics leads her to develop a detailed account of how sin against creation is always also sin against God), but their pragmatic orientation to sin-talk leads them to center primarily on the immediate experience of sin as painful or destructive in the creaturely sphere rather than on the creature's relationship to God.

28 "... my intent is not to posit an original violent act, which in effect follows the same dynamics as looking for an original Adam and Eve. Rather, it may be that violence itself is root as well as effect of sin." Suchocki, *Fall to Violence*, p. 29.

29 Suchocki, *Fall to Violence*, p. 129.

30 Ibid., p. 130.

31 Ibid., p. 131; on p. 133 she equates freedom with "self-determinacy."

32 Indeed, this focus on intent is an important feature of Suchocki's shift from God to creation as the immediate object of sin: "The drive-by murderer may or may not have an intent to take God's place, but the drive-by murderer always has an intent to destroy the well-being of another person, whether carelessly or deliberately." Suchocki, *Fall to Violence*, p. 161.

33 Suchocki, *Fall to Violence*, p. 137; cf. p. 141, where guilt is described as "a refusal to transcend the value structures that form the boundaries of one's existence."

34 Ibid., p. 145.

35 Ibid., p. 146.

36 It is important to note that Suchocki by no means rejects the possibility that genuine feelings of reconciliation might arise between victim and violator, only that such feelings are constitutive of the act of forgiveness.

37 Suchocki, *Fall to Violence*, p. 144.

38  Thus (and though Suchocki does not use this example), willing the well-being of a pedophile might include willing a situation in which he is kept from close contact with children.
39  Suchocki, *Fall to Violence*, p. 16. It is true that on the same page Suchocki identifies sin specifically with "unnecessary violence against any aspect of existence," but it is not clear that this proviso works to mitigate the moral obligation of the victim to forgive, given that Suchocki's understanding of forgiveness does not seem to preclude the use of certain necessary violence in order to curtail sinful behavior (e.g., the use of a restraining order to keep an abusive husband away from his spouse).
40  At the same time, it is hard to see how Suchocki's understanding of forgiveness works when transferred to the sphere of God's interactions with human beings. It would seem that insofar as in Suchocki's process theism God by definition always wills the maximum well-being of all entities, divine forgiveness is transformed from an act of grace to a matter of ontology, so that Suchocki's God, like Heine's, forgives sin because "that's his job." Though it is obviously not her intention, such a position would seem to open the doors to the worst sort of "cheap grace."
41  Wendy Farley sees her work as a break with the majority Christian tradition because she "place[s] suffering rather than sin at the center of the problem of evil. I do this not because I do not think sin is a problem but because I think suffering is a more serious anomaly for Christian faith." *Tragic Vision and Divine Compassion: A Contemporary Theodicy* (Louisville, KY: Westminster/John Knox, 1990), p. 12. For the classic statement of the contrast between the tragic vision and the "Adamic" emphasis on sin, see Paul Ricoeur, *The Symbolism of Evil* (Boston, MA: Beacon Press, 1967), pp. 211–78.
42  "Tragic suffering is not a consequence of a Fall or a cathartic exception that reinstates the reign of justice. Something in the constitution of the world makes an ethical passion for piety, justice, truth, or compassion self-destructive. The world order itself is implicated as the origin of tragic suffering." Farley, *Tragic Vision*, pp. 25–6.
43  "Sin is similar to tragedy in that it encompasses individual human actions in an already corrupted environment. But it is not simply tragic, it is moral. It is the willful repudiation of the stewardship that might have been the mark of humanity's relationship to God." Farley, *Tragic Vision*, p. 44.
44  Ibid., pp. 31–2. This form of existential analysis, which roots the possibility of sin in structures of creaturely freedom that precondition any concrete human choice, can be traced back through Reinhold Niebuhr to Kierkegaard.
45  Sin "corrupts the environment in which human beings must act and deceives them about their real situation … Sin becomes a kind of bondage that entangles human beings even before they choose or desire evil." Farley, *Tragic Vision*, pp. 48–9.
46  Ibid., p. 51; cf. p. 50: "Sin requires assent at some level to lies, callousness and cruelty. Consent to evil represents the transition from tragedy and bondage to guilt."

47  Specifically, if *sin* is the problem, then *forgiveness* is the solution; but, Farley argues, "abused children do not need to be forgiven." Farley, *Tragic Vision*, p. 63.
48  Ibid., p. 64.
49  "The exploration of the problem of evil must resist the temptation to absorb the problem of suffering into guilt and sin. It must also avoid the more contemporary temptation to resort to moral dualisms." Farley, *Tragic Vision*, p. 52.
50  Simone Weil, *Waiting for God* (New York: Harper Colophon, 1973 [1951]), p. 122; cited in Farley, *Tragic Vision*, p. 57.
51  Farley, *Tragic Vision*, p. 58.
52  "The conditions under which human beings must live are already corrupted by evil and are too painful to be borne ... Conflict and fragility overwhelm us. In an impenetrable mystery of freedom and tragedy, evil infects the human race." Farley, *Tragic Vision*, p. 61.
53  For this reason all three approaches to the problem of sin can be classed as exercises in natural as opposed to revealed theology. The significance of this distinction is expressed by Suchocki as a matter of "looking for answers not in Christian dogmatics, but in ... the structures of human existence" (*Fall to Violence*, p. 161). Cf. Ted Peters' contention that "the idea of original sin is an attempt to make sense out of the world in which we find ourselves. ... to interpret and explain the already existing reality of which we are a part" (*Sin*, p. 31).
54  Thus, in many respects the tragic model's emphasis on the helplessness of human beings before the power of sin is closest of the three to a traditional doctrine of original sin, even though Farley is far more suspicious than Plantinga or Suchocki of the utility of sin as a central anthropological category.
55  Henri Blocher, *Original Sin: Illuminating the Riddle* (Grand Rapids, MI: William B. Eerdmans, 1997), p. 91.
56  Importantly (and as will be explained in greater detail further on), though these circumstances are generally understood to be a permanent fixture of human beings prior to glory, the doctrine of the fall affirms that sinfulness is not logically a corollary to existence in time and space. To affirm that it was would be to indict spatio-temporal existence – and thus the material creation – as evil or defective in itself, contrary to the biblical affirmation that it is "very good" (Gen. 1:31).
57  Blaise Pascal, *Pensées*, §434 (London: J. M. Dent & Sons, 1958), p. 121. Cf. Herman Bavinck, *Reformed Dogmatics*, 4 vols. (Grand Rapids, MI: Baker Academic, 2003–), vol. 3, p. 77: "Without [original sin] we cannot comprehend ourselves, and yet it remains finally an incomprehensible mystery."

# 2

# Original Sin as Christian Doctrine: Origins, Permutations, Problems

Historical reviews of the many and various ways in which early Christians reflected on the theological significance of Genesis 2–3 testify to the long and often uneven course of development in the Christian doctrines of the fall and original sin before they took more definite form (at least in the Western churches) in the writings of Augustine. The same sort of analysis, however, also makes it clear that church teaching on these matters emerged as theologians grappled with concrete issues of Christian faith and practice. As such, they can most profitably be analyzed by focusing first of all on the theological "work" they were intended to do rather than on the exegesis or metaphysical presuppositions with which particular expressions of the doctrines may be bound up. While these latter questions certainly cannot be ignored in evaluating the place of the fall and original sin in church teaching, they are secondary to a more fundamental appreciation of the beliefs they were designed to preclude and the basic principles and convictions they were used to secure.

## The Emergence of the Doctrine

Stated summarily, the Western (or Augustinian) doctrines of the fall and original sin affirm (1) that Adam and Eve's violation of God's primordial commandment against eating from the tree of the knowledge of good and evil (Gen. 2:16–17; 3:6) caused a fundamental deformation in humanity's relationship to God, each other, and the rest of creation; and (2) that this "fall" includes among its consequences that all human beings thereafter are born into a state of estrangement from God – an "original" sin that

---

*In Adam's Fall: A Meditation on the Christian Doctrine of Original Sin*, by Ian A. McFarland.
© 2010 Ian A. McFarland.

condemns all individuals prior to and apart from their committing any "actual" sins in time and space.[1] In what remains the most exhaustive treatment in English of the history of Christian reflection on these doctrines, N. P. Williams addresses the question of internal logic by arguing that in its origin and development, "the Fall-doctrine is fundamentally an exercise in theodicy-making."[2] In other words, identifying the ultimate source of evil in the world with an act of creaturely transgression served as a means of defending the Creator against the charges of wickedness or incompetence.[3] Although the narrative in Genesis 3 represented only one possible resource for developing such a theodicy,[4] Williams shows that it had gained a solid foothold in Jewish thinking about the origin of evil by the first century.[5] Yet while the idea of the fall thus took root quite early, the emergence of the idea of original sin – that the *fact* of Adam and Eve's sinfulness and not merely its *consequences* extended to all their descendants – was much less straightforward. For example, the first-century Jewish text *4 Ezra* explicitly rejects the notion that Adam's fall in any way determines subsequent human action.[6] Nevertheless, earlier developments within Judaism do give some context to Paul's appropriation of the story of Adam in passages like Rom. 5:12–21 and 1 Cor. 15:2–22, which became the basis for the specifically Christian doctrines of the fall and original sin.[7]

The degree to which the later Christian teaching on the effects of Adam's transgression reflects an accurate exegesis of Paul remains hotly contested. More significant for Williams's thesis about the way in which the development of these doctrines was bound up with questions of theodicy, however, is the almost complete absence of any reference to Adam in the Christian literature that survives from the century after Paul's death.[8] It was only in the latter half of the second century (specifically, in the writings of Justin Martyr, Tatian, and Theophilus of Antioch) that the Paradise story re-emerged as an object of theological reflection. Though Williams attributes this sudden resurgence of interest in the figure of Adam partly to the increase in the authority of Paul that accompanied the consolidation of the New Testament canon, he surmises that the reason for attention to Paul's treatment of Adam in particular (as opposed to, say, his teaching on justification) was the theological challenge posed by Gnostic Christians.[9]

The term "Gnosticism" is traditionally used to cover a wide range of movements within early Christian history,[10] but the various groups identified (both by their opponents and, at least in some cases, by themselves) as "Gnostics" do seem to have shared a theodicy rooted in the ontologization of evil as intrinsic to the material order. For Gnostics, matter, in stark contrast to the unvarying perfection of spirit, is subject to change and decay, so that sickness, pain, and death are inevitable corollaries of material existence. It follows that the experience of evil is to some extent the responsibility of the God of Genesis 1, who deliberately formed the world of space and time.[11] Over against this perspective, theologians like Theophilus and Irenaeus of Lyons denied that evil was a necessary concomitant of materiality and cited the story of Adam in explanation of its origin.[12] In affirming the essential goodness of the material world, they defended God's power and righteousness as that world's Creator.[13] Evil was not to be understood as a reality either eternally within or alongside God, but rather as the product of creaturely rebellion against God and, as such, fundamentally contingent.[14]

These same basic principles underlie Christian reflection on Genesis 3 up to the end of the fourth century, albeit with considerable variation in opinion regarding the character of the fall, its effects, and their mode of transmission to subsequent generations.[15] This high level of variation is not surprising given the largely ad hoc character of reflection on the fall in this period. As is the case in the writings of Irenaeus (and, for that matter, Paul), references to Adam and his sin tend to be relatively brief and occasional rather than matters of sustained systematic analysis, often making it difficult to reconstruct the exact perspective of any given theologian with confidence, let alone to identify a "doctrine" held by Christians more broadly. Even Tertullian's *On the Soul*, which arguably provides the most coherent account of the effects of Adam's sin in this period, falls far short of a developed doctrine in the Augustinian sense.[16] Its primary focus is the refutation of pagan philosophical and heretical Christian ("Gnostic") views that divide the soul from the body. Tertullian's theory of the biological transmission of sin is introduced only late in the treatise, as a corollary of his belief in the inseparability of soul and body.[17] Moreover, even his strong emphasis on resulting depravity of human nature does not amount either to the denial of human freedom or to the doctrine of congenital guilt characteristic of later, Augustinian theology.[18]

In summary, the basic theological framework common to Christian theologians reading the Genesis narrative in the pre-Augustinian period included two very general convictions: first, that Adam's disobedience represented the historic occasion for the entrance of sin and death into the world,[19] and, second, that the effects of this primordial sin on subsequent generations of human beings can only be overcome through the redemptive work of Christ.[20] As noted in the preceding paragraphs, this move seems to have been motivated chiefly by resistance to Gnostic Christian and pagan philosophical schemes that traced evil to God or matter. At the same time, opposition to the perceived fatalism of these same schemes caused theologians to place great stress on human beings' capacity to avoid sin. This deep-seated belief in human freedom stood in implicit tension with the determinism of the Adamic theory of the fall, with the result that Christians' answers to the following three questions remained in considerable flux throughout the pre-Augustinian period: (1) the degree to which the Paradise story was to be interpreted literally; (2) whether the sin described there directly implicates later generations of human beings; and (3) the effect of that sin on the freedom of post-Adamic humanity. The significance of Augustine for Christian reflection on Adam's transgression can be gauged in part by the fact that his way of addressing these three issues (which, for ease of reference, I will refer to collectively as the "lapsarian questions") were as uncompromising as they remain controversial, thereby marking the transition from a loosely conceived, broadly ecumenical doctrine of the fall to a much more tightly formulated doctrine of original sin.

## The Augustinian Turn

A detailed analysis of Augustine's theology of original sin will be undertaken in the next chapter. For now it is sufficient simply to note how his thought decisively redirected Christian interpretation of the fall. This shift did not constitute a sharp break with established patterns of Christian reflection, for Augustine continued to use the doctrine in the service of theodicy: where his Pelagian opponents blanched at the idea that the newborn could be considered sinful, Augustine argued that the range and intensity of misery experienced by infants could only be squared with God's goodness if they are born guilty of sin.[21] As much as he used the fall to explain apparently unmerited suffering, however, he also argued that belief in human beings' congenital sinfulness is a necessary corollary of central Christian convictions regarding salvation: for Augustine, human beings' need of a Savior could only be consistently maintained on the supposition of their absolute captivity to the power of sin. This soteriological orientation marked a new turn in Christian reflection on the fall, in which "original sin" refers not only historically to the first sin committed by Adam and Eve (which continues to be its primary sense in Orthodox theologies), but also ontologically to the congenital sinfulness of all subsequent generations of human beings as caused by that first sin.[22] With this turn the doctrine of the fall is opened to a new dogmatic function: in addition to being used to explain why human beings suffer evil, it can be deployed to highlight their dependence on God to save them from this suffering.

The eventual triumph of Augustine's views in the West (where they were not received without objection either during his life or in the centuries immediately following his death) was bound up with this soteriological orientation. As Augustine saw matters, the human condition entailed that the three lapsarian questions listed at the end of the previous section be answered as follows: (1) Genesis 2–3 is to be read literally, as referring to actual historical events; (2) the fall described there so corrupted human nature as to render human beings congenitally guilty before God; and (3) it thereby also destroyed human beings' ability to refrain from sin by their own efforts, apart from the gift of grace.[23] No theologian prior to Augustine had addressed these issues in such stark terms: most shied away from a strictly literalistic reading of the Paradise story,[24] few spoke in terms compatible with the idea of an "original guilt,"[25] and none saw the fall as entailing a fundamental abrogation of human freedom to avoid sin. Indeed, Augustine's denial of humanity's capacity to avoid sin challenged a virtual consensus among theologians of the first four centuries, who saw human beings' freedom to choose good over evil as one of the features that most clearly distinguished Christian faith from pagan and Gnostic thought.[26]

The soteriological ground of Augustine's stance on all these points can be summarized in the principle that to qualify the depth of human sinfulness is to qualify the glory and goodness of what God accomplishes in saving human beings from the power of sin. Augustine does not emphasize human depravity for its own sake, out of some sort of theological misanthropy, but as a corollary of the good news of the gospel: that salvation is entirely a matter of grace rather than a product of human effort (Eph. 2:8). To put this in terms of probably the most contentious aspect of Augustine's teaching, if newborn infants are not guilty of sin, then the gospel doesn't apply to them. And if it doesn't apply to infants, then it is hard to see on what basis it can be assumed to apply to all persons of other ages and conditions. In short, if the good news is that *Jesus* saves, and this news is truly *for all* (Luke 2:10–11; cf. Acts 2:39), then it follows that all human beings without distinction *need* saving. For Augustine the doctrine of original sin is vital because it secures this point.

Augustine's answers to the three lapsarian questions are shaped by this soteriological orientation. If all human beings need saving from sin, and Jesus is the sole agent of salvation, then it follows that human beings are unable at any point to refrain from sin by their own efforts (question 3). And if this inability is truly characteristic of all human beings, then it must be congenital rather than acquired (question 2). At this point the issue of theodicy looms, since the claim that all human beings are congenitally sinful would seem to imply that God is the author of sin. Because Augustine shares the traditional Christian belief in the absolute and inviolable goodness of God, he rejects this conclusion and insists that human sin is the product of human rather than divine willing. Yet because the idea of congenital sinfulness means that all human beings after Adam are sinners even before they make use of their wills, Augustine finds himself able to account for the universality of human sin only on the supposition that Adam's willing of the first sin somehow implicates the wills of all his descendants in that sin. For this reason he defends a literal interpretation of Genesis 3 as an accurate historical report of sin's origin (question 1).

Augustine himself had no consistent theory as to how Adam's sin comes to be applied to subsequent generations of human beings,[27] and theologians influenced by him have come up with a range of theories.[28] As this very lack of consensus on the mechanism of sin's transmission suggests, however, the idea that Adam's sin so affects all other human beings that they not only suffer its disastrous effects (e.g., expulsion from Paradise, mortality, subjection to the passions, etc.), but also are somehow guilty of it remains the neuralgic point of the Western doctrine of original sin. Its problematic character reflects its status as the place where the soteriological framework that marks the distinctively "Augustinian turn" in Christian thinking about the fall intersects with its earlier orientation to questions of theodicy: soteriologically, the claim that human beings are saved by grace alone means that they must be born sinners; but theodicy demands that this principle of congenital sinfulness be interpreted as a matter of congenital human fault, lest anyone be tempted to accuse God of incompetence or malice in the creation of human beings.

This intersection creates difficulties that were not present in earlier theologies, and which remain largely absent in later Orthodox theologies little influenced by Augustine. Within these non-Augustinian frameworks it remains conceptually possible to view all fault as personal (i.e., as a matter of individuals' *actual* sin), even if it is conceded that human beings are in practice predisposed to sin by virtue of the psycho-physiological effects of the first sin of Adam on human nature.[29] As a result, the fall functions theodically to explain how, owing to humanity's primordial disobedience, the conditions arose within which sin has become pervasive, but it does *not* explain why individual human beings are sinners. Individual sinfulness, however much its likelihood may be increased as the result of the fall, remains a product of individual willing; consequently, the fact of human sin does not pose an immediate challenge to God's goodness.[30] By contrast, Augustine's soteriologically motivated emphasis on humanity's total bondage to sin ratchets up the tension considerably by rendering sin intrinsic to postlapsarian human nature. The fall no longer simply accounts for the environment within which human beings are more or less presupposed to commit actual sins. Although it retains that function, it now also serves to justify the claim that all human beings are sinners apart from any actual sin they commit. The resulting extension of the semantic range of the term "sin" to include not only particular *acts* that contravene God's will, but also a congenital *state* of opposition to God raises the specter of a God who makes creatures that are intrinsically evil, since they are guilty from conception and can thereafter only sin.

In summary, in the context of developing the dogmatic principle (derived from the confession that Jesus is humanity's sole Savior) that all human beings are sinners in need of salvation, an Augustinian theology needs to defend three claims regarding the fall and its effects: (1) an *ontological* claim affirming the solidarity of all subsequent generations of human beings with the first human being *in* sin, (2) a *psychological* claim that postlapsarian humanity suffers from a congenital bondage of the will *to* sin, and (3) a *moral* claim that all postlapsarian human activity unaided by grace *is* sin. If the primary motivation behind the Augustinian turn in Christian reflection on the fall is soteriological, each of these corollaries amplifies the questions of theodicy that earlier Christian theologies of the fall were intended to help resolve. Is it just of God to ascribe Adam's sin indiscriminately to all of his descendants? Or to condemn human beings for sin that they are constitutionally unable to avoid? Or to view all deeds human beings perform by their own power as equally damnable? The theological challenges posed by these questions were already the focus of opposition to Augustine during his lifetime, and they continue to set the agenda for criticism of his doctrine of original sin. Even those sympathetic to Augustine have recognized their seriousness, and some have tried to retain Augustine's soteriological emphasis on the decisive role of grace in salvation (and, with it, on universal human sinfulness) without resorting to these problematic corollaries. Before venturing a defense of Augustine, therefore, it is worth taking some time to assess whether these efforts to modify him by dispensing with these problematic aspects of his thought might save us the trouble.

## Augustinian Revisions

In the previous chapter we reviewed three contemporary proposals for recovering the category of sin in general for the present day. Each of the three attempts to revise Augustine's doctrine of original sin that we will now explore has a certain correspondence with one of those approaches. Like the "responsibility model" examined earlier, the model of original sin as lack assumes an ongoing integrity to human capacities that suggests a certain lingering ability to pursue the good and resist sin even after the fall. The model of original sin as context shares with the "participation model" an emphasis on sin as an external power that constrains and perverts human action. Finally, the attempt to conceive of original sin in existential terms shares with the "tragic model" of sin in general a belief that the fact of sin is bound up with the fundamental characteristics of finite existence. Each of these approaches arises from a position of fundamental sympathy with Augustine, but their attempts to mitigate Augustine's convictions regarding human solidarity in sin, the bondage of the will to sin, and the status of all human activity as sin results in a conception of original sin that compromises either its sinful character or its status as "original."

## Original sin as lack

The Catholic doctrine of original sin clearly displays its Augustinian roots in the magisterium's insistence on the soteriological framework within which the doctrine is properly located:

> The doctrine of original sin is, so to speak, the "reverse side" of the Good News that Jesus is the Savior of all men, that all need salvation and that salvation is offered to all through Christ. The Church, which has the mind of Christ, knows very well that we cannot tamper with the revelation of original sin without undermining the mystery of Christ.[31]

Along the same lines, it is taught that sin can genuinely be known only through revelation: since sin is fundamentally a rejection of God, knowledge of sin presupposes knowledge of God. Where this specifically theological understanding of sin is absent, sin is all too easily confused with forms of human wrongdoing that can be explained in terms of some combination of error, weakness, immaturity, or the influence of social structures that both diminishes the individual's personal responsibility for sin and at the same time undermines sin's universality by interpreting it as the product of factors that might in principle be avoided or overcome.[32]

Yet this fundamentally Augustinian framework is developed in a way that, while seeking to maintain original sin's universality, nevertheless modifies the idea that postlapsarian humanity sins necessarily and is, correspondingly, born in a condition of estrangement from God. For in Catholic theology, beginning in the medieval period, original sin is defined in terms of lack. Fundamentally, it is a loss or absence: "a deprivation of original holiness and justice" the effect of which is that humanity "is wounded in the natural powers proper to it, subject to ignorance, suffering and the dominion of death, and inclined to sin" – but not in such a way that human nature is "totally corrupted."[33] In other words, according to this account (which can be traced to Anselm but receives more fulsome development in Aquinas), original sin lies in humanity's loss of an initial gift of God – original justice or righteousness – that served to block or restrain inappropriate movements of the soul and thereby secured its proper submission to God.[34] While the privation of this original gift certainly has as one of its effects a deep-seated inclination to sin, the (negative) definition of original sin as privation implies that it is not in its essence a matter of (positive) resistance to God.[35]

The logic behind this construal of original sin is clear and in many respects compelling. After all, if the harmony at the root of original justice entails the soul's submission to God, then it must be a supernatural gift, since God's transcendence means that human beings can know God's will only as God reveals it to them, and thus by grace. At the same time, an implication of this understanding of original sin is that it simply amounts to humanity's existing according to its natural capacities and thus does not constitute a fundamental distortion of human nature.[36] To be sure, even on such a reading it remains possible to speak (as the Catholic *Catechism* does) of postlapsarian human nature being "wounded in the natural powers proper to it," since what is "proper" to human nature is determined by God's intentions for it, which Adam's disobedience has undermined.[37] Nevertheless, from this perspective genuine resistance to God is more naturally viewed as a consequence of original sin than as its content.

A further implication of this way of understanding original sin is that, while all human beings are born sinners, this does not entail that people sin always and necessarily apart from grace. This claim was explicitly anathematized at the Council of Trent,[38] and it is consistent with the claim that original sin wounds nature, since to be wounded is not to have a power taken away, but only to have it diminished. In line with this perspective, it is a noteworthy feature of Catholic teaching that original sin is not sin in the proper sense, but only analogically. At one level this affirmation can be seen as simply a means of characterizing the fact that for postlapsarian humanity original sin is "contracted" rather than "committed."[39] At another, however, it tends to lend weight to the conclusion that original sin is not really sin at all, for although it is rightly described as an inclination or disposition to evil,[40] it is not evil in itself.[41] The upshot of this position is the teaching that original sin does not cancel freedom of the will.[42] For this reason, while Catholic teaching is absolutely unambiguous in its (Augustinian) insistence that human beings are unable to save themselves from the power of sin, it combines this with the suggestions (1) that human beings are not truly sinful (i.e., genuinely turned from God) until they exercise their wills in particular deeds that mark the transition from original to actual sin, and (2) that they therefore retain some intrinsic capacity to resist (if not overcome or cancel) the power of original sin.[43]

This interpretation of original sin is clearly intended to address the theodical concerns raised by Augustine's theology. The characterization of original sin as a lack or privation helps to deflect threats to God's goodness by mitigating the extent to which original sin is viewed as sin, since a natural defect is by definition something other than an act of resistance meriting punishment; because original sin is contracted rather than committed (i.e., a state rather than an act), it cannot be understood as a "personal fault."[44] A corollary of this perspective within traditional Catholic theology is the idea of limbo (or, more properly, the *limbus infantium*) as a place reserved for infants who die unbaptized. Conventionally described as a place of natural (as opposed to supernatural) blessedness, limbo is distinct from the state of glory that is the destiny of the faithful baptized but also from the punishment of the damned – among whom Augustine explicitly included newborn children who died unbaptized.[45] Though limbo has no official dogmatic status in Catholicism and is not even mentioned in the text of the current *Catechism of the Catholic Church* (which argues that the full salvation of infants who die unbaptized is an appropriate object of Christian hope[46]), its presence in the tradition is suggestive of the way in which questions of theodicy – in this case, the specter of God damning the newborn – can lead to a subtle but real modification of the soteriological thrust of Augustinian doctrine of original sin. Where original sin is conceived as a lack or loss that affects postlapsarian human nature, it may remain true that all people need saving, but it is hard to avoid the impression that some people need it more than others.[47] Yet the idea that there are different degrees of deviation from God's will – so that those who commit actual sin acquire a level of (punishable) guilt that those afflicted only by original sin do not – undermines the Augustinian principle that all people stand equally in need of Christ.[48] Still more seriously, if original sin is not itself genuine sin (viz., active resistance to God that merits condemnation), then it is hard to see how the various actual sins that it generates can be counted as genuine either, since the congenital condition of debility under which they are committed would appear to constitute a mitigating circumstance of the highest order.[49] In short, the theodically driven attempt to qualify the confession that all human beings are sinners in need of salvation risks undermining it altogether.

### Original sin as social context

Theologians in the Reformed tradition differed sharply from Catholics, in that they viewed original sin as an active resistance to God that evoked a no less active condemnation of human beings by God.[50] At the same time, the status of unbaptized infants did not raise questions of theodicy for them, since their doctrines of election and the sacraments meant that God's eternal decision to save a person did not depend on the temporal performance of a particular rite – not even one as central to Christian life as baptism.[51] By the nineteenth century, however, many Reformed thinkers found the doctrine of original sin problematic on other grounds, not least of which was what appeared to be an unrealistic individualism that failed to take account of the ways in which human action was shaped by the broader social, cultural, and historical context within which human actors are located. From this perspective, the classical doctrine of original sin needed modification so as to bring it in line with the basic contours of human experience, including especially the psychosocial dynamics of individual growth and maturation. Attention to these matters came to be (and has been ever since) a defining feature of liberal theology, exemplified in the work of the universally acknowledged father of theological liberalism, Friedrich Schleiermacher.[52]

In line with the modern era's focus on the subject as the starting point for human knowledge and his own emphasis that human encounter with God comes indirectly, as a self-consciousness that one's status as a free agent presupposes a relationship of "absolute dependence" (*schlechthinige Abhängigkeit*) on a transcendent power, Schleiermacher defines sin in general as a painful determination of one's self-consciousness that is best interpreted as "a positive antagonism of the flesh against the spirit."[53] Despite this seemingly rather subjective understanding of sin,[54] Schleiermacher stands very much within the Augustinian tradition, for which the Christian's knowledge of sin in general and original sin in particular are experientially inseparable from the individual's experience of redemption in Christ. Thus, he is careful to state that "the first consciousness of sin" follows from "the accession of God-consciousness" and is therefore intimately bound up with "the first presentiment of redemption."[55]

Interestingly, it is precisely on the basis of this Augustinian framework, according to which original sin is bound up with the consciousness of the universal need for salvation, that Schleiermacher defends his own proposed modification to the doctrine, according to which it is understood as a function of the social context within which human beings act rather than as the result of an ontological defect intrinsic to post-Adamic human nature. As he puts it,

> What appears as the congenital sinfulness of one generation is conditioned by the sinfulness of the previous one, and in turn conditions that of the later; and only in the whole series of forms thus assumed, as all connected with the progressive development of man, do we find the whole aspect of things denoted by the term, "original sin."[56]

The upshot of this approach is an insistence that the guilt of original sin is not to be understood as an individual defect, but rather as a corruption common to the whole human race. In other words (and contrary to traditional Augustinian accounts, both Protestant and Catholic), the claim that humankind as a whole is infected by original sin is not to be understood simply as a function of the individual sinfulness of all human beings; rather, original sin pertains properly to the species, such that individuals may be said to be guilty of original sin only because they ineluctably participate in the psychosocial unity of the human race. Using this framework, Schleiermacher need not trouble with the varied speculations within the Augustinian tradition about how original sin is passed automatically from parents to their children; for him "it is transmitted by the voluntary actions of every individual to others and [thereby] implanted within them."[57] In short, we are all sinners because we are surrounded by sin.

One consequence of this move is a radical dehistoricizing of the fall. Schleiermacher argues for this in several ways. Most basically, he asserts that it would have been unjust of God to have made "the destiny of the whole human race contingent upon a single moment, the fortunes of which rested on two inexperienced individuals, who, moreover, never dreamt of its having any such importance."[58] A more complex argument revolves around the logical difficulties associated with postulating a change in nature consequent upon an individual person's decision:

> ... if the nature corrupted in consequence of [the first sin] was good, the person cannot have been good, for good cannot corrupt good; but if the nature was already bad, its corruption cannot have been brought about by the action of the person. Similarly on the other alternative: if [at the time the first sin was committed] the person no longer was good (since in corrupting the nature it acted wrongly), while the nature was good still (since it required to be corrupted), then all wrong action on the part of all later individuals must be explicable apart from the hypothesis that their nature had to be corrupted beforehand.[59]

In light of this conundrum, Schleiermacher rejects the idea that the first human beings before the fall existed in a different state than their descendants afterwards. He does attempt to retain the principle that their action set loose the course of sin in human history, but only by being the historically first instance of a psychosocial pattern that is repeated in every subsequent generation rather than by their having somehow transformed human nature. Thus, he traces the corruption of all human beings to the way in which individual human actions are shaped by the character of all other human actions that surround and precede them:

> ... in the [traditional] doctrine of the Church the first sin of the first man, and that only, is called "originating original sin," and the sinful constitution of all other men "originated original sin" – the bent and inward disposition thus bearing the name of sin equally with the act itself; but we transfer this [distinction between originating and originated original sin] to the relation between each earlier generation and the one immediately succeeding it, and maintain that the actual sin of the earlier is always the originating original sin for the later, while the sinfulness of the later generation, since it produces the actual sins thereof, is also original sin, while yet as dependent upon the sin of the earlier it is originated, and thus originated original sin as well.[60]

In short, rather than positing a psychologically unique, primordial transgression that changes human nature so as to render all later human beings congenitally sinful, Schleiermacher interprets the dynamics of human sinfulness as constant across time: every generation's sin is both determined by the previous generation and, in turn, itself determines the sinfulness of the generation that follows. Importantly, Schleiermacher wishes to maintain a basically Augustinian stance over against the Pelagian view that the only way sin can be said to be "transmitted" from one generation to the other is by the free decisions of those who come later to copy the faults of their elders. Therefore, he insists that this process is not reducible to the mere imitation of bad examples from previous generations. It involves rather a genuine and continuous deformation of the psychodynamics of human decision making, such that (in good Augustinian fashion) human beings operating within a psychosocial context of sin cannot help but sin, even though they sin willingly. The modification of the Augustinian tradition lies in the fact that for Schleiermacher the context of sin is not ontological (i.e., the product of some structural feature of the individual postlapsarian human being), and thus internal to the individual human being as such, but social, and thus an effect of the individual's multiple relationships to other human beings, past and present. In short, original sin is "common to all; not as something that pertains severally to each individual and exists in relation to him by himself, but in each the work of all, and in all the work of each."[61]

While Schleiermacher's argument is ingenious, it, too, is arguably unable to retain the full dogmatic force of Augustine's insistence on universal human sinfulness. If the Catholic interpretation of original sin as privation makes its status as sin doubtful, Schleiermacher's corporate understanding of the concept succeeds in preserving original sin's status as genuine sin at the price of making it much more difficult to see how it can be ascribed to an individual human being as his or her own.[62] Schleiermacher is inclined to see this implication of his account as a theological gain, since to view original sin as a matter of individual guilt makes the avoidance of punishment the stimulus of faith in a way that obscures the priority of the Christian's experience of Christ as both the ground of knowledge of sin and the chief motivation for resisting its temptations.[63] Yet if original sin is not finally ascribed to me as my personal resistance to God (rather than defined as a set of environmental circumstances that effectively mitigates my capacity to do otherwise) then it remains unclear to what extent I (rather than my environment) am in need of redemption.[64] In this way, a corporate understanding of original sin has as its inevitable corollary a corporate understanding of salvation that undermines the message of the gospel as God's yearning for and gracious transformation of the individual heart and mind.

### Original sin as existential inevitability

If Schleiermacher thought that original sin was only explicable as a matter of collective consciousness, according to our third modification the doctrine is to be understood very much in terms of the individual. Thus, while in this case, too, the fall is dehistoricized, this is understood in a way quite different from Schleiermacher's model, according to which each person falls because she is made to fall by the cumulative effect of others' actions. According to the third model each person falls because she makes herself to fall: existentially stretched between two poles that define the internal psychological structure of human existence, every individual inevitably "snaps" in the direction of sin. The fall remains free, and is undertaken freely by every human being in his or her own right; but it is rooted in the fundamental structure of human existence in the world.

Developed initially by Søren Kierkegaard in the mid-nineteenth century,[65] this modification of the Augustinian tradition became especially influential in the English-speaking (especially North American) world through the writings of the twentieth-century theologian Reinhold Niebuhr.[66] Human beings, it is argued, are both finite and free. As finite, they are inherently limited, being bounded by space and time and therefore constrained in the forms of existence that they are able to realize. This finitude is common to all creatures, but it is complicated for human beings by their experience of freedom, which opens them to possibilities beyond the actuality of their finite state.[67] The juxtaposition of finitude and freedom creates tension, and this tension is the existential matrix within which sin arises:

> The temptation to sin lies ... in the human situation itself. This situation is that man as spirit transcends the temporal and natural processes in which he is involved and also transcends himself. Thus his freedom is the basis of his temptation. Since he is involved in the contingencies and necessities of natural processes on the one hand and since, on the other, he stands outside of them and foresees their caprices and perils, he is anxious. In his anxiety he seeks to transmute his finiteness into infinity, his weakness into strength, his dependence into independence.[68]

The experience of freedom in the context of finitude is experienced by human beings as anxiety and invariably plays out in the futile attempt to deny that finitude.[69] Neither fear nor worry (both of which are characterized by focus on a definite object), anxiety is diffuse and ambiguous. Nor, crucially, is it rightly characterized as the *cause* of sin in a way that would lessen the guilt of the individual sinner: the move from anxiety to guilt is inevitable, but it remains free.

In short, in this existential perspective "actual sin is the consequence of the temptation of anxiety in which all life stands. But anxiety itself is neither actual nor original sin. Sin does not flow necessarily from it."[70] Indeed, far from being itself sinful, the juxtaposition of freedom and finitude does not even constitute a temptation to sin except for the person whose heart is already infected with sin.[71] This is a crucial point, since to argue otherwise would be to indict human nature as defective at best and sinful at worst, thereby undermining Christian belief in the inherent goodness of creation. Further, it would undermine belief in human freedom by rendering actual sin a natural consequence of human ontology. In direct contrast to any such claim, Niebuhr tries to argue that the inevitability of human sin actually reveals human freedom:

> The ultimate proof of the freedom of the human spirit is its own recognition that it is not free to choose between good and evil. For in the highest reaches of the freedom of the spirit, the self discovers in contemplation and retrospect that previous actions have invariably confused the ultimate reality and value, which the self as spirit senses, with the immediate needs of the self. If the self assumes that because it realizes this fact in past actions it will be able to avoid the corruption in future actions, it will merely fall prey to the Pharisaic fallacy.[72]

In other words, human freedom is experienced not in the ability to choose good over evil, but precisely in the recognition that one is responsible for one's actions in spite of (and thus in) one's inability to make such a choice. Paradoxically, the very capacity for self-transcendence that is for Niebuhr the essence of human freedom discloses humanity's constitutional *incapacity* to avoid sin.[73]

It is precisely this paradox, however, that discloses the way in which Niebuhr's approach winds up subverting the more significant paradox at the heart of the Augustinian tradition. The freedom that allows the individual diagnosis of his or her sin effectively suggests a realm of human being that is not infected by it. To be sure (and as the quotation just cited shows), Niebuhr is emphatic that the knowledge of sinfulness that human freedom enables does not in any sense include a capacity to eliminate sin from one's future actions. At the same time, he argues that human beings' capacity to recognize their own sin (as evidenced by the phenomenon of the uneasy conscience, for example) constitutes an unequivocal refutation of the idea of total depravity.[74] Inasmuch as the fall is for Niebuhr (as well as Kierkegaard) proper to the experience of every human being rather than a unique event at the beginning of human history,[75] the perfection in which humanity was created is not located in the primordial past of the species, but in the state of every human being prior to action.[76] It is in the move to action that sin invariably occurs. Thus, Niebuhr is with Augustine in affirming that everything human beings do is sin; but he departs from Augustine in insisting on a reserve that stands over against this sinfulness and which he identifies precisely with human freedom.

Of course, Niebuhr is careful to argue that the same freedom by virtue of which human beings are able to gain some knowledge of their sin is that which makes sin possible in the first place. This is part of the paradox of freedom.[77] Nevertheless, the upshot of his anthropology is to posit a permanent, if elusive and (with respect to the ability to avoid sin) ineffectual, dimension of every human being that, by virtue of its capacity to recognize and condemn one's own sin, stands over against that sin. In order to avoid the suggestion that this capacity renders human beings capable of saving themselves, Niebuhr is careful to distinguish what he calls the consciousness or memory of original perfection that arises in moments of self-reflection from the possession of such perfection.[78] Though for Niebuhr original perfection is presupposed in every action, we encounter it *only* as a memory, as that which has been lost in our action and which we are thus not able to deploy as a means of guaranteeing the sanctity of any of our future actions. Yet even if we do not have access to this perfection as a power we can bring to bear to prevent our sin, it nevertheless evidently exists as something by which we are able – apart from grace – to distinguish ourselves from our sin. To that extent (and in line with Niebuhr's denial of total depravity) it is hard to see how the conclusion can be avoided that it constitutes some element of our being that does not stand in need of redemption. Certainly, it is difficult to understand how it can be the case that human beings are congenitally sinful on Niebuhr's view, since sin is something that (in direct contrast to Augustine's teaching) is present only in act. Of course, Niebuhr is thereby able to avoid the problems of theodicy that arise in connection with the idea of inherited guilt.[79] Once again, however, the price paid for addressing this problem is a compromise of the soteriological insight behind the Augustinian turn: if human beings have any sort of purchase on sin that is not dependent on the work of Christ, then Christ is not humanity's sole Savior.

## Assessment

This chapter has argued that two theological trajectories have shaped the Western doctrines of the fall and original sin. The first, stretching back to the earliest periods of Christian theological reflection, is centered on theodicy. It focuses on the fall as a historical event that explains why human beings suffer: although the creation is intrinsically good, the actions of the first human beings disrupted it and let loose the forces of sin and death in the world. The second, developed by Augustine, is defined by soteriological concerns. It focuses on original sin as a present condition that afflicts all human beings: the proclamation of Christ as sole Savior presupposes that all human beings stand under a threat of damnation from which they need to be saved. This second thread is not rooted in a masochistic and/or sadistic enthusiasm for belittling human beings; on the contrary, it arises from the conviction that God values human life so highly as to guarantee it indefeasibly with God's own life as given in Jesus Christ. It follows that the value of a person's life is subject to no qualification based on consideration of her individual merit. In short, what I have called the "Augustinian turn" in the doctrine of original sin is born of the conviction that our salvation is a gift of God in a way that frees us from having to assess our own (let alone others') worthiness or unworthiness.

But Augustine did not simply develop this second thread independently of the first. Because he, too, was concerned with theodicy, he linked them together, arguing that original sin is the punishment justly inflicted on all humankind for Adam's primordial transgression. In line with the established Christian consensus, he was thereby able to deny that evil is a natural feature of the created order: as the consequence of willful human action, it was not the fault of God, who made all things good (cf. Gen. 1:31). Yet by virtue of the way in which he linked existing church teaching with his own soteriological interests, Augustine actually increased the theodical burden placed on the fall: since all merit eternal condemnation by virtue of their congenital resistance to God's will, no one has cause to complain that she or he suffers unjustly. In this way, for Augustine the fall not only creates the conditions under which human beings were more likely to commit sin and experience suffering, but also establishes a situation in which all human beings, by virtue of their congenital sinfulness, deserve to suffer.

Most contemporary rejections of original sin attack the doctrine because of these theodical corollaries. Far from vindicating the notion of a coherent moral order, it is argued, Augustine's teaching generates moral confusion by teaching that human beings are equally and intrinsically hateful to God, thereby undermining any basis for distinguishing different gradations of sin or for holding human beings morally accountable for sins that they cannot help but commit. The revisions to Augustine's doctrine examined above all attempt to modify him in the effort to address such concerns. They all reject the idea that original sin means that human beings are congenitally blameworthy and, therefore, fully deserving of whatever suffering comes their way. The problem is that in their attempts to modify Augustine's claim that human sin explains (and justifies) all human suffering, they propose alternatives in which, in one way or another, suffering (understood now as a given of finite existence) explains, even if it does not fully justify, sin. Humans sin because they lack original righteousness and thus are thrown back on their "natural" abilities alone, or because the character of their actions is ineluctably shaped by their external environment, or because they are unable to overcome the existential tension between their finitude and their freedom. Ironically, the result in each case is that threats to divine goodness and human freedom re-emerge in a different guise, since it is no longer sin alone (i.e., that which is utterly alien to God's intentions for creation) but the conditions of creaturely (i.e., finite) existence as such – conditions for which God is ultimately responsible and which human beings are evidently powerless to resist – from which human beings seemingly need to be redeemed.

In order to avoid these problems, the doctrine of original sin that developed in the rest of this book will eschew any attempt to explain the origins of human suffering – whether in sin or in some combination of ontological or environmental factors ontologically prior to sin – while retaining the full soteriological content of the Augustinian turn in hamartiology. In other words, I will maintain that all human beings resist God in a way that renders them objectively without hope apart from God's acting to turn their hearts to God through the free and unmerited gift of grace – but without suggesting that human beings' congenital sinfulness either illuminates or is illuminated by the fact of human suffering. It will thus be a central thesis of this book that the proper dogmatic function of original sin is limited to offering a *description of* rather than an *explanation for* the human condition apart from grace. As such, the doctrine is certainly consistent with the kind of anguished realization of one's own lostness apart from God as expressed by David in Psalm 51 and Paul in Romans 7; but (as Bonhoeffer recognized), it is misused when invoked either to promote or to diminish such anguish. Its proper role – precisely as a putatively orthodox Christian doctrine – should not be to focus attention on ourselves as good or bad, but on God. Consequently, it is not rightly used to argue from personal unworthiness to the individual's need for God, but rather to turn our attention to God as the One who in Christ has already addressed any such needs, in line with the prayer of Jehoshaphat: "We do not know what to do, but our eyes are upon you" (2 Chron. 20:12).

In short, original sin, in its proper sense as a reflex of the gospel of Jesus Christ, is rightly used to emphasize God's gracious response to human need and not to provide an etiological explanation for humanity's being in need. This is not to suggest that theodicy is a dispensable – let alone an illegitimate[80] – theological enterprise. The third part of this book will be largely occupied with the very real theodical challenges posed by Augustine's teaching, attempting to show how it is possible to reconcile God's justice with the claims that a sin may be common to the human species as a whole (the ontological claim), that individual human beings nevertheless sin willingly (the psychological claim), and that equal sinfulness does not preclude the individual's obligation to identify the particular forms of actual sin in which he or she participates (the moral claim). These efforts, however, are all merely clarifications of the internal logic of original sin, taken in its soteriological significance. In other words, their aim is to defend the doctrine's status as a self-consistent account of what is presupposed by the claim that Jesus is humanity's sole Savior. As such, they must be distinguished from every effort to ground original sin externally as either an explanation for or a consequence of the experience of human suffering. Here, too, it is necessary to hold firmly to the logic of the gospel by limiting the doctrine to an affirmation of humanity's need for salvation and resist the temptation to use it to rationalize or legitimize human suffering, which is no part of the good news.[81]

Clarifying the character of that need, however, remains decisive for a defense of original sin against the charges of incoherence that have plagued the doctrine since Augustine's day. What exactly does it mean to say that human beings "resist" God? If they do so freely, how is it that they are unable to do otherwise? And if they do so necessarily, how is it that they are sufficiently "free" to be judged responsible for that resistance? Can one appeal to a "fallen" nature as the source of the problem without undermining essential Christian convictions regarding both divine goodness and human freedom? The next three chapters will sketch an anthropological framework within which these questions can be addressed. They focus specifically on the will as the locus both of the agency through which human beings are called to relationship with God and of the sin whereby they turn from that relationship.

## Notes

1  A classic statement can be found in Article II of the Lutheran Augsburg Confession: "It is also taught among us that since the fall of Adam all men who are born according to the course of nature are conceived and born in

sin. That is, all men are full of evil lust and inclinations from their mothers' wombs and are unable by nature to have true fear of God and true faith in God. Moreover, this inborn sickness and hereditary sin is truly sin and condemns to the eternal wrath of God all those who are not born again through Baptism and the Holy Spirit." In *The Book of Concord: The Confessions of the Evangelical Lutheran Church*, ed. Theodore G. Tappert (Philadelphia, PA: Muhlenberg, 1959), p. 29. The clause specifying that original sin affects only those "born according to the course of nature" excludes Christ, whose virgin birth (as will be discussed in much greater detail in Chapter 5 below) was understood to render him immune from the contagion of original sin.

2  N. P. Williams, *The Ideas of the Fall and of Original Sin: A Historical and Critical Study* (London: Longmans, Green and Co., 1927), p. 265. Williams's conclusions contrast significantly with the earlier study of F. R. Tennant, *The Sources of the Doctrines of the Fall and Original Sin* (Cambridge: Cambridge University Press, 1903). Tennant is more inclined to see Augustine as the culmination of earlier developments, though he freely acknowledges that Augustine's doctrine (with which he personally had little sympathy) was but "one of the possible interpretations of the statements of S. Paul" (1); Williams, by contrast, sees Augustine's views as a "warping" of the "unruffled, uncorrupted thought of historic Christianity" (*Ideas*, pp. 170–1), though he concedes that it had antecedents in the thought of Tertullian, Origen, and others. For a more contemporary study that in the main follows Williams's assessment, see Elaine Pagels, *Adam, Eve, and the Serpent* (New York: Vintage, 1988), as well as the massive J. Gross, *Geschichte des Erbsündendogmas. Ein Beitrag zur Geschichte des Problems vom Ursprung des Übels*. 4 vols. (München: Ernst Reinhardt, 1960–72). Cf. also J. N. D. Kelly, *Early Christian Doctrines*, revised edn. (San Francisco, CA: Harper & Row, 1978), p. 349 and Tatha Wiley, *Original Sin: Origins, Developments, Contemporary Meanings* (New York: Paulist Press, 2002), pp. 5–6, 53.

3  Williams, *Ideas*, 35; cf. pp. 7–8. Cf. Paul Ricoeur's claim that "the etiological myth of Adam is the most extreme attempt to separate the origin of evil from the origin of the good; its intention is to set up a *radical* origin of evil distinct from the more *primordial* origin of the goodness of things." Paul Riceour, *The Symbolism of Evil* (Boston, MA: Beacon Press, 1967), p. 233.

4  Its chief competitor was the so-called "Watcher legend" of angelic seduction of human women found in Gen. 6:1–4 ("Watcher" was the technical term in Jewish apocalyptic literature for the beings described in Gen. 6:1; see 1 Enoch 6:6; 10:7–8). Williams (*Ideas*, pp. 19–28) suggests that the Watcher episode was ultimately eclipsed by the Paradise story owing to its incompatibility with the flood narrative, which would seem to imply the destruction of the Nephilim (though see *Jubilees* 7:26–39 for a later attempt to explain the Nephilim's survival, which is presupposed in biblical passages like Num. 13:33).

5  As evidence of the ascendancy of the Adamic narrative as the focus of Jewish reflection on the origin of evil in the later post-exilic period, Williams cites

Wis. 2:23–4; Ecclus. 25:24; *2 Enoch* 41 (cf. 30–2); *Apocalypse of Abraham* 23–4; *2 Baruch* 48:42; 54:15; 56:5–6; and *4 Ezra* 3:21–3; 4:30; 7:11–12, 116–18 – though he notes that the first suggestions of the doctrine of the "evil impulse" (*yeṣer ha-ra'*), which eventually replaced the idea of a primordial "fall" as the explanation for evil in rabbinic Judiasm, may also be traced to this period. See *Ideas*, pp. 52–64, 75–81.

6   See in particular *4 Ezra* 7:127–9, where the angel rejects Ezra's complaint that the results of Adam's sin extended to his descendants. See Michael Edward Stone, *Fourth Ezra: A Commentary on the Book of Fourth Ezra* (Minneapolis, MN: Fortress Press, 1990), p. 253.

7   Although the older Watcher account of the fall is presupposed in Jude 6 and 2 Pet. 1·4; 2·4, these texts had comparatively little influence on subsequent Christian teaching. For a contemporary review of the relationship between these two letters, as well as their dependence on those streams of Jewish apocalyptic in which the Watcher legend was preserved, see Steven J. Kraftchick, *Jude/2 Peter* (Nashville, TN: Abingdon Press, 2002).

8   The only exception noted by Williams is *Epistle of Barnabas* 12:5 (generally dated between 70 and 130), which refers in passing to "the transgression [*parabasis*] that happened in Eve through the serpent" (*Ideas*, pp. 171–2).

9   "… the inevitable effect of the pressure of Gnosticism upon the Church was to compel Christian thinkers to face the question of the ultimate origin of evil, and … to force them back upon a neglected element in St. Paul's teaching, namely, the doctrine of the Fall." Williams, *Ideas*, p. 184.

10  Needless to say, Williams's early twentieth-century account of the phenomenon is badly dated. For the current state of discussion, see, e.g., C. Markschies, *Gnosis: An Introduction* (Edinburgh: T&T Clark, 2003) and M. A. Williams, *Rethinking "Gnosticism": An Argument for Dismantling a Dubious Category* (Princeton, NJ: Princeton University Press, 1996).

11  Though Marcion argued from this ontological dualism that the God of the Old Testament was arbitrary and cruel, his relatively straightforward cosmology renders the overall structure of his thought rather different from that of the Gnostics. More typical of the latter is the perspective of Valentinus, who was inclined to see incompetence or ignorance rather than malice as the chief flaw of the Creator of the cosmos.

12  See Theophilus, *To Autolycus*, 2.24–6, in *Fathers of the Second Century*, vol. 2 of *Ante-Nicene Fathers*, American edn., ed. the Rev. Alexander Roberts and James Donaldson (Grand Rapids, MI: William B. Eerdmans, n.d.); and Irenaeus, *Against Heresies*, 3.18.7; 21.10; 5.23, in *The Apostolic Fathers with Justin Martyr and Irenaeus*, vol. 1 of *Ante-Nicene Fathers*, American edn., ed. the Rev. Alexander Roberts and James Donaldson (Grand Rapids, MI: William B. Eerdmans, n.d.). Note that here and throughout this book I have adopted the convention of using Arabic numerals only for referring to books, chapters, and sections of premodern texts.

13  In line with the logic of this position, Theophilus defined for the first time in the church the doctrine of creation from nothing (*ex nihilo*) as a means

of affirming the world's absolute dependence on God alone as the source of its being, thereby correlating the goodness of creation with the goodness of the Creator (*To Autolycus*, 2.10).

14   So Theophilus, *To Autolycus*, 2.17: "... nothing was made evil by God, but all things good, yea, very good – but the sin in which man was concerned brought evil upon them." Cf. Irenaeus, *Against Heresies* 4.39.2–3: "For creation is an attribute of the goodness of God ... If, however, thou wilt not believe in [God], and wilt flee from [God's] hands, the cause of imperfection shall be in thee who didst not obey, but not in [God] who called."

15   For example, this same focus on theodicy as the framework for reflection on the fall (though now in response to Manichean rather than Gnostic teaching) is found in Basil of Caesarea's homily "That God Is Not the Cause of Evils" (*PG* 31: 329–54); cited in Williams, *Ideas*, pp. 264–9.

16   While Origen's speculations in *On First Principles* include a theology of human fallenness no less focused than Tertullian's, it is not based on the Paradise story. Because Origen traces evil to a multiplicity of extra-temporal "falls" committed independently by the souls of angels, human beings and demons, rather than to a single historical event, reference to Adam is superfluous. See Origen, *De Principiis* 2.9, in *Fathers of the Third Century: Tertullian, Part Fourth; Minucius Felix; Commodian; Origen, Parts First and Second*, vol. 4 of *Ante-Nicene Fathers*, American edn., ed. the Rev. Alexander Roberts and James Donaldson (Grand Rapids, MI: William B. Eerdmans, n.d.). Williams goes on to argue that while Origen did gravitate toward a more literal reading of Genesis 3 later in his career, the effect was to render his understanding of the fall less coherent. See Williams, *Ideas*, pp. 226–30; but cf. Kelly (*Early Christian Doctrines*, pp. 181–2), who questions the idea that there was any fundamental shift in Origen's views over the course of his career.

17   Though Tertullian gives his most fulsome explanation of his traducian theory of the soul's biological transmission in chapter 27 of his *Treatise on the Soul*, the idea that every human soul is born sinful by virtue of its descent from Adam is not discussed until chapters 40 to 41 – and is promptly abandoned for a much more extensive eight-chapter analysis of dreams. See Tertullian, *A Treatise on the Soul*, in *Latin Christianity: Its Founder, Tertullian*, vol. 3 of *Ante-Nicene Fathers*, American edn., ed. the Rev. Alexander Roberts and James Donaldson (Grand Rapids, MI: William B. Eerdmans, nd.).

18   Thus, Tertullian rejects infant baptism – a practice Augustine would later correlate specifically with belief in original sin – with the words, "Why does the innocent period of life [*innocens aetas*] hasten to the remission of sins?" Tertullian, *On Baptism*, 18, in *Latin Christianity*. Cf. *A Treatise on the Soul*, 41: "Just as no soul is without sin, so neither is any soul without seeds of good."

19   Again, Origen's position in *On First Principles* constitutes a significant exception to this generalization; see note 16 above.

20   Kelly argues that in writers prior to Irenaeus Adam tends to be understood more as the prototype than as the cause of subsequent human sin; at the

same time he is inclined to see considerable convergence in the way in which both Greek and Latin theology subsequently came to understand the transmission of sinfulness from Adam to later generations. See *Early Christian Doctrines*, pp. 167–8 and 348–52 (contrast Williams, who draws a much sharper contrast between eastern "Hellenic" and western "African" theories in *Ideas*, pp. 246–9).

21  In his final writing Augustine presents the Pelagians the following theodical dilemma: "You are ... compelled to choose one of these three: either to fill Paradise with the punishments of human beings, or to say that God is unjust in the punishment of his images which the innocence of the little ones suffers, or, because these two are hateful and damnable, to acknowledge original sin." Augustine, *Unfinished Work in Answer to Julian*, 6.36 (cf. 3.77), in *Answer to the Pelagians*, vol. III, ed. John E. Rotelle (Hyde Park, NY: New City Press, 1999). Indeed, Phillip Cary argues that Augustine was initially driven to a doctrine of original sin (in his treatise *Ad Simplicianum*, which dates from around 396) by the need to account for the justice of God's rejection of Esau (Rom. 9:10–13; cf. Mal. 1:2–3). Phillip Cary, *Inner Grace: Augustine in the Traditions of Plato and Paul* (New York: Oxford University Press, 2008), p. 52.

22  Western Scholastic theologies would later draw a distinction between original sin as the originating sin (*peccatum originans*) committed by Adam, and as the sin thereby originated (*peccatum originatum*) that inheres in his descendants.

23  Cf. William Shedd's iteration of the three main components of the Augustinian doctrine of original sin: "1. The guilt of the first sin [as recorded in Genesis]. 2. The corruption of nature resulting from the first sin. 3. Actual transgressions ... which result from corruption of nature." William G. T. Shedd, *Dogmatic Theology*, 2 vols., 2nd edn. (New York: Charles Scribner's Sons, 1889), vol. 2, p. 169.

24  Augustine himself was far from doctrinaire on this point early in his career. In his early *On Genesis against the Manicheans* (388–9) he takes a basically allegorical approach that is consistent with traditional Christian strategies for explaining the evident naivety of the Old Testament narratives; and in the *Confessions* (397–8) he insists on hermeneutical flexibility: "See how stupid it is, among so large a mass of entirely correct interpretations which can be elicited from these words [of Genesis], rashly to assert that a particular one has the best claim to be Moses' view." *Confessions* 12.35 (Oxford: Oxford University Press, 1991), p. 265. While he never abandons the principle that Scripture can have multiple meanings, by the time he writes *The Literal Meaning of Genesis* (401–16) he thinks it important to affirm that the narrative of Genesis 2–3 in particular "is not cast in the figurative kind of language you find in the Song of Songs, but quite simply tells of things that happened, as in the books of the Kingdoms and others like them" precisely in opposition to those who "are not prepared to have Paradise understood literally and properly [*proprie*], but only figuratively [*figurate*]." *The Literal Meaning of*

*Genesis*, 8.2, 4, in Saint Augustine, *On Genesis*, ed. John E. Rotelle, O.S.A. (Hyde Park, NY: New City Press, 2002), pp. 346–7.

25 The phrase is Williams's (see *Ideas*, pp. 72–3). Some such conception does seem to be implicit in, e.g., Cyprian's Letter 58 ("To Fidus"), which refers to the baptism of infants as remitting not their own sins, but those of Adam. See p. 61 below.

26 See, e.g., Irenaeus of Lyons: "… all human beings are of the same nature, able both to hold fast and to do what is good; and, on the other hand, having also the power to cast it from them and not to do it" (*Against Heresies*, 4.37.2; translation slightly altered); and Gregory of Nyssa: "Thus there is in us the principle of all excellence, all virtue and wisdom, and every higher thing that we conceive: but pre-eminent among all is the fact that we are free from necessity, and not in bondage to any natural power, but have decision in our own power as we please …" *On the Making of Man*, 16.11, in Gregory of Nyssa, *Dogmatic Treatises, etc.*, vol. 5 of *Nicene and Post-Nicene Fathers*, 2nd Series, ed. Philip Schaff and Henry Wace (Peabody, MA: Hendrickson, 1995 [1893]).

27 See Chapter 5 below.

28 See Chapter 6 below for a review of some of the more significant proposals. It is worth noting that the tradition also includes conscious refusals to engage in any such theorizing. See, e.g., the 1559 *French Confession*, Article 10, in *Creeds and Confessions of the Reformation Era*, vol. 2 of *Creeds and Confessions of Faith in the Christian Tradition*, ed. Jaroslav Pelikan and Valerie Hotchkiss (New Haven, CT: Yale University Press, 2003), p. 378; cf. *The Catechism of the Catholic Church*, 2nd edn. (New York: Doubleday, 1997), §404.

29 The sixth decree of the Orthodox Synod of Jerusalem (1672) gives dogmatic definition to this point, teaching that while human beings inherit the *consequences* of Adam's sin, they are not *born* sinners (though it is important to add that the sixteenth decree of the same council nevertheless commends pedobaptism on the grounds that infants require the remission of original sin). For a contemporary interpretation of Orthodox doctrine, see Timothy Ware, *The Orthodox Church* (Harmondsworth: Penguin, 1963), pp. 227–30.

30 I do not in any way mean to imply that these non-Augustinian frameworks produce fully satisfying theodicies. Explaining suffering as a general consequence of sin leaves unanswered, for example, the question of why God allows certain persons to be afflicted with suffering on a horrendous scale while others of no greater apparent merit are spared – not to mention the question of why God should choose to create a world where suffering is possible in the first place. My only point is that the emphasis on human autonomy characteristic of non-Augustinian frameworks implies a certain ontological distance between God and human suffering that Augustine is unable to exploit (see, e.g., the way in which John of Damascus identifies the decisions of the human will as a limit to the reach of divine providence in *Exposition of the Orthodox Faith*, 2.29). Thus, within Augustine's framework sin is more than a generalized *explanation* for why suffering exists (i.e., its

more or less remote cause); it becomes an immediate *justification* for every single experience of it (i.e., every person's sinfulness means that whatever she suffers is deserved).
31 *Catechism*, §389; cf. §388, where John 16:7–11 is cited in support of the principle that the world is convicted of sin only with the revelation of its Redeemer.
32 See *Catechism*, §§386–7.
33 *Catechism*, §405; cf. §400, where original justice is defined as a state of "harmony" with God, nature, and one another in which human beings were originally created, and which was rooted in a proper order in relationships between faculties of the soul (especially reason and the passions). See also Council of Trent, "Decree Concerning Original Sin," §1, in *The Canons and Decrees of the Council of Trent*, ed. H. J. Schroeder, O.P. (Rockford, IL: TAN Books, 1978 [1941]), p. 21.
34 Thomas Aquinas, *Summa Theologiae* [hereafter *ST*], 1/2.82.1 and 3 (61 vols., Blackfriars edn. [London: Eyre & Spottiswood, 1964–81]); cf. *ST*, 1/2.81.2 (citing *ST*, 1.100.1): "original justice was a gift of grace, conferred by God on all human nature in our first parent. This gift the first man lost by his first sin."
35 To be sure, Aquinas is also quite happy to define original sin positively as concupiscence on the basis of Augustine, but this definition refers to original sin's *material* element, and thus derives from the privation of original justice, which is its logically prior *formal* element; see Aquinas, *ST*, 1/2.82.3.
36 Perhaps the most extreme formulation of this position is that of the Reformation-era Cardinal, Robert Bellarmine: "The state of man after Adam's fall does not differ much from his state in its natural purity, any more than a man stripped of his clothes differs from a nude … [for] the corruption of nature did not flow from the lack of some natural gift nor from the accession of some bad quality but only from a loss of the supernatural gift occasioned by Adam's sin." Robert Bellarmine, "De gratia primi hominis," in *Controversiis* 5; cited in Herman Bavinck, *Reformed Dogmatics*, 4 vols. (Grand Rapids: Baker Academic, 2003–), vol. 3, p. 97.
37 In this context, it is important to stress that recent Catholic theology (led by studies like Henri de Lubac's groundbreaking *The Mystery of the Supernatural*) has largely rejected the mode of distinguishing between nature and supernature characteristic of baroque Scholastic and Neoscholastic theologies, on the grounds that their concept of "pure nature," defined as a state with its own intrinsic end independent of God, misconstrues the fundamental character of human existence, which is "naturally" marked by a supernatural end and thus is not accurately conceived in isolation from grace. While this shift is important, it is worth noting that (1) even Bellarmine could speak of original sin in terms of a "corruption of nature" (see previous footnote), and (2) even contemporary Catholic writers can defend "pure nature" as a limit concept pointing to the fact that "the relationship of grace

between God and man is neither deducible from human essence, nor divine essence." Eva-Maria Faber, "Grace," in *Encyclopedia of Christian Theology*, ed. Jean-Yves Lacoste (New York: Routledge, 2005), p. 651.

38 "If any one says, that all works done before justification, in whatever manner they may be done, are truly sins, or merit the hatred of God; that the more earnestly one strives to dispose himself for grace, the more grievously he sins: let him be anathema." Council of Trent, "Decree Concerning Justification," Canon VII, in *Canons*, p. 43.

39 *Catechism*, §404; cf. §405.

40 For the character of original sin as an "inclination to evil," see *Catechism*, §§403, 405; cf. where Thomas similarly characterizes original sin as a disposition or *habitus* in *ST*, 1/2.82.1.

41 Thus, in Catholic theology (in sharp contrast to the Lutheran and Reformed traditions) concupiscence – the inordinate desire identified by Augustine with original sin – is not itself sin, but only an inclination toward sin (see *Catechism*, §405). Cf. the Council of Trent: "in the one baptized there remains concupiscence, or an inclination to sin which ... cannot injure those who do not acquiesce" ("Decree Concerning Original Sin," §5, in *Canons*, p. 23). As will be discussed further in Chapter 3 below, Augustine's own views on concupiscence are unsystematic enough to lend support to both the Catholic and Protestant positions, though he is relatively unambiguous in teaching that the fall has destroyed freedom of the will, understood as the ability to avoid sin.

42 So in the Catholic *Catechism*, §407, the postlapsarian state is described in terms of the devil having acquired "a certain domination" over humankind, but not in such a way as to destroy human freedom.

43 Thus, the Tridentine fathers clearly maintained that human beings cannot free themselves from sin, but they immediately add that "free will, weakened as it was in its powers, and downward bent [by original sin], was by no means extinguished in [human beings]." "Decree on Justification," Ch. 1, p. 30.

44 *Catechism*, §405.

45 For Augustine's uncompromising position on this question, see, e.g., *The Punishment and Forgiveness of Sins and the Baptism of Little Ones* [hereafter *PFS*], 1.55, in *Answer to the Pelagians*, I, ed. John E. Rotelle (Hyde Park, NY: New City Press, 1997).

46 *Catechism*, §1261; cf. the 2007 report of the Catholic International Theological Commission, "The Hope of Salvation for Infants Who Die Without Being Baptized," which in its preface echoes the stance of the *Catechism* but also allows that limbo remains "a possible theological hypothesis" (cited from <http://www.vatican.va/roman_curia/congregations/cfaith/cti_documents/rc_con_cfaith_doc_20070419_un-baptised-infants_en.html>).

47 Thus, the ITC document cited in the previous footnote characterizes the effects of original sin in purely passive terms: "Original sin implies a state of separation from Christ, and that excludes the possibility of the vision of God for those who die in that state." "The Hope of Salvation," §3.

48  For this reason Augustine himself explicitly rejected Pelagius' idea that infants needed baptism only to be fully incorporated into fellowship with God and not to avoid damnation. See Augustine, *PFS*, 1.25–6.
49  So Bavinck: "if original sin is not sin, all other later sins, which so readily and necessarily spring from it, cannot be sin either" (*Reformed Dogmatics*, vol. 3, p. 92).
50  Amid all their disagreements over the dynamics of human salvation, Arminians and so-called "high Calvinists" were at one in their affirmation of total depravity.
51  "We too admit that the H. Spirit ordinarily effects by baptism the things sealed in baptism. Yet we deny that the action of the H. Spirit is always tied to the act of baptism." Antonius Walaeus, *Loci communes s. Theologiae* (Leiden, 1640), p. 939; cited in Heinrich Heppe, *Reformed Dogmatics*, ed. Ernst Bizer (London: George Allen & Unwin, 1950), p. 618; cf. pp. 154–5, 164–8, and also John Calvin, *Institutes of the Christian Religion*, IV.xvi.26 (Philadelphia, PA: Westminster Press, 1960).
52  Having characterized the traditional form of the doctrine as the belief that an inherited sin is regarded as the individual's own guilt, deserving eternal punishment, Schleiermacher comments, "Nor can we regard it as other than natural that the doctrine in this form has been repudiated by many who, to avoid recognizing as guilt anything outside a man's own action, prefer to describe original sin as an evil." Friedrich Schleiermacher, *The Christian Faith* [hereafter *CF*], 2nd edn., ed. H. R. Mackintosh and J. S. Stewart (Edinburgh: T&T Clark, 1928 [1830]), §71.1, p. 286. Though Schleiermacher's position is closely associated with later developments in Protestant theology in particular (e.g., the American Social Gospel movement), broadly similar approaches can also be found in the work of Catholics such as Karl Rahner, who characterizes original sin as a co-determination of freedom by the guilt of others (*Foundations of the Christian Faith: An Introduction to the Idea of Christianity* [New York: Crossroad, 1990], pp. 110–11), and, more expansively, Piet Schoonenberg (*Man and Sin: A Theological View* [Notre Dame: University of Notre Dame Press, 1965]).
53  Schleiermacher, *CF*, §66, p. 271.
54  At the end of the section cited in the previous footnote, Schleiermacher offers a more objective definition of sin as that which "consists in our desiring what Christ contemns and *vice versa*." Even this definition, however, is presented as superior to one that focuses on violation of God's law, since for Schleiermacher knowledge of Christ, though mediated through the community and its traditions, ultimately remains internal to the self-consciousness of the Christian, the witness of which cannot be trumped by any external doctrinal or legal standard. See *CF*, §72.4, p. 299: "it is solely on … inward experience that our consciousness of the need of redemption depends."
55  Schleiermacher, *CF*, §71.3, p. 290.
56  Schleiermacher, *CF*, §71.2, p. 288.
57  Schleiermacher, *CF*, §71.2, p. 287.

58 Schleiermacher, *CF*, §72.4, p. 301.
59 Schleiermacher, *CF*, §72.3, p. 298; cf. p. 296: "the individual can act only *in accordance with* the nature of his species, but never can act *upon* that nature."
60 Schleiermacher, *CF*, §72.6, p. 304. Note that here Schleiermacher refers to the Scholastic distinction between *peccatum originans* and *peccatum originatum* described in note 22 above.
61 Schleiermacher, *CF*, §71.2, p. 288.
62 "Thus [original sin] can be called guilt with perfect accuracy only when it is regarded simply as meaning the totality of the whole race, since it cannot in similar fashion be the guilt of the individual, so far at least as it has been engendered in him." Schleiermacher, *CF*, §71.2, p. 289.
63 Schleiermacher, *CF*, §71.4, pp. 290–1.
64 As will be explained further in Chapter 6 below, it is possible to challenge Schleiermacher on this point while agreeing with him that original sin is not properly viewed as something for which the individual is held blameworthy.
65 See especially Søren Kierkegaard, *The Concept of Anxiety: A Simple Psychologically Orienting Deliberation on the Dogmatic Issue of Hereditary Sin*, ed. Reidar Thomte (Princeton, NJ: Princeton University Press, 1980).
66 A similar approach can be found in Niebuhr's contemporary, Paul Tillich, *Systematic Theology*, vol. 2 (Chicago, IL: University of Chicago Press, 1957), pp. 39–44.
67 "To the essential nature of man belong, on the one hand ... his character as a [finite] creature embedded in the natural order. On the other hand, his essential nature also includes the freedom of his spirit, his transcendence over natural processes and finally his self-transcendence." Reinhold Niebuhr, *Human Nature*, vol. 1 of *The Nature and Destiny of Man: A Christian Interpretation* (Louisville, KY: Westminster John Knox, 1996 [1941]), p. 270.
68 Niebuhr, *Human Nature*, p. 251.
69 Kierkegaard defines anxiety as "freedom's actuality as the possibility of possibility"; i.e., the experience of being opened to that which is other and more than what is presently available to the creature in its finitude. Kierkegaard, *The Concept of Anxiety*, p. 42.
70 Niebuhr, *Human Nature*, p. 250. Cf. Kierkegaard, *The Concept of Anxiety*, p. 43: "... he who becomes guilty through anxiety is indeed innocent, for it was not he himself but anxiety, a foreign power, that laid hold of him, a power that he did not love but about which he was anxious. And yet he is guilty, for he sank in anxiety, which he nevertheless loved even as he feared it ... Every notion that suggests that the prohibition tempted him, or that the seducer deceived him ... perverts ethics, introduces a quantitative determination, and will by the help of psychology pay man a compliment at the sacrifice of the ethical, a compliment that everyone who is ethically developed must reject as a new and more profound seduction." In short, while psychology can explain anxiety, sin is ultimately inexplicable – and unjustifiable.

71 Niebuhr, *Human Nature*, pp. 252–4; in this context, Niebuhr cites Kierkegaard's dictum that sin presupposes itself (see *The Concept of Anxiety*, p. 62).
72 Niebuhr, *Human Nature*, pp. 258–9.
73 "We cannot ... escape the ultimate paradox that the final exercise of freedom in the transcendent human spirit is its recognition of the false use of that freedom in action. Man is most free in the discovery that he is not free." Niebuhr, *Human Nature*, p. 260; cf. p. 263.
74 See, e.g., Niebuhr, *Human Nature*, p. 266.
75 Kierkegaard argues that Adam "is not essentially different from the race, for in that case there is no race at all; he is not the race, for in that case also there would be no race. He is himself and the race ... Through the first sin, sin came into the world. Precisely in the same way it is true of every subsequent man's first sin, that through it sin comes into the world." *The Concept of Anxiety*, pp. 29, 31; cf. Niebuhr, *Human Nature*, pp. 279–80.
76 "Perfection before the Fall is ... perfection before the act." Niebuhr, *Human Nature*, p. 278. Needless to say, Niebuhr affirms that "act" in this context includes thoughts and moods as well as physical movements.
77 "Th[e] structure of freedom is revealed in the very bondage of sin ... It is by this capacity that he is able both to sin and to have some knowledge of his sin." Niebuhr, *Human Nature*, p. 276.
78 Niebuhr, *Human Nature*, p. 277.
79 Niebuhr views the attempt to defend a historical interpretation of the fall and the corresponding efforts to account for the transmission of Adam's sin across generations as a fatal corruption of the truth of the doctrine of original sin. See *Human Nature*, pp. 260–4.
80 For a recent argument that it is illegitimate, see Terrence W. Tilley, *The Evils of Theodicy* (Eugene, OR: Wipf and Stock, 2000).
81 In addition to the book of Job, biblical refusal to posit any necessary correlation between suffering and sin is evident in, e.g., Luke 13:1–5; John 11:2–3. This is not to deny that there are places where suffering is caused by sin (Jesus himself implies as much in John 5:14; cf. Rom. 1:24–8), but they are unsystematic enough to disallow any immediate inference of sin from the fact of suffering – thereby discrediting attempts to make appeal to original sin the linchpin of Christian theodicy.

# Part II

# Reconfiguring the Debate: Sin, Nature, and the Will

# 3

# Augustine of Hippo: Willing and the Ambiguity of Desire

As noted in the previous chapter, the origin of the Western doctrine of original sin lies squarely with Augustine of Hippo. This is not to deny certain antecedents to Augustine's views among earlier generations of Latin theologians in particular. Augustine himself was quick to invoke the authority of the third-century martyr Cyprian of Carthage to support his own position. In response to a correspondent who had questioned whether it was appropriate to wait to baptize a baby until it was eight days old (on the model of the Old Testament practice of circumcising infants on the eighth day), Cyprian had replied that there was no cause to wait, since even those with the gravest sins are admitted to baptism, and

> an infant ... being lately born, has not sinned, except in that, being born after the flesh according to Adam, he has contracted the contagion of the ancient death at its earliest birth ... [and thus] approaches the more easily on this very account to the reception of the forgiveness of sins – that to him are remitted, not his own sins, but the sins of another.[1]

Yet while this text (along with some passages from Ambrose[2]) certainly bears witness to some idea of inherited sin, it is a far cry from the comprehensive and detailed reflection on the topic found in the writings Augustine produced between 412 and his death in 430 in response to the British ascetic Pelagius and his associates. Nor is there any real parallel to (or appropriation of) Augustine's views in the East, where, notwithstanding the formal repudiation of Pelagius' follower, Caelestius, at the Council of Ephesus in 431, Pelagius himself was never condemned.

---

*In Adam's Fall: A Meditation on the Christian Doctrine of Original Sin,* by Ian A. McFarland.
© 2010 Ian A. McFarland.

Augustine's insistence that human beings are born congenitally sinful and thus incapable of turning to God in faith apart from God's prevenient and unmerited gift of grace raised difficult questions about human freedom. As noted in the previous chapter, generations of Christian theologians (including Augustine himself in his early writings) had highlighted the freedom of human beings to respond to the gospel as a defining mark of orthodox faith over against both pagan and Christian forms of determinism. How could this emphasis be maintained if original sin rendered human beings utterly dependent on an unmerited gift of God for their salvation? Clearly, Augustine's doctrines of sin and grace required a profound reinterpretation of the concepts of freedom and the will.

## Augustine's Views in Outline

A detailed account of the development of Augustine's doctrine of the will is beyond the scope of this chapter, not least because many of the crucial features of his mature position emerged long before the outbreak of the Pelagian controversy.[3] Nevertheless Augustine's extended engagement with the Pelagians over the last two decades of his life provides a context within which to explore both the basic contours of and continuing tensions in his understanding of human freedom, and the account of the will with which it is bound up.

As important as the status of the will became for Augustine over the course of the Pelagian controversy, he never framed his own position as an attack on human freedom, but always as a defense of grace in the context of extreme human need.[4] Thus, his main complaint against the Pelagians was that they failed to appreciate the severity of the situation in which all human beings find themselves. His focus on original sin in the first of the anti-Pelagian writings, *The Punishment and Forgiveness of Sins and the Baptism of Little Ones*, needs to be understood in this context. Though he devotes a good deal of space to an exegetical defense of original sin, Augustine's argument is fundamentally Christological: Christians confess that Christ is the sole savior of human beings, but Christ cannot have this status unless every human being – including the newborn infants baptized in his name – are in need of saving; and since it is evident that infants have committed no sin of their own from the effects of which they need to be saved, it follows that they must be born sinful.[5] The topic of freedom comes up only in the context of explaining how it happens that congenitally sinful human beings nevertheless come to be able to avoid sin. Again, Augustine's reasoning is Christological: if the will could

## Willing and the Ambiguity of Desire

overcome sin by its own power, then Christ would have died to no purpose; therefore, it must be the case that the will is able to overcome sin only when empowered by grace.[6]

It is a crucial feature of Augustine's thinking that the will's dependence on grace does not entail any diminishment of its integrity; it is simply a corollary of the general principle that whatever good a creature does, it does by the power of God.[7] The good done by human beings is in this respect no different than the good done by non-rational or even non-living creatures; but the means by which God empowers the human creature to do good is distinctive: "God does not produce our salvation in us as if we were mindless rocks or beings in whose nature he did not create reason and will."[8] Instead, human beings' possession of reason and will means that they effect God's purposes as agents rather than (as is the case with irrational animals and insensate stones) solely by involuntary submission to the forces of instinct or physical law. Thus, "what [the human soul] has and what it receives come from God, but the receiving and the having certainly comes from the one who receives and has them."[9] God's acting is therefore not in competition with our freedom, but its essential precondition.

For the Pelagians, by contrast, the will names the *cause* of human moral action rather than simply describing the *mode* in which human activity (however caused) takes place. On the Pelagian understanding, an action cannot simultaneously be both necessary and willed, since to speak of necessity is *eo ipso* to specify a cause that is other than the will.[10] Similarly, the actions of the will cannot simultaneously be ascribed to God, except in the indirect sense that God is the one who created the will and endowed it with its powers of self-determination. Although God always sustains the will in its capacity to choose, volition is a function of the will's use of these capacities rather than of God's immediate and direct action.[11] The will is in this respect something of a mysterious entity: a creation of God that in its proper functioning is inherently (and necessarily) disconnected from God in its operation (though, somewhat paradoxically, it is God who maintains the will's capacity to operate independently of God).[12]

In comparison with the Pelagian position, for Augustine the will is a comparatively *un*problematic and not especially mysterious entity. It simply marks out human beings as the particular kind of creatures they are: personal agents.[13] Agents are beings whose actions are naturally mediated by their wills.[14] This emphatically does *not* mean that human beings have complete control over their actions (indeed, that is precisely the substance of the Pelagian view Augustine is opposing). For Augustine to say that humans will whatever they do is simply to affirm that I, as a human being, naturally describe my acts as what *I* do, even when I have no ability to choose otherwise (e.g., "I hear the car alarm outside the window," or, to cite a favorite example of Augustine's, "I wish to be happy").[15] In short, the will describes in every instance *how* human beings – precisely *as* human beings – do whatever it is they do (viz., as personal agents); but the will is not a separate factor that might constitute a causal explanation of *why* they do it.[16]

This distinction between the will as an explanation of *how* human beings do what they do and *why* they do what they do is crucial for understanding the place where the will's operation does become problematic for Augustine: namely, the fact that human beings also will evil. Here there *is* a genuine mystery associated with the will, for while Augustine insists human willing of the good comes from God, he is equally emphatic that the willing of evil does not:

> ... as the apostle says: "There is no *power* except from God ... But we never read in the holy scriptures: There is no will except from God. And it is right that scripture does not say that, because it is not true. Otherwise, if there were no will except from God, God would be – heaven forbid! – the author even of sins. For an evil will by itself is already a sin, even if the execution is lacking, that is, if the will lacks the power. But when an evil will receives the power to carry out its intention, it comes from the judgment of God with whom there is no injustice.[17]

In other words, although the will is the means by which God enables human beings to be agents of God's will, not all human willing corresponds to God's willing. To be sure (and as the final sentence of the above quotation affirms), even where human beings *will* to resist God, it is only by the power of God that they (like any creature) are able to *do* what they will. The point remains, however, that the ontology of willing is such that a gap can open between what human beings do (which is always subject to God's will) and the will with which they do it (which, in the case of sin, is opposed to God's will).

Whether in the pursuit of good or evil, however, in these passages Augustine treats the will not as an autonomous force that supervenes on human nature, but simply as the mode in which that nature subsists. God works through the will as part of the same process by which God works through every aspect of human nature to effect God's purposes, and the will's operation is thus closely correlated with other natural features of human being. Specifically, human beings will what they know and desire, and what they know and desire is a function of what God presents to our senses and how God shapes our appetites:

> ... God brings it about by the enticements of our perceptions [*visorum suasionibus*] that we will and that we believe. He does this either externally through the exhortations of the gospel ... or internally where none have control over what comes into their minds, though to assent or dissent is in the power of their will. God, then, works in these ways with the rational soul so that it believes him. For it cannot so much as believe anything by free choice [*libero arbitrio*], if there is not enticement or invitation [*suasio vel vocatio*] which it can believe. God, then certainly produces in human beings the will to believe, and his mercy anticipates us in every respect.[18]

The mystery of sin means that human beings may dissent from God's will, but even then the willing corresponds to the desire of the individual.[19] Conversely, when we turn from willing evil to willing the good, it is because God has instilled in us a desire for the good, to which our wills naturally accede.[20] And though the will only wills the good by God's grace, that grace operates with rather than against the grain of human nature by shaping the experience and desire of the individual: when we will the good, it is because God disposes us to do so – and yet it remains we who do the willing.[21]

Though the terminology deployed in the anti-Pelagian writings is variable and rarely free of all ambiguity,[22] a basic resistance to the idea that divine and human action stand in a zero-sum relationship is characteristic of Augustine's mature doctrine of the will: that God acts on the will does not annul human agency, but fulfills it. As the Pelagian controversy develops, however, Augustine finds himself persistently challenged to square this vision of human agency with his understanding of original sin. The latter is the source of the corruption that requires the outpouring of God's love in order to turn the will to the good. And yet for Augustine it is not the will as such that is corrupted by original sin. After all, the basic dynamics of human willing remain unaffected by the gift of grace: whether healed or mired in sin, the will follows desire. Moreover, Augustine agrees with his Pelagian opponents that newborn infants, though guilty of original sin, do not yet will.[23] If he nevertheless insists that infants are born sinful, it is because he locates the corruption of original sin in the desire that determines the direction of the will. His term for this corrupted desire is concupiscence, and it is as he reflects on the place of this concept in his anthropology that the fault lines in Augustine's doctrine of the will come into relief.

## Concupiscence: Humanity Internally Divided

In colloquial Latin *concupiscentia* referred to any sort of intense longing. In a specifically Christian context, Tertullian had applied it to the "lusts" of the old self described in Eph. 4:22,[24] but it is only with Augustine that it acquires the status of a technical theological term for desire that is disordered (i.e., not ordered to God, the proper object of all creaturely desire).[25] For Augustine it both is and is not to be identified with sin. On the one hand, it refers to that congenital sin that infants have "contracted through birth."[26] On the other, it refers to the persistence of the impulse to sin even after baptism has cleansed the individual of her congenital sinfulness. Thus, "concupiscence of the flesh is not forgiven in baptism in such a way that it no longer exists, but in such a way that it is not counted as sin."[27] Augustine develops this point by distinguishing between the act (*actus*) of sin and the guilt (*reatus*) associated with it. With respect to most sins (e.g., adultery), once the sin is committed, it ceases in act, but its guilt remains until remitted. In the case of concupiscence, however, the converse is the case: its guilt is remitted (and so passes away) in baptism, but concupiscence remains in act as that which continues to prompt the will to sin.[28]

Developed in this twofold way (i.e., in pre- and post-baptismal perspective), the category of concupiscence is at once the linchpin of Augustine's doctrine of original sin and a profoundly complicating factor in its exposition. It is the linchpin because it provides the anthropological ground for the soteriological concern that drives Augustine's debate with the Pelagians: the confession that Christ is the savior of all. For Augustine this confession presupposes that all human beings need to be saved, which, in turn, implies that they stand under the sentence of damnation. And they are damned because after the fall the process of human willing is so damaged that it invariably deviates from God's will unless aided by grace. Concupiscence is the reason *why* postlapsarian human willing is inherently defective: because it is led by disordered desire. Human beings continue to will even apart from God's gift of grace (they would not be human otherwise); but their willing is defective, in the same way that an eye's seeing is defective unless it is given light.[29]

This diagnosis of the postlapsarian human condition is consistent with the understanding of the will presented in the first section of this chapter: that willing is not an autonomous power of self-direction, but rather follows desire. In other words, human beings will what they want (i.e., the objects of their desire) – but what they want is something over which

## Willing and the Ambiguity of Desire 67

the will has no control.[30] Through the source and, indeed, the "law" of sin (*lex peccati*), however, the fact that concupiscence conditions – and thus is prior to – postlapsarian human willing means that it is not itself sin, strictly speaking. It can be called "sin" in an improper or loose sense "because it was produced by sin and leads to sin"; moreover, it merits eternal condemnation for those who are not baptized. But though it remains even in the baptized as a tendency that impedes their power to do good, it carries no guilt "if we do not obey it when it somehow bids us to do sinful actions whenever they [i.e., the baptized] do not consent to it for illicit works" and "is itself no longer sin."[31] In short, even though concupiscence merits damnation for the unbaptized, the fact that it is distinct from willing means that it is not in itself sin.[32]

As developed in the anti-Pelagian writings, this way of distinguishing between concupiscence and sin can lead to a bifurcation of desire and the willing, such that in some cases willing does *not* follow desire. As a result, there are situations where Augustine's resistance to the Pelagian view of the will as the autonomous ground of action is compromised by an account of the will as an instrument of control: something that stands over and directs human nature rather than as simply the modality by which human nature does whatever it does. This problem is particularly clear in his exegesis of Romans 7 in *Marriage and Desire*, in a passage that merits being quoted at length:

> We ought ... to want those [conscupiscent] desires [*desideria*] not to exist, even if we cannot attain that goal in the body of this death. For this reason the same apostle also instructs us in another passage ... "For I do not do what I want, but I do what I hate" [Rom. 7:19], that is, I have those desires [*concupisco*]. He would, after all want not to have them so that he would be perfect in every respect. "But if I do," he says, "what I do not want, I agree that the law is good" [Rom. 7:16], because the law also does not want what I do not want. The law, that is, does not want me to covet [*non vult enim ut concupiscam*], since it says, "You shall not covet" [*non concupisces*; Exod. 20:17], and I do not want these covetous desires [*nolo concupiscere*]. To this extent, then the will of the law and my will agree. But since he did not want to have desires and yet had those desires and since he was not enslaved to the same concupiscence by consenting to it, he went on to add, "It is no longer I who do it, but the sin that dwells within me" [Rom. 7:20].[33]

As a way of clarifying his point, Augustine contrasts Paul's situation with that of another, hypothetical case:

That person is, however, very much mistaken who, while consenting to the concupiscence of the flesh and definitely deciding to do what it desires, still supposes that it is all right to say, "It is not I who do it." After all, a person consents, even if one hates the fact. For these two can coexist in one person: both the hating it because one knows it is evil and the doing it because one decided to do it. But suppose that one also goes on to do what scripture forbids ... [and] carries out even with the body what one decided to do in the heart. If some should then say, "It is not I who do it, but the sin that dwells in me" [Rom. 7:20], because, when they decide and do it, they are displeased with themselves, they are so mistaken that they do not even recognize themselves. For though a person is that whole composite, namely, the heart that decides and the body that carries it out, these people still do not think that it is they themselves who do it.

Those, then, who say, "It is not I who do it, but the sin that dwells in me" [Rom. 7:20], speak the truth if they have only the desire, but not if they assent to it with their hearts or also carry out the action by means of their bodies.[34]

Augustine imagines three possible human responses to the baptized person's experience of concupiscence: first, to resist them in such a way as not to give willing assent; second, to give such assent to them; third, to act on that assent. He argues that in the second and third cases, the will is implicated, such that the person in question has moved from concupiscence (which is not itself sin) to actual sin, and must therefore take responsibility for her actions as their agent. In the first case, however, the will, though experiencing the same desires, is able to withhold its assent. Consequently, the person is not guilty of sin and is therefore justified in saying with Paul, "it is no longer I that do it, but sin that dwells within me."

Needless to say, Augustine (who repeats much of this exegesis in the slightly later *Answer to the Two Letters of the Pelagians*) is careful to note that this situation applies only to the person under grace, such that the will's capacity to withhold assent from concupiscent impulses is a gift of God and not a product of its own intrinsic power.[35] Nevertheless, one may well question the tenability of the distinction Augustine draws between the first and second cases: the person who, like Paul, covets but does not consent to those covetous impulses and the person who, though consenting, hates himself for doing so. In neither case does the person actually complete her coveting with a bodily act; in both cases, she can and must truly say, "I coveted." The difference lies in the will's relation to the impulse in question: the one whose will consents stands convicted as a sinner, because even though she abstains from the bodily act of sin, she does so "not because of the will but because of fear";[36] by contrast, the one who is acquitted wills the law of God.[37]

At this point the lines of Augustine's anthropology become difficult to follow clearly.[38] The upshot of his argument is that even though someone like Paul may experience the same concupiscent impulse as the sinner who consents to it, the fact that Paul does not so consent means that this experience is not identified with the "mind" (viz., the self as agent), but with the "flesh." To be sure, Augustine acknowledges the propriety of Paul describing himself as having been made captive to the law of sin by this impulse (Rom. 7:23), because the flesh that is the source of this captivity is not some foreign nature, "but ... our own nature is present there."[39] All the same, this captivity does not by itself make Paul a sinner. Thus, for Augustine a person's fundamental identity (i.e., *who* she is before God) is a function of the will: where it is not engaged, the self is not ultimately implicated. Yet what the will actually does in this framework (i.e., the content of its "consent" or lack thereof) remains mysterious, since, on the one hand, its consent does not necessarily lead to action (as in the case of the person who consents but does not complete the sin bodily), while, on the other, its lack of consent does not change the fact of coveting (as in the case of Paul, who confesses, "I covet," even though his will is not engaged).[40]

Thus, instead of reading Paul as a witness to the helplessness of the will in the face of distorted (i.e., concupiscent) desire, Augustine (rather implausibly) interprets his words as testifying to the will's power to resist such desire.[41] And while he insists that it has this power only owing to God's free gift of grace, the upshot is the positing of two separate "I"s that correspond to ontologically distinct parts of the Christian: the corrupt, physical "flesh" that is identified with the desires of (fallen) nature and a renewed, spiritual "will" or "mind" that successfully resists them. In dividing the self in this way, Augustine makes the will more a power *over* human nature and its desires than that aspect *of* human nature by which the individual experiences and enacts her desire as a personal agent. Moreover, by dividing the "I" of desire from the "I" of the will, Augustine ascribes sin an agency – and thus an autonomous existence – independent of the will in a way that gives some credibility to Julian of Eclanum's worry that his position veers into ontological dualism.[42]

Augustine's wrestling with the meaning of Romans 7 long antedates the Pelagian controversy; moreover, his analysis of Paul's experience of a divided will in many ways served as the basis for the rejection of his own earlier, more "libertarian" understanding of the will as a power able to trump desire.[43] Nevertheless, the exegesis of Romans 7 in *Marriage and Desire* chafes against one of the crucial features of Augustine's mature doctrine of the will: a close correlation of willing and desire (rather than a vision of the will as a power set over against desire). According to this perspective, willing and desire remain at all times distinct (as do, correspondingly, sin as a product of the will and concupiscence as its enabling condition), since if will follows desire, desire must be logically prior to willing; nevertheless, the two operate in tandem. Yet when Augustine interprets Paul's predicament as illustrating an instance where his will does *not* follow his (concupiscent) desire, this distinction becomes a division. Although Augustine connects Paul's (good) willing with his "desire" for the law, since this desire coexists with its opposite, the will is effectively suspended between them as a power that hovers over human nature and its desires rather than as the property of that nature by which human beings enact their desires as agents.

At this point, one might simply argue that Augustine's exegesis of Romans 7 does not show him at his best. After all, his argument is at least partly determined by political considerations (viz., answering the charge that his teaching on original sin slanders the saints[44]). Particularly since Augustine elsewhere insists that all Christians without exception need to pray for forgiveness,[45] his eagerness to acquit Paul of sin in this passage seems both theologically and (given that coveting is evidently cited by Paul precisely as an example of genuine sin) exegetically unnecessary. Nevertheless, if some of the features of Augustine's argument here are atypical, they point to a tension in the way he distinguishes between concupiscence and sin that is present throughout the anti-Pelagian corpus.[46] The distinction is unobjectionable as a way of making the point that humans will what they desire, but when will and desire come to be seen as two distinct and antagonistic modes of agency – so that the will's task is envisioned primarily as struggle *against* desire – the result is an oddly "Pelagian" anthropology: the will appears as a power that supervenes on and is, correspondingly, disconnected both from the self and from the nature the self instantiates.[47]

The problem is certainly not that Augustine reads Romans 7 as evidence of a divided self. It is hard to imagine how that particular chapter could be read otherwise, especially given that the theme of internal conflict is anything but anomalous in the Pauline corpus.[48] The problem – at least from the perspective of what I have identified as Augustine's most significant anti-Pelagian insight – is that Augustine here views the division in terms of a decoupling of will from desire rather than as evidence of the will's incapacity to determine the desires by which it is shaped. As a result — and in a manner directly opposed to the image of willing as the enactment of desire — the reader is given the sense that desire is an impediment to the healthy function of the will.[49] The implication that willing is properly independent of desire is only exacerbated by Augustine's account of the way in which human willing would have taken place apart from the fall.

## The Fall: Humanity Temporally Divided

In one of his more notorious pieces of theological speculation, Augustine ventures that the present experience of human (or, more specifically, male) sexuality points to the fall as the origin of humanity's ongoing struggle with concupiscence in both its pre- and post-baptismal forms.[50] Augustine focuses on the will's inability either to cause or to prevent an erection, arguing that such lack of control over so important a set of organs must represent a declension from humanity's original condition.[51] Apart from the fall, he posits, the will would have controlled the penis in the same way that it now controls the movements of the hands and feet.[52] That it should be deprived of this power is fitting punishment for Adam's primordial disobedience: the will loses mastery over the body as a penalty for having failed to exercise such mastery in Eden.[53] Thus, while Augustine believes that concupiscence comes in manifold forms and infects every dimension of human existence, its epicenter is sexual intercourse. Indeed, sex is not only the ontological point where the will's impotence is most sharply revealed, but also the ontic ground of the will's congenital captivity to sin: the reason why newborn infants are born sinners is that concupiscence (in the form of lust) is the power behind their conception and thus lies at the root of their being.[54]

Even more than in the material examined in the previous section, a crucial feature of Augustine's analysis of sex is the characterization of the will as an organ of control over nature — to the extent that the link between will and desire runs the risk of being completely sundered. Where sex is concerned, the postlapsarian will's capacity for control is virtually eliminated,[55] and desire (whether in the presence or in the absence of sexual arousal) operates independently of the will. In Augustine's vision of humanity's prelapsarian condition, by contrast, the place of desire is much less clear. On the one hand, he can speak of the prelapsarian state in a way that is consistent with a more integrated vision of will and desire;[56] on the other, he can suggest that before the fall the will's operation would have been largely independent of desire.[57] To be sure, love remains in a formal sense the ground of virtuous action for Augustine both *ante* and *post lapsum*,[58] but the emphasis placed on the will's control over the body's members tends to vitiate the role of desire in his account of prelapsarian human agency.[59] To the extent that willing becomes identified with control consciously exercised over the self (and its nature), it becomes increasingly difficult to identify the will with the self.

There are a number of problems that accompany Augustine's analysis of human sexuality,[60] but one of the most obvious is the way in which he treats the will's lack of control over sexual function as somehow exceptional, ignoring the fact it is but one of an enormous range of human biological processes that are equally removed from the realm of conscious choice: hunger, fatigue, sweating, immune response, and the like.[61] Particularly from an evolutionary perspective, it would be strange indeed to follow Augustine in viewing the "involuntary" status of such processes as evidence of declension from an original (and putatively more ideal) state of conscious control over them.[62] Their "automatic" character has positive survival value, since (for example) it is much more efficient if the body's ability to cool itself does *not* depend on a conscious decision to open one's pores. More importantly, however, the fact that such processes are not subject to conscious control need not be seen as making them any less matters of will, if the latter is understood simply as the mode by which human beings experience themselves as agents. After all, individuals naturally say, "*I* hungered," or "*I'm* sweating," using the first-person pronoun just as they do when saying things like, "*I* picked up the shovel," or "*I'm* going to the ballgame today." The degree to which these various actions are "voluntary (i.e., matters of conscious choice) varies widely, but all remain ineluctably part of one's identity (i.e., who *I* am).[63]

Augustine is, of course, very conscious of the complexities of human action. As noted in the previous section, he recognizes that a person may genuinely hate his sins and yet remain fully responsible for them. This claim is rooted in one of Augustine's most important anti-Pelagian insights: while the level of control one is able to exercise over oneself may vary across particular cases, the "I" – and thus the will – is always implicated, *because agency is a constitutive and ineradicable feature of human being.*[64] The problem comes when he fails to follow through on this insight. In allowing that Paul can defer his own responsibility for his covetousness on to sin, he limits agency to the will's conscious choice (viz., assent to the concupiscent impulse). To be sure, Augustine consistently denies that this choice is "free" in the sense of a "liberty of indifference": apart from the gift of grace a postlapsarian human being will always sin. Nevertheless, Augustine's analysis of the prelapsarian state brings him close to his

Pelagian opponents in viewing the will as essentially an instrument of control over the self rather than its mode of being as a self. He differs from them – sharply – in his estimation of how much control the will can in fact exercise in the present, but his vision of how the will was created to work is virtually indistinguishable from theirs; and this raises problems for him when he attempts to relate his doctrine of grace to the operation of the will in its pre- and postlapsarian states.

In assessing human action in the fallen state, Augustine takes his stand on two basic principles: (1) virtuous action is possible only by the gift of God's grace, and (2) this gift in no way undermines human agency. In a strictly non-competitive vision of human and divine activity, human beings have only what they receive – yet it is still they who have it. In short – and in unambiguous contrast to the Pelagian position – Augustine insists that grace empowers human agency rather than displacing it.[65] Moreover, God's means of shaping the will to the good involves transforming the individual's desires: since we can only will what we want, God sheds love on the human heart through the Holy Spirit so that the desires that prompt the will are focused on godly ends.[66]

So long as he sticks to this framework, Augustine is able to suggest an integrated model of postlapsarian human agency in which the will is "always already" related to both nature and grace (the sources of desire) rather than acting in competition with them.[67] Yet the way Augustine makes use of this framework is deeply affected by his understanding of the damage occasioned by the fall. Specifically, the reason that grace must be behind every good action is that human nature has been damaged by the fall: because concupiscence (as the penalty inflicted on humanity for Adam's primordial sin) "naturally" turns the will away from the good, grace is necessary to turn human desire – and, thereby, human willing – toward the good. Before the fall, however, concupiscence was not a factor. In what sense was grace necessary then?

As I have already intimated, when considering prelapsarian humanity Augustine operates with a much more explicitly "Pelagian" understanding of the will's freedom to choose between alternatives apart from any correlation with desire. If desire was present at all in Eden (and Augustine at least entertains the possibility that it was not), it was subordinate to the will. Consequently, there was no need for grace to shape it; on the contrary, "[a]s long as human beings remained standing in the good will endowed with free choice [i.e., before the fall], *they did not need that grace* by which they might be raised up once [after the fall] they could not rise up by themselves."[68] Of course, to say that they did not need the kind of grace appropriate to the postlapsarian condition does not necessarily imply that they needed no grace at all. How then does Augustine understand the relationship between nature, grace, and will in unfallen humanity?

Augustine explores this question in the treatise *Rebuke and Grace*. Much of his argument builds on ideas introduced in earlier writings, where (for example) he had from the beginning clearly described humanity's initial condition as one characterized by unimpeded freedom of choice.[69] As elsewhere, however, difficulties arise when Augustine seeks to work out the implications of this claim in terms of a more detailed account of prelapsarian anthropology. He describes Adam's condition as one where he had the capacity to continue in an unfallen condition by virtue of the exercise of his will.[70] That capacity evidently did not render grace utterly superfluous, because Augustine adds that Adam "had the grace in which, if he willed to remain, he would never have been evil and without which he could not have been good even with free choice."[71] Very quickly, however, the significance of this grace becomes questionable, for Augustine goes on to argue that prelapsarian grace is that whereby "the man had righteousness if he willed to," while the postlapsarian version "is more powerful, for it makes one even to will and to will so strongly and to love with such ardor that by the will of the spirit one conquers the pleasure of the flesh which has contrary desires."[72] Thus, if it is a distinguishing mark of postlapsarian willing of the good that it is immediately effected by God (so that a fallen human being cannot will the good unless immediately and directly made by God to will it), prelapsarian grace seems to be nothing more than that by which the will was given certain goods at creation,[73] including chiefly the ability to persist in goodness by its own power.[74]

On the one hand, Augustine's position seems fairly uncontroversial: he wants to claim that grace is more necessary now than it was prior to the fall. To argue otherwise (as the Pelagians seemed to do) appears to undermine the soteriological necessity of the incarnation: why would God give the supreme gift of grace in Christ if humanity's situation did not require it? On the other hand, to say that grace is more necessary now than it was in the beginning seems to imply that humanity was less dependent on God then than it is now. Augustine clearly wants to resist this latter inference, given his firm conviction that creatures are always dependent on God for everything. Thus, he argues that it is misleading to speak of Adam being less dependent on God than his descendants; it is simply that humanity's situation renders the mode of dependence different before and after the fall. Specifically, since humanity's will was created good, it did not require any additional grace to obtain the good before the fall, whereas after the fall an additional gift is necessary to overcome the will's damaged capacities.[75] From a purely logical perspective this reply is unassailable, but it nevertheless suggests that while the postlapsarian good will is at every point shaped directly and entirely by God's activity,[76] prior to the fall the will was shaped by God's activity only indirectly (viz., insofar as it had been created good) and thus somewhat less than entirely.[77]

## Assessing Augustine's Doctrine of the Will

At a moment of crisis in David Lean's film *Lawrence of Arabia*, Sherif Ali (played by Omar Sharif) reminds Peter O'Toole's Lawrence that he had once said, "A man can do whatever he wants."

"He can," Lawrence replies, "but he can't *want* what he wants."

I know of no better summary of Augustine's most revolutionary insight on the operation of the will. For all the significance that Augustine accords to the inner conflicts that mark human willing, a key feature of his mature doctrine of the will is that at a basic level human beings do what they want. Importantly, however, this point does not constitute a ringing affirmation of human autonomy; it simply reflects Augustine's belief that willing follows desire. The problem – the point of existential crisis that undergirds Augustine's analysis – is that human beings can't want what they want. It is this incapacity that is the source of the experience of the divided will: we do what we desire, invariably – but *what* we desire remains beyond our control.

Honed in response to what he understood to be the Pelagian denial of infants' need for redemption, Augustine developed this account of willing in the effort to maintain Christianity's traditional sense of human responsibility before God while at the same time rejecting any suggestion that human beings are at any point able to live under God independently of God. Because all postlapsarian human beings (Christ excepted) are born sinners meriting eternal damnation, they can come to faith and do good works only because God makes them faithful and loving. Whether or not they receive this grace from God, however, human beings do what they do willingly, and thus as responsible agents.

Augustine's opponents (especially Julian of Eclanum) saw these claims as indistinguishable from the kind of fatalism that Christians had always rejected. But Augustine firmly rejected the implication that his claims about grace's shaping of human action vitiated freedom of the will, though the plausibility of this claim rests on an equally firm rejection of the Pelagian model of freedom as independence from God. For Augustine our wills are engaged whatever the degree of choice we may exercise over our actions. Because of the kind of beings we are, we cannot disavow our acts as *our* acts, however much we may recognize the many ways in which they are conditioned by forces beyond our control (which is why Augustine sees no contradiction in the idea of involuntary sin[78]). But if all acts are equally willed, not all are equally free. There is a crucial difference between the confessions, "I sinned" and "I believe," such that the latter bears witness to a genuine freedom of the will not present in the former. The difference does not lie in the fact that faith entails a greater degree of individual autonomy. On the contrary, insofar as Augustine understands sin as the mark of a fundamental disjunction between creature and Creator, it is in sin that we manifest the greater existential "independence" from God – but the result is, paradoxically, an experience of bondage, in which we somehow fail in enacting our identities as agents truly to be ourselves. For Augustine it is when we are least on our own that we experience ourselves as genuinely free beings, whose agency discloses most fully who we are, because we can only be ourselves when our agency is shaped by the Creator who is the ever-present source and guarantor of our selfhood.

This position allows for a fairly low-flying understanding of the will as that by which a human being is an agent. To will is simply to experience oneself as an "I" and, correspondingly, to acknowledge one's actions as "mine." Over against the Pelagian understanding of the will as a power of choice detached from (however much it may be influenced by) both human nature (which it governs) and God (whom it is free either to obey or disobey), Augustine suggests that the will is intimately connected to both. Because for Augustine willing is shaped by desire, it is an integral part of human nature, which is the seat of those desires (e.g., for health and happiness). But insofar as those desires are also shaped by grace (since, for example, it is only as and when God graciously makes God's self present to the individual as an object of desire that she is able to love God), the will is also subject to God. From this perspective, the will is not (as the Pelagians taught) a power by which we govern our lives. Rather than leading, it follows: we will what we are inclined to will, whether by nature or grace; and in so willing, we both experience and acknowledge our lives in all their many dimensions of action and passion as our own.

The contrast between Augustine's position and that of his opponents on this point is seen in Julian of Eclanum's claim that willing arises *in* human nature, but not *from* it.[79] Augustine finds this claim utterly incredible, since it so removes the will from the realm of creaturely causation as to make it impossible to understand how it can be spoken of as a human will at all:

> The world, of course, came to be from nothing, but with God as its maker. For if it did not have God as its maker, it could not have come to be from nothing at all. If, then, the will in a human being or in his free choice came to be out of nothing, who made it? ... Or is it among the things which began to exist the only one made by no one, the only one sprung from nothing? Why, then, is a human being condemned on its account, since the evil will of which he was only the recipient, but not the cause, came to be in him without his willing it? But if, so that he was rightly condemned, the evil will came to be in him because he willed it, why do you deny that the will of that man came to be from him, when you do not deny that it came to be because he willed it and could not have come to be without his willing it?[80]

By separating the will from nature and making it a source of action over and above the nature in which it is found, Julian ends up divorcing one's agency from one's humanity: willing is no longer an expression of one's nature, but a kind of mysterious force operating independently of it.[81] Correlatively, when willing is seen in this way as *choosing between* desires rather than as *following* desire, it becomes impossible for an actor to give a rational account of his or her actions, since by definition no motive or set of motives can explain the final decision of the will.[82] Over against this position, Augustine argues that the will is far more meaningfully understood as a function of nature that, in its operation, makes that nature personally manifest as an agent. Holding to this insight, the ideal situation is not one in which the will directs nature like a ghost in a machine, but rather one in which will is experienced as fully integrated into nature as part of it.[83]

The difficulties we have identified in Augustine's position are the result of a failure to hew consistently to this metaphysically unambitious account of willing. If the strength of his doctrine lies in his depiction of the will as that by which human beings experience their nature and receive God's grace as self-conscious agents, his account comes under strain whenever the will is separated from nature and grace as an independent factor in human action. As described in the second and third sections of this chapter, this separation becomes prominent in the later anti-Pelagian writings, as Augustine attempts to refine his account of the relationship between the postlapsarian will and concupiscence on the one hand, and to explain the dynamics of prelapsarian willing on the other. In both cases,

Augustine veers toward an understanding of the will that is oddly Pelagian in its equation of the will with a power of choosing that seemingly operates independently of nature and grace.

In the first case, Augustine attempts to distinguish between (postbaptismal) concupiscence and sin by arguing that the agent's experience of concupiscence (e.g., coveting) only counts as sin when the will assents to it. Where this assent is absent, the person does not sin, even though she may confess, "I covet." Here a split is opened up within the self, since the "I" who (unwillingly) covets is distinct from the "I" who wills to obey God's law. Furthermore, instead of the will following desire, it chooses between conflicting desires. And though its capacity to choose the good over the evil is attributed by Augustine wholly to God's grace, by making the will an instrument of control over nature, the defining feature of which is the power of choice, he raises the question of how it is possible to speak of sin where this power is absent.[84]

Things become still more problematic when Augustine turns his attention to the dynamics of human willing before the fall. Since he views concupiscence as punishment for the fall, it is not surprising that it does not figure in his account of unfallen human willing. But it is one thing to eliminate *disordered* desire as a factor in the prelapsarian state and quite another (at least from the perspective of Augustine's more anthropologically integrated accounts of willing) to suggest that the will originally operated independently of *all* desire, as Augustine seems at least inclined to do. Moreover, when speaking of paradise, Augustine also separates the will's operation from the direct activity of God. Because the will was not yet corrupted by the fall, it did not need the immediate intervention of grace to hold to the good – and thus could do so simply by exercising the power with which it was endowed at creation. Its operation in this way decoupled both from natural impulse and divine grace, the prelapsarian will is accorded the same characteristics ascribed to it by the Pelagians.

To be sure, in sharp contrast to the Pelagians Augustine insisted that the will no longer enjoys this original state of freedom of choice. Nevertheless, to the extent that the metaphor of control continues to form the background of his understanding of the will, his account of human sinfulness in general and of original sin in particular is unstable. Because sin is identified with an act of the will choosing one particular desire or course of action over another, it becomes very difficult to sustain a doctrine of universal sinfulness, since (by Augustine's own admission) not all human beings have the capacity to choose.[85] Moreover, to the extent that he makes the capacity to choose the defining feature of the will, Augustine compromises his more integrated account of nature, will, and grace in favor of a model in which the three appear in a kind of zero-sum tension with one another. As will be shown in the following chapter, the strengths of Augustine's views appear in much sharper relief when the distinction between willing and deliberate choice implicit in much of Augustine's anti-Pelagian writing is developed with greater consistency than Augustine himself managed to achieve.

## Notes

1  Cyprian, Letter 58 ("To Fidus"), in *Fathers of the Third Century: Hippolytus, Cyprian, Caius, Novatian*, vol. 5 of *Ante-Nicene Fathers*, ed. Alexander Roberts and James Donaldson (Edinburgh: T&T Clark, n.d.). From the earliest stages of the Pelagian controversy, Augustine cites this text repeatedly to stress the pedigree of his position. See *The Punishment and Forgiveness of Sins and the Baptism of Little Ones* [hereafter *PFS*], 3.10; *Answer to the Two Letters of the Pelagians* [hereafter *ATL*], 4.23; cf. *The Deeds of Pelagius* [hereafter *DP*], 25; *Marriage and Desire* [hereafter *MD*], 2.51; *Unfinished Work in Answer to Julian* [hereafter *UWJ*], 1.50, 52; 2.164. All translations from these and other works from Augustine's anti-Pelagian corpus are taken from the *Answer to the Pelagians, I–IV*, ed. John E. Rotelle, vols. I/23–25 of *The Works of Saint Augustine: A Translation for the 21st Century* (Hyde Park, NY: New City Press, 1997–9). Any modifications are noted, with the Latin taken from the appropriate volumes of the CCSL.
2  See especially *De paenitentia* 1.13, cited in Augustine, *The Grace of Christ and Original Sin* [hereafter *GCOS*], 2.47; *ATL*, 4.29; *UWJ*, 1.52, 126; 2.1, 208; 3.37 and *passim*.
3  For a masterful account of the evolution of Augustine's understanding of the will, see James Wetzel, *Augustine and the Limits of Virtue* (Cambridge: Cambridge University Press, 1999). See also Phillip Cary's more recent study, *Inner Grace: Augustine in the Traditions of Plato and Paul* (New York: Oxford University Press, 2008).
4  This is not an insignificant point: as is particularly clear in the later treatises *Grace and Free Choice* and *Rebuke and Grace*, Augustine's chief theological concern throughout the Pelagian controversy was not to disparage the human power of self-determination, but rather to insist that human intransigence is no obstacle to God's power of redemption.
5  Augustine, *PFS*, 1.18–27, 33, 39, 55; 2.37, 47–8; 3.7–8. Cf. the slightly later *Nature and Grace* [hereafter *NG*], 60: "If we admit that the small and the great, that is, wailing infants and old grey heads, need this savior and that medicine of his, namely, that the Word became flesh in order to dwell among us, the entire question under dispute between us has been resolved."
6  Augustine, *PFS*, 2.5. See *UWJ*, 2.101 for a pithy summary of this basic Christological principle in the last of Augustine's anti-Pelagian writings.

7 See Augustine, *PFS*, 2.30, with reference to 1 Cor. 4:7.
8 Augustine, *PFS*, 2.6.
9 Augustine, *Spirit and the Letter* [hereafter *SL*], 60; cf. Augustine's comments on 2 Tim. 2:20–1 in *UWJ*, 1.134: "Hence, both of these are true: God prepares the vessels for glory, and they prepare themselves. For in order that human beings may do this, God does it, because in order that human beings may love, God first loves them."
10 For Augustine's understanding of Pelagius' and Caelestius' views, see *NG*, 34, 54 and *The Perfection of Human Righteousness* [hereafter *PHR*], 2. Pelagius' own beliefs are hard to know with certainty, given the fragmentary character of his extant writings. He seemingly wanted to avoid a facile opposition between grace and free will (see Augustine, *GCOS*, 1.8), but nevertheless stated: "that we really do a good thing, or speak a good thought, proceeds from our own selves" (quoted by Augustine in *GCOS*, 1.17). Augustine recognized that Pelagius was chiefly concerned to avoid the suggestion that sin originates with God (see *GCOS*, 1.18), but finds his reasoning confused and his public affirmations of the necessity of grace disingenuous.
11 See Augustine, *NG*, 11, 53, 59; *DP*, 5–8, 30, 42, 65; and *GCOS*, 1.3–8. By contrast, Augustine insists that "free choice itself belongs to the grace of God … not only insofar as it exists, but also insofar as it is good, that is, insofar as it turns to carrying out God's commandments" (*PFS*, 2.7). Cf. the discussion in *UWJ*, 3.106.
12 Julian of Eclanum went so far as to describe freedom of choice as that by which the creature is "liberated from God" (*emancipatus a Deo*) in *UWJ*, 1.78 (translation altered).
13 Thus, though in *SL*, 58, Augustine designates the will as a "neutral power" (*media vis*) that "can either turn to faith or fall into unbelief," this fact is for Augustine testimony to the will's *incapacity* to direct itself rather than evidence of its autonomy. Thus, the fact that the will can incline either way is precisely the reason why "human beings cannot be said to have this will by which they believe in God, unless they have received it, since at God's call it arises from the free choice which they received as part of their nature when they were created" (translation altered).
14 See Augustine, *SL*, 31.
15 See, e.g., Augustine, *NG*, 54–5.
16 "There is no faculty of will, distinct from desire, which we use to determine our action." Wetzel, *Augustine*, p. 8. As will be discussed in greater detail in the following two sections, Augustine is not always fully consistent on this point. Thus, Cary's claim that for Augustine will is "a power of choosing that is not reducible to … desire" (*Inner Grace*, p. 42) can certainly find support even in some of Augustine's most mature writing. But, far from reflecting an innovation on Augustine's part, it is in such passages that his interpretation of the will corresponds more closely to earlier Christian ways of emphasizing human self-determination.
17 Augusine, *SL*, 54 (translation altered).

18  Augustine, *SL*, 60. In Augustine's later writings emphasis on God's internal transformation of desire largely displaces reference to the mix of external and internal stimuli found in this quotation. See J. Patout Burns, *The Development of Augustine's Doctrine of Operative Grace* (Paris: Études augustiniennes, 1980), pp. 7–15. Cf. Cary, *Inner Grace*, p. 70.

19  "Since a human being can be without sin in this life, when God's grace helps the human will, I could easily and truthfully give as an answer to the question why no one is without sin: Because they do not will to be. But if someone asks me why they do not will to be, the question becomes a long one. I will, nonetheless, give a short answer … Human beings do not will to do what is right, either because they do not know whether it is right or because they find no delight in it … But it is due to God's grace helping the human will that we come to know what is hidden and find pleasing what was not attractive." Augustine, *PFS*, 2.26. Of course, *why* God does not shape the knowledge or desire of a person so as to correspond to God's will remains for Augustine an impenetrable mystery. See, e.g., Augustine, *SL*, 60; cf. *Grace and Free Choice* (hereafter GFC), 45.

20  Thus, we will the good by the operation of the Holy Spirit, who "substituting good desire [*concupiscentiam bonam*] for evil desire [*concuipiscentia mala*], that is, pouring out love in our hearts." Augustine, *SL*, 6.

21  "For, if it is not the work of God, because it is done by us or because we do it with his gift, then it is not God's work that the mountain is moved into the sea, because the Lord said it was possible through the faith of human beings." Augustine, *SL*, 63.

22  For example, in the quoted passages from *SL*, 60 Augustine's way of describing God's action in terms of enticement and invitation seems to preserve a distinction between a divine action on the will and the human response to that action. Nevertheless (*pace* Cary), the fact that Augustine can speak of God directly moving the will need not be taken as antithetical to the idea of moving the will by shaping desire: insofar as willing follows desire, for God to elicit our desire is *eo ipso* for God to turn the will.

23  See, e.g., Augustine, *MD*, 2.45; cf. *PFS*, 1.24.

24  See Tertullian *On the Resurrection of the Flesh*, 45, in *Latin Christianity: Its Founder, Tertullian*, vol. 3 of *Ante-Nicene Fathers*, ed. the Rev. Alexander Roberts and James Donaldson (Grand Rapids, MI: William B. Eerdmans, n.d.).

25  Augustine also recognizes a "praiseworthy spiritual desire [*concupiscentia*] by which one desires [*concupiscitur*] wisdom" (*MD*, 2.52 [citing Eccl. 6:21]; cf. *SL*, 6, cited in note 20 above); but this is very much a marginal use of the term in his corpus.

26  Augustine, *GCOS*, 2.17, in *Nicene and Post-Nicene Fathers* [hereafter *NPNF*], 2nd Series, ed. Philip Schaff and Henry Wace (Peabody, MA: Hendrickson, 1995 [1893]) 5, p. 243.

27  Augustine, *MD*, 1.28; cf. *PFS*, 2.4: "Concupiscence … is present in little ones at birth, though its guilt is removed when little ones are baptized. It

remains for the combat that is life, but it does not punish with damnation those [viz. infants] who die before engaging in that combat ... But in the case of baptized adults who have the use of reason, whenever the mind consents to that same concupiscence in order to sin, it is due to one's own will. After the destruction of all sins and after the removal of that guilt as well [i.e., baptism], by which it held them in bonds from their origin, it remains in the meanwhile for the combat that is life ... [until] when peace has been achieved [in glory], there will remain nothing more to be conquered."

28  Augustine, *MD*, 1.29.
29  See Augustine, *PFS*, 2.5. The analogy between light and the eye on the one hand, and grace and the will on the other, is a favorite of Augustine's; see also *DP*, 7. For the Platonic roots of Augustine's ocular analogies, see Cary, *Inner Grace*, pp. 10–14.
30  The simile of the eye and light is apropos here: even as the eye can only see where light is present, but the eye cannot generate the light by which it sees, so the will can only will rightly when right desires are right. Cf. *PFS*, 1.57 (in *NPNF* 5, p. 37), where the "evil of sin with which every human being is born" (viz., concupiscence) is such that "it does not arise when the mind wants and does not quiet down when the mind wants."
31  Augustine, *MD*, 1.25; cf. *PFS*, 2.4.; *GCOS*, 2.44; *UWJ*, 1.71.
32  See Augustine, *ATL*, 1.27: "even if it is called sin, it bears that name, not because it is a sin, but because it was produced by a sin, just as writing is said to be the hand of a certain person, because the hand produced it."
33  Augustine, *MD*, 1.30 (translation altered).
34  Augustine, *MD*, 1.31 (translation altered).
35  See Augustine, *ATL*, 1.21–2.
36  Augustine, *ATL*, 1.15.
37  Cf. the summary of the same point in Augustine, *MD*, 2.6.
38  Julian points out the problems with Augustine's analysis in *UWJ*, 1.71.
39  Augustine, *ATL*, 1.20.
40  Cf. Augustine, *UWJ*, 6.8: "The righteousness ... of this life does not mean that we have no defect, but that we diminish our defects by not consenting to them and live in temperance, justice, and piety by resisting them."
41  It should be noted that in *De verbis Apostoli*, 5 Augustine gives more attention to the essential unity of the flesh and the spirit as the dual locus of the human "I."
42  In this context, it is important to contrast the situation Augustine describes in Rom. 7:20 with his understanding of Paul's claim in 1 Cor. 15:10 that the agent of his good works is "I ... [yet] not I, but the grace of God that is with me." In the latter case, the will empowered by God conforms to God's works; in the case of the activity of sin, it is precisely the will's lack of engagement that is crucial. Thus, while in 1 Corinthians 15, it is both I *and* not I (i.e., the believer is the agent, though his agency is completely dependent on God), in the case of concupiscence it is sin to the *exclusion* of

the I (i.e., no agency is ascribed to the believer). See the discussion in Augustine, *GFC*, 12. Augustine's interpretation of Romans 7 remains consistent, throughout his subsequent writing (see especially *UWJ*, 5.59).

43 See Wetzel, *Augustine*, p. 166: "The graced Paul who fails to reconcile his habits of the flesh with his own consent to the spirit not only emerges at the heart of Augustine's polemic against the Pelagians, but he also lurks ... at the threshold of Augustine's conversion."

44 See Augustine, *ATL*, 1.13, 24. Cf. *UWJ*, 3.179.

45 See, e.g., Augustine, *PFS*, 2.24; *SL*, 65; *NG*, 42; *PHR*, 24; *On the Gift of Perseverance*, 8; *UWJ*, 1.98; indeed, the point is made with particular force just a few chapters after his exegesis of Romans 7 in *ATL*, 1.28: "I would say that no one in this life is without sin ... [because] while we remain in the infirmity of this life, we do not cease daily to commit those sins which are daily forgiven, if we pray with faith and act with mercy."

46 See, e.g., Augustine, *PFS*, 2.4, which is discussed more fully below.

47 Wetzel characterizes Augustine's interpretations of Paul in *MD* and *ATL* as a "compromise with Pelagian views" that harks back to his own earlier work (especially the *Expositio quarundam propositionum ex epistula ad Romanos* of 394). See *Augustine*, p. 174.

48 In this context, it is worth noting that Augustine also makes frequent reference to Gal. 5:17 ("For the what the flesh desires is opposed to the Spirit, and what the Spirit desires is opposed to the flesh; for these are opposed to each other, to prevent you from doing what you want") throughout the anti-Pelagian works. See, e.g., *MD*, 1.25 and *UWJ*, 1.72.

49 "Because Augustine has Julian's complaint in mind when he rereads Romans 7 ... he focuses more attention on what [Paul's] delight [in the law] facilitates – refusing consent to perverse desires – than on the delight itself. As a result, he obscures the direction in which his own theology of grace is evolving." Wetzel, *Augustine*, p. 175.

50 While Augustine attempts to link his claims here to the Genesis narrative in *GCOS*, 2.41, he concedes the lack of direct biblical support for his account of prelapsarian sex.

51 See, e.g., Augustine, *GCOS*, 2.40.

52 See, e.g., Augustine, *MD* 1.7; *UWJ*, 2.42, 45.

53 For Augustine, in the fall "the rational soul ... emerged as disobedient to its Lord, so that it experienced the disobedience of its own servant, the flesh." *PFS*, 2.36; cf. *GCOS*, 2.39; *ATL*, 1.31; *The City of God against the Pagans*, ed. R. W. Dyson (Cambridge: Cambridge University Press, 1998), 14.17.

54 See, e.g., *UWJ*, 2.122, where concupiscence is described as "the defect from which original sin is contracted."

55 It is not completely absent, however, for though without the ability either to produce or to prevent an erection, the will retains control over the use of one. See Augustine, *MD*, 1.8; *UWJ*, 1.68; cf. the discussion of the ability of the virtuous to exercise some control over the passions in *City of God*, 14.19.

56  Thus, he contrasts concupiscence as it now exists with "the sort of concupiscence that would have existed there [viz., in paradise] if it ought to have existed there" *UWJ*, 3.187. See also 3.167, where he argues that in glory concupiscence will be healed (i.e., transformed from disordered to ordered desire) rather than simply destroyed.

57  In *UWJ*, 1.68, Augustine posits that in Eden "either sexual desire did not exist ... or it was absolutely never aroused against the choice of the will." See also 4.39, where he speculates that before the fall "concupiscence of the flesh would have been such that it would not have arisen unless the soul ... willed it" (cf. 5.15). Again, what bothers Augustine in such passages is evidently the will's inability to control the fact of desire, even where it is able to govern activity consequent upon desire. Thus, while Julian wants to distinguish between "natural" concupiscence of the flesh associated with sexual arousal and "evil [viz., immoderate] concupiscence" characteristic of gross sexual sins (*UWJ*, 3.209), Augustine views the evil of concupiscence as intrinsic and not simply a matter of how it is used: "An excess of desire ... is sinful, but its impulse is also a defect" (*UWJ*, 4.41; cf. 21).

58  In *GCOS*, 2.40, Augustine argues that in contrast to humanity's present condition, where conception is effected "by the heat of passion," apart from the fall "it would yield to the command of peaceful love."

59  Augustine's refusal to come to a firm decision over the status of desire in the prelapsarian state is evident in the fact he says of concupiscence that "it is either a defect or has been damaged" (*UWJ*, 5.17; cf. 5.14).

60  One egregious problem is its lack of fit with female sexuality. How useful can a diagnosis of the postlapsarian human condition be, when the connection between sexual arousal and reproductive function on which it is based does not apply to half of the human race?

61  Augustine does not, of course, limit concupiscence to sexuality, but he does not typically connect it with any other involuntary aspects of physiology (see, e.g., *UWJ*, 4.28). The closest he comes to exploring these other dimensions of human existence is in *City of God*, 13.22, where he suggests that in the resurrection humanity will continue to eat, even though food will no longer be *necessary*. It would seem to follow that food might nevertheless legitimately be *desired*, but this conclusion is only implied rather than explicitly stated.

62  In this context, it is interesting to note that, in contrast to the situation among human beings, sexual desire among animals "is not something evil precisely because in them the flesh does not have desires opposed to the spirit" (*UWJ*, 2.122; 4.38). One might ask why Augustine could not posit the same of prelapsarian human beings instead of arguing that desire was either absent or under the control of the will.

63  The fact that one may not "want" to sweat in a particular situation (e.g., because it is embarrassing) is not inconsistent with this point. Though it might seem to undermine the claim that willing follows desire if a person sweats though not "wanting" to, this is no more problematic than Augustine's

insistence that the sinner who hates his sin nevertheless sins willingly. In both cases it is simply necessary to reject the idea that desire, broadly conceived, is (any more than the willing that follows it) a matter of conscious control. For a sweating person to say he does not want to sweat is in this sense analogous to an alcoholic who falls off the wagon saying he does not want to drink: neither event would take place unless there was an underlying desire, and the expression of "not wanting" is simply a wish that the desire were not present. Certainly any talk of a nervous person "desiring" to sweat must include the recognition that such "desire" is very different even from the desire for a drink on the part of an alcoholic whose drinking is ruining his life (not to mention from a parent's desire for the well-being of her child); but to completely depersonalize such functions is to risk falling into an anthropological dualism, in which it is somehow more correct to say, "*This body* is sweating," than "*I* am sweating." Much of the conceptual difficulty here is blunted if agency is not understood as entailing a level of control that includes the capacity to have acted differently.

64  Along these lines, Augustine affirms that the "freedom of the will ... with which human beings were created and are created, remains unchangeable, for by it we all will to be happy, and we cannot not will this." He immediately adds, however, that "this freedom does not suffice for anyone to be happy" (*UWJ*, 6.12). In short, while we never even after the fall lose the characteristic of agency (i.e., the experience of oneself as an "I" with particular, conscious desires), we do not maintain the capacity to enact that agency as we wish.

65  As already noted, Pelagians could acknowledge a non-competitive relationship between grace and human agency only by limiting grace's role to that of sustaining the will's existence and capacities, whereas Augustine insisted that grace's operation extended to the very act of willing. See note 11 above.

66  "... the love of God produces the courage of Christians ... which is 'poured out in our hearts,' not by a choice of the will which comes from us, but 'by the Holy Spirit who has been given to us' [Rom. 5:5]." Augustine, *UWJ*, 1.83. See also 1.107: "From this necessity of slavery [to sin, God] sets us free who not only gives commandments by the law, but also bestows love by the Holy Spirit so that the delight of sin may be conquered by the delight of that love."

67  I owe this way of putting the matter to Charles T. Mathewes, *Evil and the Augustinian Tradition* (Cambridge: Cambridge University Press, 2001), p. 103.

68  Augustine, *UWJ*, 1.83 (emphasis added).

69  See, e.g., Augustine, *MD*, 1.9. This idea can actually be traced back to the period before Augustine's encounter with Pelagius to the anti-Manichean treatise *Against Fortunatus*; see the discussion in William Babcock, "Augustine on Sin and Moral Agency," *Journal of Religious Ethics* 16 (1988), p. 40.

70  Augustine, *Rebuke and Grace* (hereafter *RG*), 28.

71  Augustine, *RG*, 31.

72  Augustine, *RG*, 31.

73  Augustine, *RG*, 29.
74  So God "gave [Adam] a help without which he could not remain in that will even if he willed to, but left it up to his free choice to will it." Augustine, *RG*, 32.
75  As Augustine puts it, Adam in his prelapsarian state "did not ... need grace to receive the good because he had not yet lost it." *RG*, 32.
76  Thus, in receipt of grace "we have not only the help without which we cannot remain, even if we will, but also a help so great and so excellent that we do will it." Augustine, *RG*, 32.
77  Augustine himself compares prelapsarian humanity's need for grace to its need for food, i.e., something "without which we do not live, not [something] that makes us live." *RG*, 34. Cf. ch. 35, where Augustine states that the saints in the present have a greater freedom than Adam did before the fall, since while they still sin, they are by the gift of persevering grace prevented from falling away from the faith even though they continue to commit lesser sins.
78  Augustine makes use of the category of involuntary sin (generally with specific reference to Romans 7) as a means of emphasizing against the Pelagians the impotence of the will to avoid sinning on its own. In line with our earlier criticism of Augustine's interpretation of Romans 7, the description of sin as involuntary in these passages can be faulted as inconsistent with Augustine's general denial that culpable human action is ever a matter of compulsion (i.e., lack of agency) even in the postlapsarian state (see, e.g., *UWJ*, 1.101). From this perspective, a more consistently "Augustinian" reading of Paul's situation would not be that he fails to do what he desires, but that his most fundamental desires are not what he wants them to be. Augustine comes close to acknowledging this equivocation in his talk of involuntary sin in *SL*, 53.
79  Cited in Augustine, *UWJ*, 5.56.
80  Augustine, *UWJ*, 5.56.
81  Thus, Alistair McFadyen concludes that Pelagius "saves the freedom of the will at the cost of being able to say that the will is in any sense *personal*," in *Bound to Sin: Abuse, Holocaust and the Christian Doctrine of Sin* (Cambridge: Cambridge University Press, 2000), p. 170, n. 6.
82  "The theory of the will as the power of choice, informed by but independent of desire, makes every action to some degree unintelligible, for if the theory were true, no action would ever be sufficiently explained by its motives. We would have to add the agent's free-floating choice of motives to complete the explanation." Wetzel, *Augustine*, p. 8; cf. p. 216. See also Mathewes, *Evil*, p. 54: "The explanation of our actions then ends invariably in the raw existentialist claim 'so I willed it'. But that ends up rendering one's identity a riddle; for why should I, a reflective, deliberative agent, identify myself with this willing 'I'?"
83  One might draw an analogy here to the way in which in the early stages of learning a language, one has to "will" (i.e., make a deliberate, conscious

effort) to understand what is spoken or written as language, while once fluency is achieved this happens automatically – without it being any less the case that in a given instance my understanding a given phrase as Italian is something I "will" (i.e., something "I" do, even though it may well escape any act of conscious choice and, indeed, may well be experienced as something I cannot help doing).

84   To put it bluntly, it is much less problematic to speak of newborn infants as sinners when sin is seen as a constitutive feature of postlapsarian human agency than when it is specifically identified with a capacity that infants evidently do not have.

85   The tension between Augustine's "Pelagian" and anti-Pelagian characteristics emerges with particular clarity in the way original sin is related to choice: even though original sin is present in each member of post-Adamic humanity independently of choice, his agreement with the Pelagians that sin arises only from choice forces him to argue for inherited sin, for inasmuch as "a little one does not have a will for sinning … a little one would not have sin if that man had not sinned by the will from whom the little one contracted it" (Augustine, *UWJ*, 4.116). In short, by deriving sin from the will's libertarian power to choose, Augustine is forced to commit to a particular account of natural history and a still more questionable account of sin's transmission.

# 4

# Maximus the Confessor: Willing Is Not Choosing[*]

Maximus the Confessor lived for a long time in the very same regions of northern Africa where Augustine served as bishop, albeit two centuries after the latter's death.[1] Although there is no evidence that he was directly familiar with Augustine's writings,[2] he was broadly sympathetic to Western (i.e., Latin) theological concerns.[3] Like most Orthodox writers before and since, he shared little of Augustine's passion for the doctrine of original sin and showed no inclination to endorse the latter's views on post-lapsarian humanity's congenital sinfulness. He was, however, happy to affirm the catastrophic effects of Adam's transgression in very traditional terms:

> After the transgression pleasure [*hēdonē*] naturally preconditioned the births of all human beings, and no one was by nature free from a birth subject to the passion associated with this pleasure; rather, everyone naturally [*phusikōs*] paid for it with sufferings and subsequent death.[4]

The passions introduced by the fall had wreaked havoc on the human condition by subjecting the body to the tyranny of the passions, but while Maximus goes on to add that this situation makes the human exercise of freedom in obedience to God very difficult (*aporos*), that very terminology seems to suggest that it is not impossible in the way that Augustine

---

[*] Chapter 4 is a revised version of the article "'Willing Is Not Choosing': Some Anthropological Implications of Dyothelite Christology," first published in *International Journal of Systematic Theology* 9, no. 1 (January 2007), 3–23, Wiley-Blackwell.

---

*In Adam's Fall: A Meditation on the Christian Doctrine of Original Sin*, by Ian A. McFarland.
© 2010 Ian A. McFarland.

claimed. For Maximus (as for the broader Greek tradition going back to Irenaeus) postlapsarian humanity's subjection to passion may severely compromise its capacity to obey God, but does not seem to eliminate it.

In spite of his adherence to a traditional (i.e., non-Augustinian) understanding of the fall, however, Maximus develops a doctrine of the will that has important points of resonance with the innovations characteristic of Augustine's anti-Pelagian position. This is by no means to overlook the significant differences between the two positions. Not only is it virtually impossible to imagine Maximus endorsing Augustine's insistence on the postlapsarian will's congenital inability to avoid sin, but the two writers approach the topic from very different perspectives. Augustine's concerns were overtly soteriological and shaped primarily by his doctrine of grace. Maximus' ideas, on the other hand, were forged in the context of Christological controversy and were strongly influenced by trinitarian categories. Thus, while Augustine depends heavily on speculative reconstructions of Adam's prelapsarian state for his understanding of the essential character of the will, Maximus' context leads him to focus on Christ as the touchstone for his views on human willing.

One crucial effect of this difference in approach is that Maximus defends a much more consistently close coordination of will and nature than does Augustine. Most famously (and as will be explored in much greater detail in the section of this chapter that deals with Maximus' interpretation of Christ's willing), Maximus views Christ's fear at the prospect of death – precisely the kind of reflexive action that Augustine was inclined to view as evidence of humanity's fallenness – as evidence that Christ possessed a will that was both fully human and (given Maximus' conviction that Christ did not suffer the effects of original sin) undamaged. In making this argument, Maximus draws on a history of Christological reflection that goes back to Cyril of Alexandria. At about the same time that Augustine was writing his later anti-Pelagian treatises, Cyril's Nestorian opponents were charging that his doctrine of a "natural union" (*phusikē henosis*) of divine and human in Christ implied that the Word was compelled involuntarily to become incarnate, "since what is natural is necessary" (*anagkastikē gar hē phusis*). Cyril responded as follows:

> ... they insist that what pertains to nature is at all times and in every respect subject to the laws of necessity ... But if it is true that human beings are by nature rational, does it follow that they are rational involuntarily or by compulsion [*aboulētōs kai ēnagkasmenōs*]? What then? Will they argue that the God of all is not God by nature? That God is not by nature holy, righteous, good, life, light, wisdom, and power? But does it follow that

God is all these things involuntarily and by necessity [*aboulētos kai hōs ex anagkēs*]?[5]

One can find similar arguments in Augustine,[6] but while he uses them to show the logical compatibility of responsible willing and natural necessity (whether applied to the goodness of God or the perversity of human beings), Cyril invokes it precisely to argue that talk of "necessity" is misplaced when it comes to characterizing the actions of natures that are rational and (therefore) possess a will, arguing that "nothing natural is involuntary in a rational nature."[7] Far more than is the case with Augustine (who, as noted in the last chapter, thought "liberty of indifference" characteristic of the unfallen human will), willing is here decoupled entirely from the capacity to choose between alternatives. As Maximus develops the point in his own work, willing is simply the way in which rational beings (whether human, angelic, or divine) enact their natures. Thus, while Augustine thought that the capacity to choose between good and evil was integral to humanity's prelapsarian condition (and thus a defining feature of the human will as originally created by God), Maximus, in perhaps his most technically precise analysis of human volition, insists that "willing is not choosing."[8] Because willing is instead an expression of nature (*phusis*), it is not the source or ground of individual identity (*hypostasis*). And if identity is not reducible to the will, then the will's lack of alternatives with respect to sin either now or in glory may not constitute the kind of threat to human integrity that modern Westerners are inclined to fear.[9]

## Maximus' Christology in Context

In order to appreciate the significance of Maximus' argument, it is necessary to give some sense of its context: the sixth-century monothelite controversy that was finally resolved only after Maximus' death at the Third Council of Constantinople in 680–1. Perhaps none of the ancient ecumenical councils is less familiar to contemporary Christians, and initial acquaintance with the issues with which it dealt may lead many to the conclusion that its obscurity is richly deserved. After all, the various factions all confessed the Nicene doctrine of the Trinity, and all accepted the Chalcedonian principle that Christ was consubstantial with God in his divinity and consubstantial with us in his humanity. Nor did the council's debates have the kind of clear implications for the daily life of the church that marked the iconoclastic controversy in the following century. Indeed, the central issue under debate emerged almost by accident in the course of an extended process of theological and political negotiation designed to secure unity among the churches of the Byzantine Empire. On these grounds the great historian Adolf von Harnack claimed the whole episode "essentially belongs to political history" and dismissed the deliberations of 680–1 as "the Council of antiquaries and paleographists," whose definitions and anathemas were shaped more by a desire to please the Emperor than by theological conviction.[10]

The monothelite theology condemned at the Council had its roots in imperial efforts to reconcile with those churches that had broken with Constantinople over the two-natures Christology of Chalcedon.[11] Patriarch Sergius of Constantinople worked hard through the early decades of the seventh century to promote a compromise position, according to which Christ was to be confessed as possessing two natures in line with the decrees of Chalcedon, but as having just a single composite operation or mode of activity (Greek *monē energeia*). Though this "monoenergist" position did prove acceptable to at least some anti-Chalcedonians, it met with stiff opposition from the staunch Chalcedonian monk Sophronius, who in 634 became Patriarch of Jerusalem. In the face of this resistance, Sergius backed off, referring the matter to Pope Honorius I with the suggestion that all attempts to enumerate Christ's *energeiai* be proscribed. In his response Honorius concurred, but also set the stage for further controversy by making a fateful reference to "the one will of our Lord Jesus Christ" in the context of affirming Sergius' view that it was impossible for two wills to exist together in one and the same person.[12]

In speaking of one will in Christ, Honorius may have wished only to deny that Jesus experienced any conflict in willing.[13] Whatever his intent, however, the doctrine that Christ had a single will (Greek *monē thelēsis*) was the centerpiece of a renewed attempt at rapprochement with the anti-Chalcedonian churches promulgated in an imperial edict (the *Ecthesis*) of 638. This "monothelite" theology met with resistance from the same quarters as its monenergist precursor, and though Honorius died before being able to respond to criticism of his reference to Christ's one will, his successors condemned the phrase as heretical. This opposition led the next emperor, Constans II, to issue a further decree (the *Typos*) forbidding debate over the number of Christ's operations or wills alike. Nevertheless, continued support for the monothelite position by successive patriarchs in Constantinople, combined with Maximus' refusal to allow the question of the number of Christ's wills to be passed over in silence, guaranteed that controversy over the interrelated categories of will and operation in Christ would continue.

## Dyothelite Christology in Outline

At first glance perhaps the most surprising thing about the monothelite controversy is that the claim that Christ had one will proved controversial at all. As we have already had occasion to observe, the early church placed a premium on the importance of human free will as a means of opposing both pagan fatalism and the perceived determinism of various Christian Gnostic groups. The will could be named using a wide range of terms,[14] but there was virtual consensus in the patristic period that it was both the basis of human ability to respond to God and the means by which creature and Creator would be united in glory.[15] Against this background, it is easy to appreciate how Honorius might have failed to see anything either innovative or especially controversial in his reference to the one will in Christ. Indeed, even Maximus himself, who would become the chief intellectual architect of the dyothelite response to monothelitism, could in the years before the outbreak of the controversy speak of the goal of human life as one of deification, in which human and divine wills are made "identical ... in a union of relation."[16]

Of course, even in this early quotation the fact that Maximus speaks of a "union of *relation*" suggests that even in glory an *ontological* distinction between the divine and the human remains. In fact, there is little evidence that Maximus' views on deification underwent any fundamental shift as a result of the monothelite controversy.[17] For example, there is no change either in his material claim that deification is a state in which human wills are shaped directly by God's will, or in his more formal grounding of theological anthropology in Christology. Already in the short essays that make up the relatively early *Ambigua ad Ioannem*, the reference point for Maximus' account of the deified will is the story of Christ in Gethsemane – the same text that is the linchpin of his later, dyothelite theology.[18] At the same time, his language in these early treatises lacks the precision of his later theology, so that at one point Maximus can speak of the glorified state in seemingly monenergist terms that he will later find it necessary to clarify.[19] In this way, the monothelite controversy did not so much alter the Confessor's basic theological convictions as it provided the occasion for him to clarify the terms in which human freedom and integrity were to be described and understood. Though cast in a highly technical Christological idiom, the results are in their own way no less significant for the Christian understanding of the relationship between nature, grace, and human salvation than Augustine's anti-Pelagian writings.

Maximus' dyothelite theology is often explained in highly schematic terms that obscure its anthropological significance. The standard textbook account takes syllogistic form: the Council of Chalcedon had established that Christ was to be confessed as one hypostasis in two natures; the will is a feature of nature rather than hypostasis; therefore commitment to Chalcedon demands that Christ be confessed as having two wills. This summary is accurate as far as it goes, but it begs the question of why the will should be associated with nature rather than hypostasis. Here, too, it is possible to present the decisive arguments in fairly short order. The first is more soteriological in character. Working from the well-established principle that Christ cannot redeem what he has not assumed, one argues that Christ must have assumed a human will to have effected its redemption, concluding that whatever Christ assumes pertains to the nature by definition.[20] The second depends on an appeal to consistency in the use of theological terms. According to this argument, the monothelite claim that Christ has but one will corresponding to his one hypostasis implies that God has three wills corresponding to the three trinitarian hypostases; but this is inconsistent with the belief that God has only one will, which corresponds to the one divine nature and thus is common to all three divine hypostases.[21]

While the logical force of these arguments is undeniable, neither is particularly effective in illuminating the anthropological implications of the dyothelite position. Indeed, it might seem at first glance that the correlation of will with nature rather than hypostasis purchases theological consistency at the price of psychological plausibility. Most basically, what sense does it make to speak of two wills in Christ if – as both monothelites and Maximus agreed – there is in Christ only one willing agent (viz., the divine Son)?[22] And the confusion seems only to be increased when it is recognized that Maximus' dyothelite argument includes a further distinction within human willing between the "natural will" (*thelēma phusikon*, or simply *thelēma*) and the "gnomic will" (*thelēma gnomikon*, or simply *gnōmē*).[23] According to Maximus, all human beings possess both a natural and a gnomic will; yet while he insists that Christ's full humanity dictates that he, too, has a natural will, he repeatedly denies that Christ has a gnomic will.[24] Given that Maximus explicitly associates the gnomic will with the powers of deliberation and decision – effectively with the ability to choose between options – his defense of Jesus' consubstantiality with the human race risks being subverted from the outset, since the significance of Jesus' solidarity with us in possessing a natural will seems inconsistent with the denial that his willing is marked by those features connected with choice that we are inclined to view as most central to human freedom.[25]

## Maximus' Analysis of the Will

In order to address these concerns, it is necessary to explore in greater detail why Maximus introduced the distinction between natural and gnomic wills. Prior to the monothelite controversy, Maximus treats *thelēma* and *gnomē* as synonyms and, correspondingly, has no difficulty in ascribing a *gnomē* to Christ.[26] Already in one of his earliest extant writings, however, there is a foreshadowing of the later distinction. Maximus describes humanity's end as "to have one *gnomē* and one *thelēma* with God and with one another," while at the same time noting that the fall has blocked this process by introducing a division within the will that causes us "to turn from the natural movement ... to what is forbidden."[27] This contrast between the will's "natural movement" on the one hand and its capacity to turn from nature on the other parallels the later distinction between the natural and gnomic wills. It was only in confronting the monothelite identification of Christ's will with his divine hypostasis, however, that Maximus found it necessary to cast this distinction in technical terminology.

As already noted, Maximus' immediate theological concern in confronting monothelitism was to affirm the theological principle that Christ could only redeem the will if the will were part of the nature that he assumed in the incarnation. This correlation of the will with nature is the basis for the category of the natural will. And though the claim that the will was a constitutive feature of human nature had the effect of reducing the will to one among many such faculties, no diminishment of the will's significance was thereby intended. On the contrary, Maximus is quite clear that the natural will is the most significant of humanity's faculties, since it "holds everything together," and "we exist in and through it" in a way that is not true of other aspects of our nature.[28] Indeed, the supreme importance of the natural will in Maximus' anthropology is illustrated by its persistent identification with human agency (*autexousia*). Nevertheless, Maximus' analysis of the natural will suggests that such agency is distinct from freedom of choice.[29] For Maximus the primary manifestation of the natural will is in our natural appetites:

> For by this power [of the will] alone we naturally desire being, life, movement, understanding, speech, perception, nourishment, sleep, refreshment,

as well as not to suffer pain or to die – quite simply to possess fully everything that sustains the nature and to lack whatever harms it.[30]

Clearly, we do not desire sleep or food because we choose to do so; on the contrary, Maximus' whole point is that such desires are *natural*. They do not need the presence of a will to manifest themselves, as is clear from the fact that animals, too, naturally seek life and avoid death. What is distinctive about human beings is what it means for them to desire something naturally. For whereas other sentient beings desire rest or flee pain by instinct (and thus by compulsion), human beings do so "in and through" the will (and therefore freely):

> For that which is rational by nature has a natural power that is a rational appetite [*logikēn orexin*], which is also called the will [*thelēsis*] of the intellective soul. And by this power we reason willingly [*thelontes logizometha*]; and when we have reasoned, we desire willingly [*thelontes boulometha*].[31]

In short, for Maximus the natural will is that property whereby we do whatever we do as responsible agents rather than mechanically or by instinct. It follows that if Christ is confessed as fully human (i.e., a genuinely human agent rather than a divine ghost in a biochemical machine), he must have a human natural will.

What then of the gnomic will? In line with the description of the fall in his early letter to John the Cubicularius, Maximus understands sin as the product of a *gnōmē* that has turned from what is natural; yet it would be a mistake to conclude that he simply identifies the gnomic will with fallenness, since he has no difficulty acknowledging that it can conform to God's will.[32] Yet if the gnomic will is not inherently sinful, it is intimately connected with the *possibility* of sin, for it is understood in terms of the capacity to choose between options – including especially good and evil. Maximus associates this capacity with a will that does not enjoy the eschatological state of immediate conformity to God's will, arguing that short of this state willing is a complex process that moves from desire (*boulēsis*) through deliberation (*boulē* or *bouleusis*) to the actualization of the results of deliberation in choice (*prohairesis*).[33]

Deliberation is crucial to Maximus' understanding of the gnomic will. It is correlated with the ignorance and doubt that are characteristic of the will that has not yet been deified: we deliberate about those things which are within the scope of our will, but the implications of which are unclear to us – and under the conditions of history, that includes everything that we will.[34] Because our deliberation can go either well or badly, we have the capacity to deviate from our natural end, and our willing is, correspondingly, mutable. Though inseparable from our nature as responsible agents, the gnomic character of our willing under conditions of historical existence leaves open the possibility of deviating from that nature. In the fall this possibility was actualized in a way that continues to render human beings disposed to sin.[35] Whether or not we sin in any particular instance, however, our status as pilgrims dictates that our earthly actions are invariably characterized by the process of gnomic deliberation and choice.

At this point it is possible to speak more precisely about the relationship between the gnomic and natural wills. For Maximus the gnomic will is a mode (or *tropos*) in which individual human beings will rather than an inherent property (or *logos*) of the will as a constitutive feature of human nature.[36] In other words, the gnomic will is not a separate power that exists alongside the natural will; it is simply a name for how willing takes place. In the same way that hypostasis is defined as the *tropos* (i.e., mode of being) of a particular *logos* (i.e., type of entity), so the gnomic will refers to the mode in which the natural will is instantiated by human hypostases prior to its eschatological transformation into a condition of immediate conformity to God's will.[37]

In this context, Maximus' denial that Christ has a gnomic will derives from his conviction that Christ does not suffer from the kind of ignorance and uncertainty that we do; for this reason, he wills without deliberation and decision. Crucially, however, Christ's willing lacks these characteristics not because his humanity is essentially (i.e., with respect to its *logos*) other than ours, but only because his human nature is already deified and thus wills in a mode (or *tropos*) different than ours:

> But as for the Savior's willing according to his human nature, even though it was natural, it was not bare [*psilon*] like ours, any more than his humanity as such is, since it has been perfectly deified above us in union, because of which it is actually sinless.[38]

Because *gnomē* is a *tropos* of the will, it is not analytic either to the act of willing or to the nature of the will. Instead, *gnomē* is a feature of the will only when willing hypostasized under conditions of ignorance and doubt. Since Christ's human will is, by virtue of its enhypostatization by the Second Person of the Trinity, fully deified, it is permanently oriented to God in a way that obviates any need for deliberation.[39] Christ's individual experience of willing is therefore different from that of all other human beings; but it does not compromise Christ's consubstantiality with us, because the latter is a function of the will's *logos* rather than its *tropos*.[40]

In short, in the same way that Christ's having a genuinely human body is not compromised by the fact that the agent who is the subject of his bodily movements is God, neither is the claim that his incarnate acts are humanly willed compromised by the fact that God is the subject of the willing. As a property of human nature, the humanity of the will – like that of the mind or body – is logically distinct from (and thus ontologically unaffected by) the divinity of the hypostasis.

## Maximus' Interpretation of Christ's Willing

Because the gnomic will names merely a mode of willing and not the essence (or *logos*) of the will itself, the lack of a *gnomē* does not mean a dissolution of human agency. Again, the driving purpose behind Maximus' introduction of the distinction between natural and gnomic wills was precisely to defend the principle that Christ's fully deified humanity included a human will – and thus genuinely human willing – notwithstanding the fact that this will did not operate by means of the processes of deliberation and choice. The way Maximus uses Scripture to defend the doctrine of Christ's human will makes this clear. For though the soteriological issue of Christ's consubstantiality with human beings serves as the dogmatic foundation of Maximus' dyothelitism, it is only by attending to the biblical texts Maximus uses to substantiate and illustrate his position that his understanding of the will's place in theological anthropology becomes clear.

Maximus' exegetical arguments for a distinct human will in Christ rests on the contention that the Bible depicts Christ willing things that cannot coherently be ascribed to the divine nature: "How ... if the incarnate Word did not himself will naturally as a human being ... did he voluntarily [*hekousiōs*] and willingly [*thelōn*] submit to hunger and thirst, labour and weariness, sleep and all the rest?"[41] This line of argument is developed at some length in the *Disputation with Pyrrhus*, where Maximus cites a range of texts from the Gospels as support for the existence of a distinctly human will in Christ, arguing in each case that Christ is depicted as willing something that cannot be referred to divinity and so must be ascribed to Christ's human nature. For example, he argues that Christ's wandering around Palestine must be viewed as a function of his human will, since the omnipresence of the divine nature makes it absurd to speak of Christ willing his own physical movement from one place to another according to his divinity.[42] The force of Maximus' exegetical logic in these passages comes across with particular clarity in his interpretation of Phil. 2:8:

The divine Apostle says of him in the Epistle to the Hebrews [*sic*]: "He became obedient to the point of death – even death on a cross." Was he obedient willingly or unwillingly? If unwillingly, then it should be described as compulsion [*turannis*] and not obedience. But if willingly, obedience is not a property of God but of human beings, as the divine Gregory [of Nazianzus] says (in agreement with the Fathers): "God is neither obedient nor disobedient, for such matters pertain to subordinates and those under authority."[43]

Obedience cannot be ascribed to the divine nature. Therefore, insofar as Christ willed to be obedient, he must have done so according to his human nature. And for Maximus it is essential to say that Christ's obedience was a matter of will; otherwise Christ would not be fully human, since human beings, as rational creatures, do what they do willingly rather than by instinct or compulsion.

As important as such passages are to building his case, the exegetical center of Maximus' dyothelite Christology is (as already noted) the agony in the garden.[44] The *crux interpretandum* in this story is the relationship between Christ's initial petition that the cup pass from him and his subsequent acquiescence to the Father's will.[45] Monothelites read this prayer as depicting a displacement of the human will by the divine. In response, Maximus argued that both aspects of Christ's prayer are to be ascribed to his human will: as a human being, Christ recoiled from death (in line with the inherent disposition of the natural will); but it was also as a human being that he overcame this fear in obedience to the divine will (since obedience pertains to the human rather than the divine nature):

> ... he was in truth and properly a human being: to this his natural will bears witness in his plea to be spared from death ... And again that the human will is wholly deified [*diolou tetheoto*], in its agreement with the divine will itself, since it is eternally moved and shaped by it and in accordance with it, is clear when he shows that all that matters is a perfect verification of the will of the Father, in his saying as a human being, "Not mine, but your will be done," by this giving himself as a type and example of setting aside our own will by the perfect fulfilment of the divine, even if because of this we find ourselves face to face with death.[46]

Given that Christ's two petitions clearly differ in content, one cannot help asking how they can both be ascribed to the same human will, if – as Maximus insists – Christ's lack of a gnomic will precludes the possibility that doubt and deliberation be used to account for the shift from resistance to acceptance.[47] As the quoted passage suggests, Maximus' answer rests on making a distinction between what is natural to human will (in this case, avoidance of death) and the movement of the same will inasmuch as it is "wholly deified" and thus fixed immovably on God. Working within this framework, Maximus insists that though Christ's two petitions are clearly different from one another, the fact that God, as the common author of created nature and deifying grace, is the source of both movements of the will means that this difference cannot be interpreted in terms of the process of choosing between sin and righteousness characteristic of gnomic deliberation.[48] Nor is it permissible to see Christ's eventual acceptance of the cup as indicating the overshadowing or bracketing of his humanity, since Maximus insists that deification produces no change with respect to nature.[49] Instead, the movement from rejection of the cup to its acceptance illustrates a progression from human nature as it operates according to its own powers and nature that, as enabled to transcend those powers through grace, fulfils the particular calling of the individual within God's wider plan for a deified humanity.[50]

This distinction between the natural power (*logos*) of Christ's human will and the particular way (*tropos*) it moves in Gethsemane parallels the distinction between the natural and gnomic wills. There are, however, three crucial and interrelated differences, two of which we have already had occasion to note. First, the deified will is permanently fixed on God's will, in contrast to the inherent mutability of gnomic willing, which is a function of the ignorance and uncertainty of a will that is not so fixed. Second, this difference in the will's basic orientation means that the processes of deliberation and decision which are an intrinsic feature of gnomic willing are not found in the deified will. Finally, while the distance from God that is definitive of gnomic willing means that in itself its freedom of choice consists in the possibility of willing that which is *against* nature (and which is therefore opposed to God), the freedom of the deified will consists in the God-given capacity to will that which is *beyond* but – crucially for Maximus – *not against* nature.[51] In other words, the gnomic will has the capacity either to follow nature or to sin.[52] By contrast, the deified will's deviation from its "natural" object is not sin, because it is not a rejection of nature; on the contrary, it wills whatever it wills (in this case, the cup of suffering) precisely out of obedience to the God who is recognized as the author of human nature and thus as the one whose calling must be understood as a fulfillment of that nature even as it exceeds that nature's intrinsic inclinations and capacities.[53]

Thus, although the *tropos* of Christ's will in Gethsemane is certainly a function of his hypostatic particularity (i.e., of his particularity as the incarnate Word), it is not a product of a gnomic will: instead of being the product of gnomic deliberation and decision, it has its origin directly in the will of God. The divine will "moves and shapes" Christ's human will; but this will, in turn, accepts this moving and shaping in an act of obedience that both reflects and constitutes its deification.[54] Moreover, this unswerving orientation to God, far from undermining the willer's particularity, actually secures it in a way analogous to what we have already seen in Augustine's account of grace. Thus, Christ is never more Christ than in his acceptance of the cup; and, indeed, he would not be Christ apart from it. The deified will remains both free and distinctively human, because God draws the individual to Godself not by cancelling or overriding human willing, but rather by giving the will the grace to desire an object that exceeds its natural capacities. In this way, the will is presented with an object that it could not desire on its own, but which by God's grace it is able to accept as its most proper desire.[55]

## Anthropological Implications

Inasmuch as Maximus conceives of deification as the proper end of human nature as such, it should come as no surprise that he does not view the characteristics of Christ's deified humanity as unique to him. On the contrary, because Christ is fully human it follows that the willing of all deified human beings (viz., the saints in glory) will have the same structural features that mark his willing during his earthly ministry.[56] The parallels are clear in Maximus' characterization of the saints' experience of deification:

> At that time there will be no *prohairesis* (as in the law of nature that now prevails), since every uncertainty regarding things will fall away, and there will be in an active desire [*orexis energēs*] that is single and cognitive for whatever nature renders desirable [*tois ... kata phusin orektikois*]. And this desire, having marvelously attained the pure, mystical enjoyment of that which is naturally to be desired ... finds its satisfaction in the infinite extension of its appetite for enjoyable things.[57]

Gnomic choice (*prohairesis*) will disappear from human experience, but while this means that among the saints there will be revealed "one common will with respect to the *logos* of nature, difference will remain with respect to the *tropos* of motion."[58] In other words, the eschaton preserves the individual integrity of each person: in no case is will at odds with nature (as is the case at least potentially where the gnomic will is active), but, as with Christ, deification means that the various objects of human willing will transcend – without opposing – nature as God draws each individual to her or his own particular calling.[59] There is an important contrast with Augustine here, for whom (as James Wetzel observes) speculation about the perfection of paradise makes sin that aspect of our identities that gives us individual character.[60] Correlatively, insofar as grace overcomes sin by restoring and, indeed, improving upon this primordial perfection, it eclipses the role of the will in a way that risks making the life of the blessed appear a featureless gray. By contrast, Maximus' articulation of the category of the natural will in the context of Christ's prayer in Gethsemane provides a model of grace that mitigates this risk, because it depicts a capacity for moral development that is not limited to overcoming sin. In other words, the struggle of Christ in Gethsemane provides a model of genuinely human labor, growth, and adventure that is not dependent on sin – resulting in an understanding of the operation of grace that does not render the will invisible.

As with Christ, so with all other human beings the distinction between nature and hypostasis is crucial here as a framework for interpreting the distinction between the natural and gnomic wills. Insofar as it pertains to the hypostasis, gnomic will is not a distinct property (*logos*) of human being. With respect to *logos*, human beings have but one – natural – will both now and in glory; and it is this natural will that constitutes them as free and responsible agents. *Gnomē* is a *tropos* of willing that marks individual hypostases of the human nature so long as that nature remains undeified. Deification establishes a new mode of willing in which gnomic deliberation is replaced by a direct and undeviating orientation to God.

This model of deification makes it easier to see how Maximus' understanding of glory is consistent with a continuing vision of human beings as free and responsible subjects. As that feature of human nature by which human beings can and must own their actions as precisely theirs (i.e., as that which is rightly predicated of their individual "I's"), willing is properly conceived as the natural *mode* but not the *source* of human action. This basic principle is true whether or not the will is deified. Just as the fallen person claims rightly her actions (whether eating, fornicating, or praying) as her own, so the glorified person will rightly claim her actions (e.g., loving God) as her own: in both cases, "I willingly did x," will be the correct form by which an individual describes her actions. The mode by which this willing action is accomplished, however, differs radically before and after deification. The undeified will operates by means of deliberation and decision, culminating in choice (*prohairesis*); in the deified will, by contrast, these processes are rendered redundant as the will is moved and shaped directly by God.

In this way, the power of self-determination characteristic of gnomic willing turns out to be an index of the willer's *distance* from God.[61] The deified will is not self-determining in this way, but it is free, since Maximus' construction of the will is one in which the abolition of gnomic distance from God by grace takes away nothing from the integrity of willing. For the will to be moved and shaped directly by God in glory is not for it to be compelled, any more than the fact of its being moved and shaped by nature in the present life (in, e.g., the impulse to pursue what is life-preserving and flee what is life-threatening) is a matter of compulsion. Indeed, Maximus' strict correlation of the will with human nature means that the human experience of glory must involve the will if it is to be genuinely human in the first place. And if the example of Christ in Gethsemane shows that to will rightly means obeying God's will, the same story makes it abundantly clear that when this happens the human will is not simply overridden – let alone displaced – by God's. It accords with this Christological model that other human beings are called by God to will destinies that are equally transcendent of their natural appetites and equally unique to their own hypostatic particularities. The deified will is unable to sin because it is fixed on God; but because God's being is infinitely rich and the divine will for each rational creature unique, what obedience to God's will means concretely will differ for each person – and discovering what it means is an adventure that is not so much terminated as fully enabled by deification.

In short, Maximus' understanding of deification suggests that while the will is the *means* by which we live out our identities before God (i.e., as rational creatures we are who we are willingly), it is not the *source* of those identities. Their source is God, such that the fulfillment of what it means to be human is to have one's own will fixed steadily on God's. Maximus' insistence against the monothelites that Christ had a human will shows that this understanding of the place of the will entails no diminishment in the importance of the will as a constitutive feature of a distinctly Christian anthropology. On the contrary, his position is distinguished from that of his opponents precisely by his insistence that it is impossible to speak of humanity where there is no human will. Willing for Maximus defines our humanity as much as rationality does; indeed, it has a good claim to being the focal point of human existence, insofar as it is that feature of our being that defines our many passions and actions as ours. The will defines us as subjects able to respond to God in love, trust, and obedience – and thereby to participate in the divine life.

But if the will is central to our nature as human beings able to love God, it is not what defines us as particular hypostases who, having been loved by God, are called to love God in return. To be sure, we love God willingly — and no more so than when we have been deified — but who we are as individual hypostases is not to be identified with our wills any more than it is with any other aspect of our shared nature as human beings. If in the eschaton there will continue to be, as Maximus insists, genuine difference among human beings, this will not be a function of their natural wills as such: with respect to *logos*, all human wills will be united in their immutable focus on God; their difference will be a function of *tropos* — the various ways in which those wills will individually be moved and shaped by God. Crucially, however, this variation will not be then (as it is now) a function of our wills' gnomic mutability, but of their individual conformity to a divine will.[62] It is, in short, God who makes the saints who they are — though it must be immediately added that the saints accept and live out these identities willingly in the same way that Christ willingly accedes to the will of the Father in the garden.

In effect, gnomic will amounts to something like freedom of choice; but for Maximus this freedom is emphatically not to be identified with human nature as such. On the contrary, it is characteristic only of our humanity in its earthly state and, far from defining what it means to will, it describes only a particular mode of willing that for Maximus is at best penultimate and at worst (and in fact) predisposed to sin. In effect, *gnomē* in the present life occupies the place that is taken by God in the state of glory. But this very fact signals that for Maximus the drive to self-determination characteristic of gnomic willing is not to be identified with the self in the present — any more than God will be identified with the self in heaven.[63]

Thus, for Maximus the gnomic will is that power which most immediately shapes our identity here and now, even as God is the power that will do so in the state of glory. Since all our willing in the present life is invariably gnomic in character, our virtues are as much a product of *gnomē* as our sins — and Maximus is quite clear that deification is not realized apart from by ascetic cultivation of the virtues in the present life.[64] Nevertheless, even in the present it is ultimately the gift of divine grace rather than any inherent capacity of the *gnomē* that brings the saints to their appointed end.[65] The gnomic will is incapable of securing human identity before God on its own because (unlike the natural will, which is moved by its own inherent — and therefore God-given — appetites) it does not have any content: as a mere mode of willing it is in itself empty, directionless, and (therefore) mutable.[66] Thus while the effects of gnomic willing continue to mark human hypostases even once the *gnomē* itself has been transcended in the state of glory,[67] the this-worldly limit of gnomic willing rules out its being interpreted as either the source of or the key to human identity.

Appreciating the character of the gnomic will as a mode of realizing hypostatic identity but not as the source of that identity allows an important anthropological distinction to be made between claiming one's actions as one's own and taking credit for them as self-generated. As just noted, the gnomic will is intrinsically devoid of content. Its objects come to it from without, either (positively) from divine promptings and the intrinsic drives of human nature, on the one hand, or (negatively) from the soul's disordered passions, on the other. From this perspective, the idea that human beings make themselves is true only to the extent that they drift away from their natural end toward self-destruction. By contrast, insofar as human beings follow their nature, they are emphatically not self-made, but God-made – and never more so than in their deification. At the same time, because what God first makes and then deifies are human beings – rational, responsible, self-conscious agents – the saint's relationship with God is a manifestation of her freedom as one who, by grace, not only knows and loves God, but does so willingly.[68]

## Conclusion

If willing is not about choosing, then lack of choice with regard to sin, whether now or in glory, says nothing in itself about our integrity as free and responsible beings. The will is not, on this reading, the guarantor of our specific *hypostatic* identity, but rather that *natural* faculty by which our appetites and acts, many of which are functionally indistinguishable from those of other animals, acquire their distinctly human character. Thus, my hunger is the same as my dog's insofar as its basic physiology is concerned, but I can claim (and, indeed, cannot honestly avoid claiming) my hunger as my own in a way that my dog cannot – even though I am no more able than my dog not to hunger when I have not eaten for a time. Of course, I am also distinguished from my dog by my ability to deliberate and decide with respect to the way in which I satisfy (or refrain from satisfying) my hunger, but for Maximus this distinction is not of final significance for my identity as a human being. If I am saved, there will come a time when my willing will no longer be characterized by deliberation and decision; but I will not be any less human. On the contrary, it is Maximus' contention that only then will my calling and destiny as a human being have been fulfilled.

This distinction between willing and choosing cuts against any anthropology that equates humanity with radical self-determination. Theologically, the doctrine of creation renders such visions of radical autonomy problematic, since they imply that value is to be assigned to the capacity to distinguish ourselves from our natures, as though our integrity depended on our being essentially other than God made us.[69] Over against this perspective, it is worth highlighting Maximus' characteristic way of pressing home the implications of Chalcedon. Taking up a phrase from Leontius of Byzantium, he speaks of the two natures "from which, in which, *and which* Christ is."[70] The last clause is crucial because it highlights the fact that Christ's hypostasis – and thus his integrity as a human being – is not the function of a further "something" (*logos*) that exists over and above the natures, but simply the way (*tropos*) that those natures are personally instantiated in the rabbi from Nazareth. *What* Christ is, is simply his two natures. *Who* Christ is – the divine Word – is a matter of hypostasis, but to make this point is not to add any ontological content to Christology; it is simply to specify *how* the human and divine natures concretely subsist.[71] The fact that the answer to this "how" is "divinely" does nothing to compromise Christ's humanity for Maximus, because the integrity of human nature is a matter of *what*, and not who (or how) an entity is. In short, a given *logos* may be instantiated according to a range of possible *tropoi*. The full humanity of the will is thus unaffected by whether the *tropos* by which it operates is gnomic deliberation or the immediate presence of God characteristic of deification.

This technical distinction allows the will to be understood as a matter of nature instead of as some kind of ontological reserve whereby we stand over against our natures. To be sure, in concrete acts of willing we may violate our natures through the (gnomic) willing of sin or transcend them through the willing of our divinely given callings (either gnomically in the present or by virtue of deification in glory); but for Maximus the fact of our humanity is independent of these particular processes, which merely name various ways in which we go about living out our humanity. Because our humanity has its natural end in a life with God that exceeds its natural capacities, it is in our nature to transcend our natural capacities. But for Maximus (more clearly than for Augustine) this does not imply that it is our task to try to master – let alone resist – our nature through self-generated acts of will. On the contrary, our attempts to do so are precisely the source of our misery, since it is in and through rather than despite our nature that God wills to bring us to that life that perfects nature.

Our capacity to will is part of our nature. Indeed, for Maximus willing stands at the center of our nature, rendering us responsible agents rather than creatures of instinct. It follows that the will, too, is subject to deification; moreover, because the will has a particular role in rendering our being specifically human, deification necessarily implicates the will – to the extent that only when deified do our wills operate with what Maximus views as their proper freedom, untrammeled by uncertainty, doubt, and ignorance. Once again, this is not to say that deification is an achievement that we either merit or maintain by our own effort; but it is to recognize that deification, as both a process and a state, is something in which our will is ineluctably engaged. We love and know God by grace, but by grace it is nevertheless we who, willingly, love and know God.

This way of conceiving the will is a direct consequence of Maximus' decision to associate the will with nature rather than hypostasis. Against his opponents, Maximus insisted that it was impossible to follow Chalcedon and confess that Christ existed in two natures while denying that he had a specifically human will. Yet this affirmation of the will as a property of human *nature* invariably relativizes its significance for the individual human being's *hypostasis*. To be sure, who we are as particular individuals is inseparable from our wills; but the same could be said of our minds, bodies, and all other intrinsic properties of human nature: we are who we are in and through our bodies, minds, and wills. Indeed, given the will's particular place within human nature, we may even go so far as to say that the kind of bodies and minds we have is to some extent a function of the will, since the will directs them; but the will itself, as an inherent property of human nature, can no more be viewed as the source of hypostatic identity than the body is. As part of human being, will is the (natural!) *context* within and through which we live as persons, but not the *source* of personhood. Founding our personhood is not an achievement of the will (even though it is done willingly), but a matter of grace.[72] Willing is not itself the object of the will, but simply the mode in which we do whatever it is we do. The content of willing – and thus the hypostatic particularity of how our humanity is realized – comes to the will from without. Though it is realized by and through the will, it is not the will's own creation.

It follows for Maximus that our fulfillment as human beings comes when our wills are fixed on God in such a way that their movement is continually and invariably one of obedience. Short of glory, our wills lack this constancy. Because they act gnomically, they both can and do swerve in profoundly unnatural directions. Far from being a sign of the will's freedom, however, this "capacity" is for Maximus a sign of its instability:

insofar as it is not moved and shaped by God, it is moved and shaped by other forces. Its power of choice is thus not a sign of perfection. On the contrary, it reflects the willer's ignorance of and distance from God. Correspondingly, the will's healing involves the willer's recognition that her identity is secured by God rather than by her own capacities. In short, the will's task is not to create personal identity, but to (willingly!) receive it, knowing that the infinite richness of the God who is its giver promises a content that is ever new, surprising, and more fully one's own than anything of one's own creation.

This interpretation of the will's place in theological anthropology directly addresses some of the conceptual difficulties that threaten the coherence of Augustine's anthropology of willing. Though it cuts against some of his own most penetrating criticism of the Pelagian thinking, Augustine frequently reverts to an equation of willing with choice in a way that makes the will a *tertium quid* suspended between nature (the source of those desires the will needs to control) and grace (the source of those desires to which the will properly subjects itself). Thus, when Augustine argues that the prelapsarian will had the capacity to obey God without any immediate gift of grace, he invariably suggests that the gift of grace after the fall entails a compromise of human autonomy, in which God has to intervene to create a good will in a way that would not have been necessary for unfallen humanity. Still more problematically, his lingering tendency to understand willing as the power to choose forces him to concede that infants lack will and thus (because for Augustine sin is at root a product of freedom of choice) requires him to indulge in a hefty degree of special pleading to be able to make a coherent case for their status as sinners.

Maximus' more thorough integration of willing and nature addresses both these problems. If will is implicated in every expression of a rational nature, then its attribution to infants is no longer dependent on their capacity to make self-conscious choices. Likewise, Maximus' schema posits a consistency in God's relationship to the will across history that avoids Augustine's implication that human beings are more dependent on grace after the fall than beforehand: whether pre- or postlapsarian, human glorification is equally a matter of grace, even if grace has more to overcome in the wake of Adam's transgression. Moreover, while Maximus' understanding of postlapsarian human willing neither envisages nor requires Augustine's vision of a fallen humanity unable to avoid sin, it certainly allows for it. If the integrity of the will remains intact when we become unable to sin in glory (as both he and Augustine affirm), there seems nothing inherently problematic about affirming that genuine agency is preserved in circumstances where sinning is unavoidable.

As promising as Maximus' doctrine of the will may appear for shoring up Augustine's understanding of original sin, however, further reflection suggests serious obstacles to any proposed marriage of the two theologies. As Augustine himself was very aware, the doctrine of original sin is credible only if the categories of nature (as God's good creation) and will (as the source of creatures' deviation from God) are kept distinct. But surely one of the consequences of Maximus' integration of will and nature is to render this sort of distinction untenable: if sin is a function of the will (viz., its deviation from God's will for the creature), *and* the operation of the will is simply an expression of human nature, then the doctrine of original sin (viz., the assertion that the will is congenitally opposed to God) seemingly implies that human nature as such has become evil. It follows either that God is not the creator of human nature (the Manichean position), or, worse, that God – precisely *as* the creator of human nature – is also the creator of sin.[73] Clearly, neither of these alternatives is consistent with Christian belief in God as the indefectibly good Creator of all that is, thereby raising the real possibility that Maximus' analysis of human willing, far from providing resources for supporting Augustine's doctrine of original sin, only highlights its fundamental incoherence. It will be the task of the next chapter to address this challenge by pursuing further the implications of Chalcedonian Christology for the doctrines of the fall, sin, and the human will.

## Notes

1. Fleeing the turmoil that followed the Persian siege of Constantinople in 626, Maximus arrived in North Africa no later than 630 (perhaps as early as 628) and remained there until he departed for Rome in 646 in the midst of the monothelite controversy.
2. For a review of this intriguing question, see G. Berthold, "Did Maximus the Confessor Know Augustine?" in *Studia Patristica* 17 (1982), 14–17.
3. For example, Maximus defended the *filioque* and (as discussed in note 13 below) attempted to give an orthodox interpretation to Pope Honorius I's claim that Christ had only one will – though the need to secure Rome's support for dyothelite Christology cannot be ignored as a contributing factor in Maximus's sympathetic interpretations of Western positions.
4. Maximus the Confessor, *Quaestiones ad Thalassium* [hereafter QT] 61, in *On the Cosmic Mystery of Jesus Christ: Selected Writings from Saint Maximus the Confessor* (Crestwood, NY: St. Vladimir's Seminary Press, 2003), p. 133 (translation altered). Interestingly (and again in contrast to Augustine), at the beginning of this piece Maximus implies that humanity's fall followed immediately upon its creation (*hama toi genesthai*). See *CCSG* 22:85.

5   Cyril of Alexandria, *Apologeticus contra Theodoretum pro duodecim Capitibus*, 3 (*Patrologia Graeca* [PG] 76:405D–408A).
6   "If it is evident that [as Julian argued] whatever is natural is not voluntary, it is, then, not natural that we will to be alive and well, that we will to be happy. Who would dare to say this but you?" Augustine, *Unfinished Work in Answer to Julian* [hereafter *UWJ*], 4.92, in *Answer to the Pelagians*, III, ed. John E. Rotelle (Hyde Park, NY: New City Press, 1999).
7   "Mēden phusikon einai in tēi noerei phusei akousion." Maximus quotes the passage in his *Disputatio cum Pyrrho*[hereafter *DP*] (PG91:296A). By contrast, Protestant theologians, operating in an Augustinian context, maintained a firm distinction between moral and natural desires, on the grounds that the latter *were* involuntary. See the discussion in William G. T. Shedd, *Dogmatic Theology*, 2nd edn. (New York: Charles Scribner's Sons, 1899), vol. 2, pp. 120–5. For a mediating position that emphasizes the varying degrees to which an action is voluntary, see Austin Farrer, *The Freedom of the Will* (New York: Charles Scribner's Sons, 1958), pp. 109–15.
8   "Ouk estin oun prohairesis hē thelesis." Maximus the Confessor, *Opuscula Theologica et Polemica* [hereafter *OTP*] 1 (PG91:13A).
9   Note that Augustine's insistence that "will is an act of nature" (*UWJ*, 5.40) over against the Pelagian idea that it is in but not of nature parallels some of the ideas later developed by Maximus. In a very different theological context, Shedd notes that choice or volition "is common to man and the animal creation; inclination or self-determination [i.e., will] belongs only to man, and other rational beings." Shedd, *Dogmatic Theology*, vol. 2, p. 140.
10  Adolf Harnack, *History of Dogma* (London: Williams & Norgate, 1898), vol. IV, pp. 254, 259. Without denying the importance of politics in setting the stage for the debate, Harnack's dismissal of the theological seriousness of the controversy is belied by the stiff resistance put up by monothelite bishops at III Constantinople. Nevertheless, the basic thrust of Harnack's opinion continues to draw support from Catholic scholars in particular; see, e.g., the judgment of Filippo Carcione that the monothelite debate was "più verbale che sostanziale." "Enérgheia, Thélema e Theokínetos nella lettera di Sergio, patriarca di Costantinopoli, a papa Onorio Primo," *Orientalia Christiana Periodica* 51:2 (1985), 263–76.
11  While these churches are usually called "Monophysite," this term is not especially apt, for while the anti-Chalcedonian churches do confess that in Christ two natures have been united to form one (*mia phusis*), they deny that Christ has one nature only (*monē phusis*) in a way that would compromise his consubstantiality with humankind.
12  "unam voluntatem fatemur Domini nostri Jesu Christi," in Honorius, Epistle 4 ("*Ad Sergium Constantinopolianum Episcopum*") in *Patrologia Latina* [PL]80: 472A. Sergius' letter to the Pope had not contained an explicit reference to "one will."
13  See the discussion by Paul Verghese, "The Monothelite Controversy – A Historical Survey," in *The Greek Orthodox Theological Review* 13:2 (Fall 1968),

110    *Reconfiguring the Debate*

       197–8. Verghese basically reiterates the line of argument taken by Maximus, who defends Honorius' language as orthodox in *OTP* 20 (PG91:238C–239C) and *DP* (PG91:329A–B). A less positive assessment of Honorius is given by Demetrios Bathrellos (*The Byzantine Christ: Person, Nature, and Will in the Christology of Maximus the Confessor* [Oxford: Oxford University Press, 2005], pp. 77–9), who argues that Maximus' defense of the Pope is not altogether consistent and was probably driven as much by political as by theological considerations.

14    A variety of Greek terms were used to refer to this capacity, including *prohairesis*, *boulesis*, and *autexousiotēs*, alongside Maximus' own preferred terms, *thelema* and *thelesis*. Bathrellos (*Byzantine Christ*, pp. 118–19) argues that Maximus' preference for *thelema* is a function of its prominence in key Gospel texts like Luke 22:42 and John 6:38. For further discussion of the history of the key terms, see John Madden, "The Authenticity of Early Definitions of Will (*Thelesis*)," in *Maximus Confessor. Actes du Symposium sur Maxime le Confesseur Fribourg, 2–5 septembere 1980*, ed. Felix Heinzer and Christoph Schönborn (Fribourg: Éditions Universitaires, 1982), pp. 61–79.

15    Polycarp Sherwood argues that in the seventh-century church "a spirituality which places the summit of holiness in the unity of [divine and human] wills ... was in large measure common property." Polycarp Sherwood, *An Annotated Date-List of the Works of Maximus the Confessor*, Studia Anselmiana, fasc. XXX (Rome: Herder, 1952), p. 3.

16    *Commentary on the Our Father* [PG90:900A], in *Maximus Confessor: Selected Writings*, ed. George C. Berthold (New York: Paulist Press, 1985), p. 114.

17    For an exhaustive defense of this claim, see the magisterial study of Jean-Claude Larchet, *La dvinisation de l'homme selon saint Maxime le Confesseur* (Paris: Les Éditions du Cerf, 1996).

18    Marcel Doucet, in "La volonté humaine du Christ, spécialement en Son agonie. Maxime le Confesseur, interprète de l'Écriture," in *Science et Esprit* 37:2 (1985), 123–59, makes the case that Maximus' basic belief in the integrity of Christ's human will antedates the outbreak of the monothelite controversy.

19    In *Ambiguum* 7 (PG91:1076C), Maximus describes the state of glory as one in which the human being has "attained the divine activity [*theias ... energeias*], and indeed become God by deification." In *OTP* 1 (PG91:33D–36A) Maximus explains that in so writing he did not mean to "take away the natural activity [*phusikēn ... energeian*] of those who experience this," but only to stress that deification was a product of divine rather than human capacity. In this context, it is worth pointing out that in *Ambiguum* 7 (PG91:1076B) Maximus does explicitly deny that deification amounts to a "dissolution of human agency [*autexousiou*]."

20    Maximus makes this argument in *DP* (PG91:325A), paraphrasing the dictum given classic form in Gregory of Nazianzus, Epistle 101 ("To Cledonius Against Apollinaris"). Cf. *OTP* 16 (PG91:196D).

21  Maximus makes this point in *DP* (PG91:313C–316B); cf. *OTP 3* (PG91:53C).
22  For Maximus' insistence on the Logos as the unique subject of Christ's willing in either nature, see, e.g., *DP* (PG91:289B); cf. *OTP 7* (PG91:80B–C). Bathrellos points out that Maximus' position was not consistently maintained in subsequent dyothelite Christology, with both the Sixth Ecumenical Council and (at least on occasion) John of Damascus making the two natures rather the single hypostasis the subject of willing in Christ. See *Byzantine Christ*, pp. 184–5.
23  Maximus also uses the term *thelesis* for the natural will (see, e.g., *OTP 1* [PG91:12C]); and he regards the phrase "prohairetic will" (*thelema prohairetikon*) as equivalent to the gnomic will in *OTP 1* (PG91:28D) and *DP* (PG91:329D).
24  See, e.g., *OTP 7* (PG91:81C–D) and *DP* (PG91:308D–309A, 329D).
25  This criticism of Maximus is made in Raymund Schwager, *Der wunderbare Tausch: zur Geschichte und Deutung der Erlösungslehre* (München: Kösel, 1986), pp. 157–8.
26  See, e.g., *Commentary on the Our Father*, in *Maximus Confessor*, p. 104 (PG90:877D).
27  Maximus, "Letter 2" [PG91:396C–397A], in Andrew Louth, *Maximus the Confessor* (New York: Routledge, 1996), p. 87.
28  *OTP 16* (PG91:196B); cf. *OTP 1* (PG91:12C).
29  See, e.g., *DP* (PG91:304C): "agency, according to the Fathers, is will." Cf. 301B–C (where Maximus cites the authority of Diadochus of Photike) and *OTP 15* (PG91:147C). "Agency" is preferable to "self-determination" or "freedom of choice" as translations for *autexousiotēs* precisely because Maximus contrasts *autexousiotēs* as the defining feature of the natural will from the gnomic qualities of *prohairesis* (*OTP 1* [PG91:13A]) and *authairesis* (*OTP 16* [PG91:192B–C]), both of which much more clearly have the sense of freedom of choice.
30  *OTP 16* (PG91:196A).
31  *DP* (PG91:293B); cf. *OTP 7* (PG91:77B).
32  See, e.g., *OTP 16* (PG91:193B). This distinction between the exercise of the gnomic will and sin shows that Maximus does not subscribe to an Augustinian version of fallen humanity as *non posse non peccare*.
33  *OTP 1* (PG91:13A–16C). Though Maximus gives a more detailed elaboration of the stages of volition in the subsequent sections of this *Opusculum*, this basic sequence is not affected. For a comprehensive analysis, see Lars Thunberg, *Microcosm and Mediator: The Theological Anthropology of Maximus the Confessor*, 2nd edn. (Chicago, IL: Open Court, 1995), pp. 218–26.
34  *OTP 1* (PG91:16D–17B); cf. *DP* (PG91:308D, 329D).
35  "What happens through the fall is that a perversion of man's capacity for self-determination takes place ... which predisposes man for its constant misuse ... That is to say, it forms in man a sinful disposition of will (*gnome*)." Thunberg, *Microcosm and Mediator*, p. 227; cf. *OTP 20* (PG91:236D): "for

the nature did not change [because of the fall], but its motion was perverted, or rather (to speak more accurately) it exchanged one motion for another."

36  See, e.g., *OTP* 3 (PG91:48A), where Maximus draws a parallel between the natural and gnomic wills on the one hand, and the capacity to speak and the act of speaking on the other.

37  See *DP* (PG 91:308D), where *gnomē* is explicitly defined as "a *tropos* of use, not a *logos* of nature" (*tropos ousa chrēseōs, ou logos phuseōs*); cf. *OTP* 3 (PG91:53C), *OTP* 10 (PG91:137A), and *OTP* 16 (PG91:192B–C), where "the self-determining impulse" of the gnomic will is defined as "not of nature but … of person [*prosopou*] and hypostasis."

38  *OTP* 20 (PG91:236D). *Psilon* here presumably means something like "on its own," with the implication that Christ's will was from conception suffused by grace in a way that the rest of humanity's is not.

39  "The human will of God [incarnate] … having received being in unity together with God the Word, had a motion that was without hesitation but had instead fixed [*stasimon*] motion in accordance with the natural appetite or will; or, to speak more precisely, there was in him an unmoving condition [*stasin*] in accord with his absolutely pure, completely deified subsistence [*ousiosin … pantelōs theotheisan*] in God the Word." *OTP* 1 (PG91:32A); cf. *OTP* 7 (PG 91:80D) and *OTP* 20 (PG91:236A).

40  Some monothelites rejected the ascription of a human will to Christ on the grounds that it would imply ignorance (see *OTP* 19 [PG91:216B–C]). The terms of Maximus' dyothelitism imply not so much a flat-out rejection of this charge as its deflection by conceding that ignorance is a feature of gnomic will but denying that Christ willed gnomically. To put it another way, from Maximus' perspective the monothelite charge rests on a failure to recognize that *gnomē* refers to a *tropos* rather than the *logos* of the will.

41  *OTP* 7 (PG91:77A).

42  *DP* (PG91:320D–324A); cf. *OTP* 15 (PG91:157C–159B). A helpful schematization of this series of exegetical arguments is found in Doucet, "La volonté humaine du Christ," p. 126.

43  *DP* (PG91:324A–B; the citation from Gregory comes from his *Fourth Theological Oration*); cf. PG91:293B, where Maximus also rejects the idea that Christ's human nature is moved by necessity (*ēnagkasmenon*).

44  Christ's prayer in Gethsemane (Matt. 26:36–46 and pars.) is the focus of *OTP* 3 (PG91:45B–56D), 6 (PG91:65A–68D), and 7 (PG91:69B–89B) and is referred to at various other points in Maximus' dyothelite corpus (though, oddly, it does not come in for explicit discussion in the *Disputation with Pyrrhus*, beyond a brief allusion at PG91:297B).

45  For a helpful review of earlier patristic exegesis of the Gethsemane episode, see Bathrellos, *Byzantine Christ*, pp. 140–6.

46  *OTP* 7 (PG91:80C–D). The translation is by Louth, *Maximus the Confessor*, p. 186.

47  See, e.g., *DP* (PG91:308D).
48  *OTP* 3 (PG91:48D).
49  *OTP* 7 (PG91:31D); see also *OTP* 4 (PG91:60C): "His willing is with respect to natural being [*on phusikon*] entirely like ours, but it is above ours in that it is divinely shaped [*tupoumenon* ... *theikōs*]."
50  *OTP* 3 (PG91: 48C); see also *OTP* 7 (PG91:84A–B). Cf. Adam G. Cooper (*The Body in St. Maximus the Confessor: Holy Flesh, Wholly Deified* [Oxford: Oxford University Press, 2005], p. 152), who writes that "Christ's human nature is affirmed, since its *logos* ... remains completely intact and natural. At the same time, it is transcended, since the *tropos* ... in which that nature ... is freely lived out and encountered at the level of the contingent and particular is supernatural."
51  So in *OTP* 6 (PG91:65A) Maximus insists that the move from the first to the second petitions is a matter of "perfect accord [*sumphuia*] and agreement [*sunneusis*]."
52  This is not to deny that the lives of the saints are also marked by ascetic practices directed to a supernatural end, and these must be seen as a matter of gnomic willing insofar as no saint is fully deified in this life and the non-deified will is *eo ipso* gnomic with respect to its *tropos*. Nevertheless, for Maximus such movements, though necessarily mediated through the *gnomē*, have their source in divine grace that allows for the "setting aside of [merely] human, fleshy properties" (*DP* [PG91:297A]) rather than autonomous decisions of the gnomic will. Apart from grace the gnomic will can deviate from created nature only to what is unnatural and thus sinful.
53  As Larchet puts it (*La divinization de l'homme*, p. 593), "la divinization, tout en ne pouvant pas être accomplie par la nature elle-même, se trouve cependant dans la continuité de celle-ci en tant qu'elle est sa finalité, et constitue donc son accomplissement, la nature étant, si l'on peut dire, naturellement ordonné au surnaturel." See also p. 681.
54  This is not to say that Christ in any way increases – let alone achieves – his deification in Gethsemane; but it is to stress that for Maximus deification combines steadfastness with movement and is therefore not a static condition. See, e.g., *The Church's Mystagogy* 19 [PG91:696B–C], where Maximus characterizes human experience of the glorified state as "the identity of an inflexible eternal movement around God" (in *Maximus Confessor*, p. 202).
55  Does this process by which the object of willing transcends the merely natural not entail choice? It depends on how the term is understood. If "choice" means the psychological processes by which we in this life (i.e., gnomically) choose between alternatives, then the deified will does not choose. If, however, "choice" is simply used to refer to change in the object of willing, without any speculation regarding the psychological processes by which this takes place, then there can be no objection to speaking of "choice" – though the choosing in question is one of which we have no

experience prior to the consummation. See, in this context, Bathrellos, *Byzantine Christ*, 151, n. 302: "*prohairesis is a particular kind of choice or decision that ... depends on deliberation and goes hand in hand with mutability, sinfulness, etc. To exclude ... prohairesis from Christ as man means to exclude this particular kind of choosing and deciding, not choosing and deciding as such.*" Cf. Hans Urs von Balthasar, *Cosmic Liturgy: The Universe According to Maximus the Confessor* (San Francisco, CA: Ignatius Press, 2003), pp. 254–5 and Joseph. P. Farrell, *Free Choice in St. Maximus the Confessor* (South Canaan, PA: St. Tikhon's Seminary Press, 1989), p. 161, n. 15.

56 Of course, though Jesus shares our humanity's *logos*, he is unique with respect to the *way* his humanity is lived out as the humanity of the incarnate Word (i.e., his *tropos*). Thus, Maximus writes that the "natural aspects of the will are not attached to the Lord in the same way as they are to us. For though he truly hungered and thirsted, he did not hunger and thirst in the mode [*tropoi*] that we do, but in a mode above us, because it was voluntary [*hekousiōs*]" (*DP* [PG91:297D]). The point seems to be that while we no less than Christ hunger willingly (i.e., our experience of hunger is part of our existence as agents), our hungering is a necessary feature of our non-deified existence in the way that it is not for Christ. Cf. Augustine's suggestions regarding the saints' use of food in glory in *City of God*, 13.22.

57 *OTP* 1 (PG91:24C).

58 *OTP* 1 (PG91:25A). This view of *prohairesis* as a contingent feature of human being contrasts sharply with the significance accorded the term in later Stoicism, where it is an inalienable mark of human freedom and dignity (see, e.g., Epictetus, *Discourses*, I.1). It is similarly different from Pelagius, whose vision of freedom of the will seems far closer to the "prohairetic" character of Maximus' gnomic will than to the freedom the Confessor associates with the deified human natural will.

59 "Thus the world above will reach its fullness; the members will be united with their head, each according to his merit [*kat'axian*]. Through the constructive skill of the Holy Spirit, every member will have a place appropriate to it ... So each of us will bring to completion the Body that itself brings all things to completion in each of us, filling everything and itself brought to fullness by all things." *Ambiguum* 31 (PG91:1280D–1281A), cited in von Balthasar, *Cosmic Liturgy*, p. 358 (translation altered). The idea, again, is not that will is the means by which a particular place is earned, but that each place is a function of the particularity of the individual agent.

60 Augustine "meant grace to individuate the soul and restore to it the identity it was losing in sin. We can still wonder, however, whether human entrance into the cosmic plot of redemption, whose ending has all the saints bear the image of God, does not in retrospect lend the life of sin an identity and interest all their own." James Wetzel, *Augustine and the Limits of Virtue* (Cambridge: Cambridge University Press, 1999), p. 211. Augustine's claim that "the evils contracted by sin are left to us for the contest of faith" (*UWJ*,

6.26) pushes in this direction by implying that there would be no contest or growth apart from sin. See also his suggestion – quite different from the implications of Maximus' anthropology – that in Eden there would have been no labor involved in learning, as though all labor were in itself a defect of the fall (in *UWJ*, 5.3, 6.9). For Julian's challenging of Augustine's contention that labor would have had no place in paradise, see *UWJ*, 6.27.

61  Maximus defines the gnomic will as self-determining impulse (*authairetos hormē*) in *OTP* 14 (PG91:153A–B); cf. *OTP* 16 (PG91:192B–C) and *QT* 2 (*CCSG* 7.51).

62  It needs to be conceded here that insofar as every human being's place in God is for Maximus evidently proportionate to the desire for God felt during life (*hekastou ... methexontos, hoson epothēse* according to *OTP* 1 [PG91:24C]), the gnomic will is clearly a factor in determining the precise character of each person's experience of deification; but insofar as among the saints the gnomic will is not an alternative to grace (as though deification were earned), but rather a filter through which it operates, God remains the ultimate author of individual human destiny.

63  Maximus can say that insofar as the deified individual "has placed himself completely in God alone" she "both is and is called God" (*Ambiguum* 7 [PG91:1084C]) but the context makes it clear that there is no question of ontological identity (cf. *Ambiguum* 41 [PG91:1308B]).

64  See, e.g., *DP* (PG91:309C–312A).

65  See *DP* (PG91:297A): "Moses and David and whoever has been made open to the divine operation were moved by his direction in the putting aside of human and fleshly properties."

66  See *OTP* 1 (PG91:13A), where gnomic *prohairesis* is distinguished from natural will on the grounds that while the latter is "a simple desire that is rational and intrinsic to the life-process" (*haplē tis orexis, logikē te kai zotikē*), the former is "a compound of desire, deliberation, and decision" (*orexeōs kai boulēs kai kriseōs sunodos*).

67  Bathrellos (*Byzantine Christ*, p. 157, n. 337) rightly cites *OTP* 1 (PG91:24D–25A) in support of this point: "To whatever extent anyone has desired, to that extent he participates in that which has been desired." Cf. the citation from *Ambiguum* 31 in note 59 above (though the latter antedates Maximus' engagement with monothelitism).

68  For Maximus "it is obvious ... that the grace of the Holy Spirit in no way leaves the natural faculty unengaged ... but rather grace begins to make the natural faculty active again, leading it via the use of modes harmonious with nature towards the comprehension of divine things." *QT*, 59.95–9 (*CCSG* 22.51), cited in Cooper, *Body*, p. 58.

69  It is not hard to see the serpent's temptation of Eve in precisely these terms: though she is already "like God" by nature (Gen. 1:27), she is persuaded that this is inadequate insofar as it is not something that she claims for herself over and above her nature.

70 This phrasing is found in *OTP* 1 (PG91:36C), 6 (PG91:68A), and 19 (PG91:224A); *Ambigua* 5 and 27 (PG981:1052D and 1269C); and *Epistles* 12 and 15 (PG91:488C and 573A); cf. *DP* (PG91:289B), *OTP* 9 and 19 (PG91:121B and 224A). For a discussion of the derivation and significance of the three clauses, see Bathrellos, *Byzantine Christ*, pp. 108–11.

71 Note that this is not to reduce the hypostasis to the natures, but rather to insist on the ontological distinction between the two. See the discussion in Felix Heinzer, *Gottes Sohn als Mensch: Die Struktur des Menschseins Christi bei Maximus Confessor* (Freiburg: Universitätsverlag Freiburg Schweiz, 1980), pp. 117–32.

72 Balthasar makes this point nicely, describing deification as a process by which: "the free moral act … is changed progressively into the act of God himself, who lifts us out of our own freedom into his" (*Cosmic Liturgy*, pp. 325–6).

73 Julian repeatedly attempts to force Augustine into precisely this alternative. See, e.g., *UWJ*, 4.2.

# 5

# The Status of Christ's Will: Fallen or Unfallen?*

The foregoing examination of Maximus the Confessor had a great deal to say about the will, but very little to say about original sin. At one level, this is hardly surprising, since the categories of the fall and original sin do not play the same prominent role in the Greek theological tradition out of which Maximus comes as they do in Augustine's theology. Indeed, the categories Maximus brings to bear on human willing sidestep the divide between pre- and postlapsarian willing that is a central feature of the Augustinian doctrine of original sin. Though it is true that for Maximus the torrent of passions unleashed by the fall affects the conditions under which the will operates, it does not produce the fundamental perversion of postlapsarian human willing that is so central to Augustine's understanding of human fallenness. Indeed (and as noted at the very end of the previous chapter), this aspect of Maximus' thought constitutes a critical point of dissonance between the two thinkers, since it undermines the distinction between will and nature upon which Augustine relies to avoid the charge that his doctrine of congenital sinfulness impugns the inalienable goodness of creation.

The aim of this chapter will be to resolve that dissonance by developing further the Christological principles deployed by Maximus in the monothelite controversy. Writing before the Council of Chalcedon, Augustine could not draw on this conceptual framework. As a result, at the same time that he sought on the one hand to link the will more

---

\* Chapter 5 is a revised version of the article "Fallen or Unfallen? Christ's Human Nature and the Ontology of Human Sinfulness," first published in *International Journal of Systematic Theology* 10, no. 4 (October 2008), 399–415, Wiley-Blackwell.

---

*In Adam's Fall: A Meditation on the Christian Doctrine of Original Sin*, by Ian A. McFarland.
© 2010 Ian A. McFarland.

closely to nature as a means of stressing their common dependence on grace, he found himself on the other having to separate them, since he had no other means of avoiding the implication that original sin rendered nature itself perverse than to identify the will as a locus of sin distinct from nature. In order to avoid this difficulty, I will contend that the categories of nature and person provide a framework within which it is possible to say that nature – including the will – is congenitally fallen without implying either that nature is evil or that God is the author of sin. This conclusion will be defended by reflecting on whether in taking flesh the Word assumed a fallen or an unfallen human nature. Though at first glance this question may sound like the epitome of theological hair-splitting, careful consideration of its implications clarifies the relationship between sin and human nature in a way that can help acquit Augustine's doctrine of original sin from the charge of fostering any sort of Manichean dualism.

Both sides of the debate over the character of Christ's human nature take their bearings from passages within the same biblical book: the letter to the Hebrews. On the one hand, it records that Christ "had to become like his brothers and sisters in every respect [*kata panta*], so that he might be a merciful and faithful high priest in the service of God … Because he himself was tested by what he suffered, he is able to help those who are being tested" (Heb. 2:17–18). This principle – that Christ's conformity to the human condition is a necessary condition of his working to save it – was later echoed by Gregory of Nazianzus in his protest against Apollinarian denials that Christ had a human mind distinct from the divine Word: "For that which he has not assumed he has not healed; but that which is united to his Godhead is also saved."[1] In brief, for human beings to be brought into genuine communion with God, it is necessary for God to have entered into the most intimate possible solidarity with human nature (cf. Gal. 4:4–5).[2]

On the other hand stands the claim that Christ, though "in every respect [*kata panta*] … tested as we are," was nevertheless "without sin" (Heb. 4:15). While Christ's communion with humankind includes the most profound sharing of human vulnerability, this experience of vulnerability does not lead him to share in human sin (cf. 1 Pet. 2:22; 1 John 3:5). In short, Christ is an exception to the anthropological rule that "all have sinned and fall short of the glory of God" (Rom. 3:23; cf. v. 10 and Ps. 14:2–3). Moreover, this exceptionalism has generally been viewed by Christians as no less crucial to Christ's saving work than his solidarity with the human condition: in order for Christ to be the agent through whom human beings are reconciled with God, he needs to be free of that sin by which all other human beings are estranged from God. Calvin's language is typical here: "... no man, unless he belonged to God, could serve as the intermediary to restore peace. But who might reach to him? Any one of Adam's children? No, like their father, all of them were terrified at the sight of God."[3] In other words, for all Christ's solidarity with us, his role as redeemer requires some point of discontinuity with the rest of humankind.

The debate over whether Christ's human nature is fallen or unfallen arises from theologians' differing intuitions regarding the implications of these two basic principles of the Christian doctrine of the incarnation. The dilemma can be cast as follows: is the assumption of a fallen human nature necessary in order to affirm that Christ became like us "in every respect," sin excepted; or does the assumption of a fallen human nature imply a sinfulness that precludes Christ's ability to effect our reconciliation?[4] In what follows, I will argue that the implications of Chalcedonian Christology require that this second question be answered in the negative, and that (in response to the first) it is therefore dogmatically permissible to affirm Christ's assumption of a fallen human nature. This argument will rest on careful delimitation of the way in which the Chalcedonian categories of "nature" and "hypostasis" (or "person") relate to the hamartiological concepts of "fallenness" and "sin."

## The Question in the Tradition

To the extent that Christians understand sin as the creature's moral deviation from God's will, it is not surprising that they have rejected the idea that Christ's identification with the human condition includes participation in sin. And if Christ does not participate in sin, it would seem to follow that the nature he assumed was not fallen; for despite the considerable range of opinion within the tradition regarding the precise effects of the fall on human nature, there is virtual consensus that such effects are a consequence of sin. Thus, insofar as Christ has no share in the sin of Adam, it would seem to follow that he has no share in the nature-deforming consequences of that sin. In short, if fallenness is a symptom of sinfulness, then it becomes difficult to affirm a fallen nature where there is no sin.

Though this line of reasoning has been extremely common, the scope of Christian reflection on this topic is far too extensive to allow for anything more than the most cursory of summaries here. My aim will be only to highlight the general characteristics of three significant periods, beginning with the patristic era, where the question is not formulated as sharply as it came to be later on. The example of Gregory of Nyssa is in many ways typical. In his *Life of Moses* he cites Paul's claim in 2 Cor. 5:21 that God made Christ "to be sin" as evidence that Christ "was invested with our sinful nature [*tēn hamartētikēn phusin*]."[5] Yet later on in the same treatise, he cites Rom. 8:3 to draw (seemingly) just the opposite conclusion: even as that which was raised up by Moses in the wilderness was "a likeness of the serpent and not a serpent itself," so Christ took on only the "likeness" of sinful flesh in the incarnation.[6] Gregory clearly wants to affirm the closest possible identification of Christ with the rest of humanity, sin excepted; but his language leaves it unclear exactly how his application of this principle maps on to the later question of the fallenness of the human nature assumed by Christ.[7]

A second period of reflection on Christ's human nature emerged in the wake of Augustine and his doctrine of original sin. In response to the views of Pelagius and his followers, Augustine proposed a description of the fall's effects that, as we have seen, was unprecedented in its severity. For him, much more clearly than for any of his predecessors, Adam's transgression did not simply afflict human beings with a propensity (however strong) to sin, but rendered them congenitally sinful – and thus incapable of following God's will apart from grace. Because the will was now bound in such a way that postlapsarian human beings are unable to avoid sin, fallenness is directly equated with sinfulness in a way that is not so clearly the case in earlier theology. Consequently, Augustine is the first theologian whose theological anthropology provides the basis for a relatively clear affirmation that the human nature assumed in the incarnation was unfallen: "he alone, having become man, while remaining God, never had any sin and did not assume sinful flesh, though he assumed flesh from the sinful flesh of his mother. Whatever of the flesh he took from her, he either cleansed it to assume it or cleansed it by assuming it."[8] Quite simply, given the principle that the fallen nature necessarily produces human sin, if Christ was sinless, then the nature ("flesh") he assumed could not have been fallen.

In medieval Europe the influence of Augustine's teaching on original sin elevated the principle that the human nature assumed by Christ was unfallen to a matter of virtual consensus.[9] Thus, around the turn of the eleventh century Anselm of Canterbury combined staunch affirmation of Christ's consubstantiality with humanity with an equally firm insistence that Christ's human nature was not mortal (and thus, by implication, unfallen), justifying this conclusion on the grounds that "mortality belongs to the corrupt not to the pure nature of man."[10] He justifies the claim that Christ was not naturally mortal on soteriological grounds, arguing that Christ's life could only count as a gift to God (as Anselm's understanding of the atonement as a voluntary offering of "satisfaction" to God demands) if its ending were a matter of Christ's own willing rather than necessity.[11] At the same time, he insists that this denial of mortality does not vitiate Christ's full humanity, since "neither corruptibility or incorruptibility ... belongs to the integrity of human nature."[12] In short, human nature, however badly damaged by the fall, cannot have been destroyed by it (since otherwise human beings would cease to be human); therefore, Christ's sharing human nature does not require his assumption of fallen humanity. That he should have been fully human does not depend on his having taken on the damage that has accrued to human nature as a result of the fall.

Though Thomas Aquinas differs from Anselm in viewing mortality as inherent in the materiality of incarnation,[13] he, too, draws from the confession of Christ's sinlessness the conclusion that he assumed human nature "in the same purity that it had in the state of innocence" and thus without any intrinsic liability to the disabilities suffered by postlapsarian humanity.[14] Like Anselm, he is thus faced with the problem of explaining how he can affirm Christ's consubstantiality with the race of Adam apart from sharing in the effects of the fall inherited by all the rest of Adam's descendants. In order to square this circle, Thomas makes use of Aristotelian biology to draw a distinction between the (fully human) *nature* Christ received from his mother and the supernatural origin of his (divine) *hypostasis*. While Christ is fully human by virtue of the Adamic substance he inherits from his mother, his hypostatic identity is simply that of the Second Person of the Trinity and thus is not – as is the case for other human beings – received via the male semen that forms the inert maternal matter into a particular human hypostasis. In short, because the contagion of sin (and thus the fallenness of human nature) is transmitted paternally, Christ can be sinless (and his nature therefore unfallen) because he lacks a biological father.[15]

The same sorts of considerations also shaped the thought of Protestant orthodoxy through the post-Reformation period. Thus, the position of the Lutheran scholastics largely echoes that of Aquinas: while Christ as human "participates in all the natural weaknesses to which human nature is subject since the Fall – He participates therein ... not in consequence of a natural necessity, but in consequence of His own free will ... for, as He was ... not begotten of a human father, his human nature did not inherit any of the consequences of Adam's sin."[16] The weaknesses characteristic of the postlapsarian state cannot be intrinsic to Christ's humanity, because they are "punishments [that] accompany sin," and Christ is sinless.[17] And though Reformed theologians were less inclined to attribute Christ's immunity from sin to his lack of paternity, they agreed that his subjection to the "penal infirmities of our nature"[18] was not due to any inherent corruption of his flesh.[19] At the same time, both traditions insisted that while the assumption of these "infirmities" was voluntary with respect to Christ's *person*, it was necessary for his saving *work* of mediation.[20] To be able to die on our behalf, Christ had to be subject to suffering; but the assumption of this and other postlapsarian weaknesses had to be distinguished from the assumption of humanity as such, since Christ had no part in the sin for which they were punishment.[21]

In short, the majority tradition of Western Christianity in particular has not thought it possible to affirm both that Christ had assumed a fallen human nature and that he was without sin. From the nineteenth century, however, a number of influential theological voices have challenged this consensus in a way that constitutes a third approach to the question of whether or not Christ's human nature was fallen. Karl Barth, while holding with the tradition that Christ was sinless, did not see this confession as inconsistent with the claim that his solidarity with the rest of humanity extended to his assumption of the consequences of sin (viz., fallenness) that burdened the rest of postlapsarian humanity.[22] He defended this position by reference to Paul's assertion that Christ became "a curse for us" (Gal. 3:13) and that God "made him to be sin who knew no sin" (2 Cor. 5:21), as well as by the more general consideration that Christ can be genuinely with and for us before God only if he is "all that we are and exactly like us even in our opposition" to the divine.[23] Likewise, Hans Urs von Balthasar is emphatic that the "Son of God took a human nature in its fallen condition."[24] For both theologians, if the human nature Christ has assumed is not fallen, then the effects of the fall on human nature are not healed. While their position cannot be said to have carried the day, it has proved enormously influential in contemporary academic theology.

## Preliminary Assessment

Crucial to any assessment of this debate is a clear statement of what fallenness entails. For if to be fallen simply means to be susceptible to suffering and death, then Christ's possessing a fallen human nature would follow from the creedal confession that Christ "suffered death and was buried." Yet classical Catholic and Protestant theologians alike show that it is possible to affirm Christ's susceptibility to the penalties of the fall while strenuously denying that Christ's nature shares the postlapsarian condition of the rest of Adam's descendants. In this context, one way to specify more clearly the content of fallenness is to define it in terms of a nature that is *intrinsically damaged*, as it was precisely the ascription of any such qualities to Christ's human nature that the theologians of the medieval and Reformation periods (and even the patristic era[25]) were particularly keen to avoid.

As this brief historical review has already suggested, there is good prima facie theological reason to want to avoid the idea that Christ assumed an intrinsically damaged human nature; for if such damage is understood as punishment for sin, then it is not clear how Christ can have a damaged nature without being a sinner. Moreover, insofar as there has been virtual consensus among Christian theologians that one consequence of the fall is an increased propensity to sin, ascribing Christ a fallen human nature would risk making his sinlessness less psychologically credible.[26] Finally (and, again, as already noted in connection with Anselm), denying that Christ assumed a damaged nature does not in any way qualify his consubstantiality with the rest of us, since damage to a nature is by definition not intrinsic to the nature in the way that (for example) the characteristics of having an intellect or will are.[27] Thus, one cannot defend the claim that Christ assumed a fallen nature by appealing to the soteriological axiom of Gregory of Nazianzus; for if the effects of the fall are a matter of damage to human nature, they are by definition not constitutive of that nature and thus do not need to be assumed in order to redeem it.[28]

At the same time, something *like* Gregory of Nazianzus' soteriological axiom seems to be at work when (for example) Heb. 2:14 associates Christ's sharing in our nature ("flesh and blood") with his sharing in our mortality ("that through death he might destroy him who has the power of death, that is, the devil"), even if the fact that mortality and corruptibility are not defining features of human nature means that the application cannot be a straightforward one. Here it is important to recognize that though it is difficult to see how one could insist on soteriological grounds that Christ *had* to assume a fallen human nature, this does not rule out the possibility that he *did* in fact assume one. As Thomas argues in the Christological sections of the *Summa Theologiae*, the details of the economy of salvation are largely a matter of God acting according to what is fitting or seemly (*ex convenientia*) rather than from necessity (*ex necessitate*). For example, that the Second Person of the Trinity should have been the one to assume flesh and that God should have chosen the passion as the means of reconciling the world to God's self are both treated by Thomas as matters of fittingness rather than necessity.[29] Could not the fallenness of Christ's human nature be defended on such terms?

In formulating an answer to this question, it is important to note that though many theologians have thought it important to argue that Christ assumed an unfallen human nature, very few have been attracted to the idea that he assumed a fully glorified one.[30] While this point may seem to be self-evident (since a glorified nature is incapable of dying and even the staunchest supporters of Christ assuming an unfallen nature have not wanted to mitigate the reality of his suffering and death), it is not demanded by the principle that only what is assumed is redeemed. On the contrary, Anselm's argument against the necessity of Christ's assuming a fallen nature applies here as well: being glorified or not does not define human nature as such any more than mortality or immortality does. But while a human being is equally human whether in Eden, expelled from it, or raised to glory, human nature is nevertheless marked by certain characteristic features in each of these phases of the economy. Thus, before Adam and Eve sinned, all human beings had an unfallen nature; after this primal transgression and before the parousia all have a fallen one; with Christ's return all will have a fully glorified one.[31] In other words, human nature has a temporally indexed dimension marked by particular qualities (e.g., mortality) uniquely associated with each of these different historical periods, even though these qualities do not define human nature as such (i.e., human beings are truly human in all three states).[32] Because Christ came to be among *fallen* human beings so that he could be (as both Hebrews 2 and 4 agree) tested *as they were*, it would seem appropriate that he would share the damaged condition in which postlapsarian humanity experiences testing.[33] In short, it seems fitting (though not strictly necessary) that he should have assumed a fallen human nature.

Thomas suggests how one might proceed to defend this position when he argues that it was fitting for Christ to assume the *defectus* of fallen humanity, on the grounds that "human nature is unknown to us except as subject to these bodily disabilities, [so that] if the Son of God had taken on a human nature without them it would seem as if he were not a real man."[34] One could go beyond what Thomas himself states by arguing that to view Christ's susceptibility to the disabilities of postlapsarian humanity as anything other than an intrinsic feature of his human nature would render his exhibition of these disabilities quasi-Docetic. For while it would not follow from this position that Christ's temptation and suffering were illusory (Docetism in the strict sense), they would nevertheless be different from ours in a crucial respect, since their basis would not lie immediately in the temporally indexed qualities of the humanity he assumed, but would rather be a voluntary modification of them.[35]

And yet this line of reasoning can be challenged on two fronts, both connected with the Christian confession of Christ's sinlessness. First, it remains unclear that it is coherent (at least on a Western doctrine of original sin) to maintain that Christ had a fallen nature unless he was also a sinner. Second, while even Anselm was cautious about affirming that Christ was ontologically incapable of sin,[36] Christians have wanted to affirm that he did not avoid sin merely by happenstance. Yet if (as theologians on both sides of the fallen/unfallen debate generally want to affirm) Christ lived a life in which his human will was at every moment preserved from sinning (so that, in classical Augustinian terms, he was in a state of *non posse peccare*), then his will was not merely "unfallen" in a prelapsarian sense (since, according to the classic Augustinian position Adam and Eve were created *posse non peccare*, and thus capable of sin in a way that Christ was not) but actually possessed one of the defining characteristics of *glorified* humanity.[37] The implications of this belief are serious, for it is hard to see what sense it might make to speak of Christ possessing a damaged human nature when his will – an essential feature of that nature according to the decisions of the Third Council of Constantinople – is held to be morally indefectible.

## The Problem of Christ's Will

As a way of addressing this problem, it is useful to begin by exploring the question of what might be implied by the claim that Christ's human will was glorified during his earthly ministry, when his body was not. Recall the following quotation from Maximus the Confessor, previously examined in Chapter 4: "But as for the Savior's willing according to his human nature, even though it was natural, it was not bare like ours, any more than his humanity as such is, since it has been perfectly deified above us in union, because of which it is actually sinless."[38] Maximus does not believe that the deification of Christ's human will rendered his human body impassible; for Maximus (as for Thomas) Christ's body is not glorified until Easter.[39] With this point in mind, the quoted passage seems best interpreted as teaching that by virtue of the fact that his hypostasis was divine (i.e., none other than the Second Person of the Trinity), his human will did not subsist in isolation from God ("bare like ours") but was at every point shaped by God's will. Consequently, whatever he did as a human being, from hungering and sleeping to suffering and dying, was a function of his obedience to God's will. Thus, insofar as he was genuinely human, he was subject to the natural passions of human existence, like thirst, weariness, and even fear in the face of death; but because his will was (again, by grace and not by virtue of any alteration in essence) united with God's in each of these acts, he submitted to each of these realities freely and not by compulsion.[40]

In order to see how this understanding of Christ's person does not fall into a Docetism according to which his material existence was only a sort of divine play-acting, it is necessary to attend to the peculiarity of the will among all the components of human nature. The deification of the body involves transformation of its physical properties in order to render it incapable of suffering and death. By contrast (and as Maximus takes pains to insist), to speak of Christ's will as deified does not imply any such structural alteration: as a piece of human nature, the deified will differs from the non-deified will only in its relationship to God (i.e., in its mode of operation).[41] This difference reflects the ontologically odd status of the will as the feature of human nature that gives this nature a kind of open-ended indeterminacy. This is not because our wills allow us to determine or to override our natures. To argue that way would be precisely to succumb to the Pelagian understanding of the will as some sort of ontological reserve standing over against human nature rather than as part of it. The will is not a power we have over our natures (since we will what we desire, and we do not control what we desire), but rather identifies the fact that we live out our nature as agents who (and to be an agent is precisely to be a "who") are always implicated in our nature in a way that makes it impossible to view it as simply given. In short, human nature's open-endedness is a function of the fact that a human being is some*one* rather than some*thing*, and thus not adequately or fully described in terms of *what* she is.

The phenomenon of sin further displays this ontological oddity of the will. As both Maximus and Thomas agree, human beings hunger, grow tired, experience fear in the face of danger, and the like because these phenomena are natural consequences of material embodiment that cannot be altered except by the wholesale transformation of human bodies through the resurrection. They are, in other words, ontologically determinate features of human being under conditions of earthly existence prior to glory and, as such, constitute the determinate "whatness" of our nature in time and space.[42] By contrast (and following the Augustinian insight that human willing follows desire), the reason human beings sin is that their desires are perverse. But when it comes to explaining *why* those desires are perverse, the only answer that can be given is, "Because we are sinners" – that is, in terms of the "whoness" (or, in the language of classical theology, the individual hypostasis) – that is the mark of a created nature with a will.[43] In this way (and as a further example of the correlation of will with human nature's open-endedness), the will, as that aspect of my nature (i.e., my whatness) where my status as agent (i.e., my whoness) is revealed, discloses a limit to all attempts to account for my being solely in terms of what I am (i.e., my nature).[44]

When this same sort of analysis is applied to Christ, the fact that his hypostasis (i.e., *who* he is) is the Second Person of the Trinity (i.e., divine) means that things come out differently. In brief, while we sin because we are sinners, Christ does not sin because, as the divine Word (i.e., a hypostasis of the Trinity), he is not a sinner.[45] In contrast to the rest of us, Christ's will is glorified. To say this is simply to describe the effects of Christ's hypostatic identity (his whoness) on the way he lives out his human nature (i.e., his incarnate whatness): because he is God, his human will is at every point turned toward God and therefore is continuously and uninterruptedly shaped by God's will for him. Crucially, this claim does not imply that there is any difference between the intrinsic qualities of his will and ours of the sort that would need to be acknowledged if it were claimed that during his earthly ministry Christ's body was glorified. In contrast to the glorified body (which, e.g., changes from being material to spiritual), the glorified will is indefectible not because of any change in its internal properties, but simply because of its changed relation to God.

In other words, because Christ's sinlessness is a function of his hypostasis and not of his human nature, the fact that his will was deified says nothing about the character of the rest of his nature and is does not constitute a conceptual obstacle to the idea that the human nature he assumed was fallen.[46] Nor, contrariwise, does the assumption that the human nature he assumed was fallen imply that he was sinful – even on an Augustinian understanding of original sin. This is because sinfulness, though an existential corollary of the fallen will, is properly attributed to hypostasis rather than nature in its fallenness. For while the will is a constitutive element of human nature and therefore participates in that nature's fallenness, sinfulness is a matter of the concrete disposition of the will as personal agency and is therefore function of the I (i.e., of the individual hypostasis). Now, in all post-Adamic humanity (Christ excepted), this is a distinction without a practical difference, since the fall, as something which damages the whole of human nature,[47] necessarily includes the will as a part of that nature. Since the will is that by which the agent turns to God, for every human hypostasis damage to the will entails a turning away from God that renders the hypostasis sinful – even though the logic of willing is such that the hypostasis, as the I who wills, cannot lay the blame for sin on her nature without thereby subverting his or her status as an agent whose being is irreducible to the qualities of that nature.

By contrast, the fact that Christ's hypostasis is divine means that its character cannot be linked to the qualities of his human nature in the same way.[48] On the contrary, because his human nature, following the terminology of mature Chalcedonian theology, is anhypostatic (i.e., has no identity or whoness other than that of the Second Person of the Trinity), the fact that his human will is fallen is bootless: its hypostatization by the divine Word means that its relation to God is such that even when assuming a nature afflicted by postlapsarian corruption, it cannot sin.

## Theological Implications

This defense of the claim that Christ assumed a fallen human nature while remaining sinless suggests several basic principles for theological anthropology in general and the doctrine of original sin in particular. First, it allows a distinction to be drawn between *fallenness* and *sinfulness* as predicates in relation to the Chalcedonian categories of *nature* and *hypostasis*, respectively. Quite simply, fallenness is a property of nature and sin of hypostasis (or person). Though writing long before the course of the Christological controversy had led to the refinement of Chalcedonian terminology, Basil of Caesarea writes in terms suggestive of the distinct yet complementary roles of the nature and person in Christ's work of reconciliation: "Just as the death which is in us through Adam was swallowed up by the Godhead, so was the sin taken away by the righteousness which is in Christ Jesus, so that in the resurrection we receive back flesh neither liable to death nor subject to sin."[49] In other words, mortality – a symptom of the fallenness of the human *nature* – is overcome by immortality of the divine *nature*, while the sinfulness of individual human beings is overcome by the righteousness of the incarnate divine *person*.

Thus, even as nature and hypostasis are ontologically incommensurable categories, so are sinfulness and fallenness. A nature can be damaged (and thus fallen); but a nature cannot sin, because sin is ascribed to agents, and thus is a matter of the hypostasis.[50] At this point, however, the ontological oddity of the will obtrudes. Insofar as the will is a feature of human nature, a fallen human nature implies a fallen will. Yet because the will's fallenness – even though formally a matter of nature – is experienced by the individual human being *hypostatically* as one's own sin rather than as damage that exists apart from or independently of individual agency, fallen nature generally correlates with the fact of a sinful hypostasis.[51] In no other aspect of humanity's makeup does damage to the nature implicate the hypostasis in the same way.[52]

Nor does this correlation between fallen will and sinful hypostasis apply to Christ. Whereas the rest of us can do only what our natures permit (though it is always *we* and not our natures who do it), Christ is not so constrained. Because the divine Word who Christ is, is prior to (even if indissolubly united with) his human nature, the sinlessness of his (divine) hypostasis nullifies the fallenness of his (human) will. This does not make his will any less human; it simply reflects the fact that where the will (as opposed to, say, the body) is concerned, fallenness is a matter of relationship rather than intrinsic qualities. Because Christ hypostatically is God, he cannot will humanly other than what he, as very God, wills divinely. His will remains fully human, but by virtue of its hypostatic union with the divine, it remains the one aspect of Christ's earthly human nature whose fallenness is overcome by virtue of the mere fact of incarnation.

Second (and following immediately on from the distinction between fallenness and sinfulness), the affirmation that Christ had a fallen human nature implies that talk of sinful *natures* is best avoided, since even a nature so damaged as to be "fallen" remains good and not evil.[53] However badly damaged it may be, our nature never separates us from God.[54] On the contrary, because (in line with belief in creation from nothing) a created nature only exists as it is sustained in its existence by God, if such a nature exists at all, that existence is testament to an ongoing relationship to God based in God's affirmation of the creature as good in its nature. The assumption by Christ of a fallen human nature simply reinforces this basic point: if the nature that God assumes is itself damaged and yet is taken on by God as God's own humanity, then the damage our natures suffer is clearly not an occasion for divine revulsion. Insofar as we are at all, we are loved by God; no aspect of our nature stands in the way of or in any way mitigates God's love; on the contrary, every such aspect is during the course of our existence a constantly renewed testimony to that love.[55]

Third (and as will be developed in greater detail in Chapter 7), the claim that Christ's human nature was fallen provides a framework for affirming the congenital sinfulness of postlapsarian humanity without subscribing to implausible (and pastorally harmful) accounts of congenital blameworthiness. Insofar as sin is a function of hypostasis, *who* we are is the source of our alienation from God as surely as *what* we are is unceasingly loved by God. At first glance, this position appears to bring into relief all that is most problematic about Christian hamartiology by affirming divine love of fallen humanity simultaneously with divine hatred of all fallen human beings because of their status as sinners. Jesus alone escapes this judgment by virtue of his sinlessness. Precisely here, however, the relationship between sin and fallenness disclosed through Christological analysis provides a corrective. As that which separates us from God, no sin – including original sin – can be termed "natural" in the strict sense, since nature is by definition that which *connects* us to God.[56] Sin is, rather, a function of the individual human hypostasis, and to concede this is to recognize that human beings are responsible for sin – that the "I" participates in and does not merely suffer the separation it entails. Indeed, the structure of sin is such that it implicates even those who are sinned against in estrangement from God.[57] And yet all this does not require that sin be interpreted as a matter of guilt that calls for blame, because the original sin that, in Augustinian perspective, is the ground of all actual sin is fundamentally an ontological rather than a moral category. It is, in other words, *not* in itself the kind of act for which one might be blamed or rightly feel guilt. Indeed, it is not an *act* at all (which is why it can be thought of as congenital) but rather the ground of all our acts apart from the transforming power of grace. In this way, we sin *because* we are always already sinners; but because our sinfulness is logically prior to our acting, our actions are a symptom rather than the source of our sin. Instead, our sinfulness turns out to be deeper than those individual acts of the will for which guilt and blame may well be appropriate responses.

Fourth (and as will also be discussed further in the next chapter), this way of talking removes the understanding of the transmission of original sin both from a purely biological model of genetic transmission (which would seem to undermine any meaningful talk of human responsibility for sin) as well as Reformed models of imputation (which preserve human responsibility at the price of making the morally problematic assumption that God attributes Adam's guilt to Adam's descendants). Both these models effectively conflate fallenness and sinfulness in a way that is inconsistent with their correlation with nature and hypostasis, respectively. How then do we come to be "guilty" of original sin? As already noted, one can speak of a fallen will insofar as the will is an essential feature of human nature in all its states, including that of postlapsarian "fallenness." Yet the ontology of the will disallows the reduction of sin to an external determination that would vitiate individual responsibility, since to speak of willing is precisely to acknowledge agency. As a sinner, I cannot help but acknowledge that my will is fallen. But when it comes to asking *why* I am a sinner, there is simply no answer. As Augustine recognized, it is a mystery:

> The will, of course, comes from something, and it is not forced to exist. And if we should not ask for its origin, we ought not to ask for its origin, not because the will does not come from something, but because it is obvious where it comes from ... For the will comes from the one whose will it is ... the will of the human being from the human being; the will of God from God. Even if God produces in a human being a good will, he, of course does this so that the good will comes to be from the one whose will it is.[58]

Doctrinally, Christians are committed to denying that God made them sinners (all the more since the ontology of the will militates against any passing off of my agency to a third party). Therefore, reference to the will's "fallenness" does not work as an explanation of *my* sin in particular; at most it specifies the anthropological context within which the universal and congenital character of sin is affirmed. In this way, the will turns out to be less the *cause* of my sinfulness than the *place* where my sinfulness is experienced and known. The sinfulness itself is a mystery – a function of who I am that finally resists causal explanation.

Crucially, in Christ the mystery of sin is met by the greater mystery of God's mercy toward sinners. And this greater mystery does have an assignable cause: God's love. If Christ's possessing a fallen human nature is not soteriologically necessary, it is an appropriate manifestation of this love, for by displaying solidarity with us to the point of assuming a nature that is damaged, God both reveals and qualifies our status as sinners. Though as sinners we have damaged human natures, the fact that Christ can assume this nature without sin shows that this damage is a symptom rather than a cause of our separation from God. In sharing our nature without sharing our sin, Christ reveals sin as a function of the will that is nevertheless prior to any act of the will, and thus allows it to be understood as an ontological rather than an axiological category. Far from letting us off the hook, however, the revelation that sin is a matter of who rather than what we are reveals the depth to which we are implicated in sin even as it vindicates the ineradicable goodness of our created whatness. Contrary to the charges typically leveled against Augustinian construals of original sin, postlapsarian human beings are neither ontologically evil nor morally passive automata. That we remain nevertheless bound to sin is a mystery of our being the magnitude of which is, thankfully, known to us only as it is overcome by the even greater mystery of the one who was made like us in all respects yet without sin.

Needless to say, this sketch of some implications of bringing Chalcedonian categories to bear on Christian hamartiology remains a long way from constituting a defense of the doctrine of original sin. Indeed, at best the last three chapters constitute a kind of ground-clearing operation: providing a series of terminological and doctrinal clarifications that address some of the basic challenges to the internal coherence of the doctrine, as well as its compatibility with other fundamental Christian convictions relating to human freedom and the inalienable goodness of the creation. The task of providing a robust account of the doctrine's positive significance for Christian theology remains. In order to provide such an account, it will be necessary to develop the ideas summarized over the last few pages in order to engage a further set of challenges to original sin that were not addressed by Augustine – challenges relating to its scientific credibility, its implications for the victims of sin, and its compatibility with Christian commitments to the pursuit of social justice. These matters will be the focus of the third part of this book.

## Notes

1 Gregory of Nazianzus, Letter 101 ("To Cledonius Against Apollinaris")," in *Christology of the Later Fathers*, ed. Edward R. Hardy (Philadelphia: Westminster, 1954), p. 218. The passage continues: "If only half Adam fell, then that which Christ assumes and saves must be half also; but if the whole of his nature fell, it must be united to the whole nature of him that was begotten, and so be saved as a whole."
2 Irenaeus may have been the first to enunciate this principle, which became a commonplace of patristic theology: Christ "did through His transcendent love, become what we are, that He might bring us to be even what He is Himself." *Against Heresies* 5 (Preface), in *The Apostolic Fathers*, vol. 1 of *The Ante-Nicene Fathers*, ed. Alexander Roberts and James Donaldson (Grand Rapids, MI: William B. Eerdmans, n.d.), p. 526.
3 John Calvin, *Institutes of the Christian Religion* 2.12.1, ed. John T. McNeill. (Philadelphia, PA: Westminster Press, 1960), p. 464.
4 For an excellent discussion of the points of agreement uniting those on both sides of the fallen/unfallen debate, see Kelly M. Kapic, "The Son's Assumption of a Human Nature: A Call for Clarity," *International Journal of Systematic Theology* 3:2 (July 2001), 164–6.
5 Gregory of Nyssa, *The Life of Moses* 2.32 (New York: Paulist Press, 1978), p. 62 (PG44:336B).

6   Gregory, *The Life of Moses* 2.275, p. 124 (PG44:413D–416A). Cf. *Against Eunomius*, 6.1, in *Dogmatic Treatises, etc.*, vol. 5 of *Nicene and Post-Nicene Fathers*, 2nd Series, ed. Philip Schaff and Henry Wace (Peabody, MA: Hendrickson, 1995 [1893]), p. 183 [PG45:713C], where Gregory interprets the "sin" of 2 Cor. 5:21 as nothing more than a synonym for "flesh." I am grateful to an anonymous reader of an earlier draft of this chapter for alerting me to this last text.

7   The same ambiguity is seen in the "Address on Religious Instruction" (in *Christology of the Later Fathers*, ed. Edward R. Hardy [Philadelphia: Westminster, 1954], p. 305), where Gregory affirms that in the incarnation "this sick creature of earth" had to be "united with the divine" – but only to oppose a Docetist denial Christ's physical birth. See also Maximus' complex account of the character of the human nature assumed by Christ in *Quaestiones ad Thalassium* 21 (*CCSG* 7: 129), where reference is made to Christ's having assumed both Adam's original condition *and* the liability to passions resulting from the fall. This lack of fit between the rhetoric of the fathers and the character of later controversies renders Thomas Weinandy's attempts to show that Christ's assumption of a fallen human nature was a matter of consensus in the patristic period unpersuasive. See Thomas Weinandy, *In the Likeness of Sinful Flesh: An Essay on the Humanity of Christ* (Edinburgh: T&T Clark, 1993), ch. 3. The same reservations apply to T. F. Torrance's claims in *The Trinitarian Faith* (Edinburgh: T&T Clark, 1995), pp. 153–4.

8   Augustine, *The Punishment and Forgiveness of Sins and the Baptism of Little Ones*, 2.38, ed. John E. Rotelle, O.S.A. (Hyde Park, NY: New City Press, 1997). See also *Unfinished Work in Answer to Julian* [hereafter *UWJ*], 4.59–60, where Augustine insists that Christ "had integrity without any corruption, rectitude without any depravity, good health without any desire for sin," immediately adding that it is blasphemous to "make the flesh of Christ equal to the flesh of other human beings," since Christ "came, not in sinful flesh, but in the likeness of sinful flesh." Interestingly, one other patristic text that offers a seemingly clear and unambiguous affirmation that Christ's human nature did not suffer the effects of the fall is the infamous "monothelite" letter of Pope Honorius I (Epistle 4 ["*Ad Sergium Constantinopolitanum Episcopum*," PL80:472A–B); cf. p. 91 above.

9   Julian of Norwich, writing outside of the mainstream of monastic and university theology, would seem to constitute a notable exception to this trend. See her *Showings*, Long Text, (New York: Paulist Press, 1978), ch. 51.

10  Anselm, *Why God Became Man*, 2.11, in *A Scholastic Miscellany: Anselm to Ockham*, ed. Eugene R. Fairweather (Philadelphia: Westminster, 1956). He makes the same point in the later treatise *On the Virginal Conception and Original Sin*.

11  Anselm, *Why God Became Man*, 2.11.

12  Anselm, *Why God Became Man*, 2.11.

13 "In terms ... of the kind of necessity that follows on being material the body of Christ was faced with the necessity of death and other kindred disabilities [*aliorum huiusmodi defectuum*]." Thomas Aquinas, *Summa Theologiae* [hereafter *ST*], 61 vols., Blackfriars edn. (London: Eyre & Spottiswood, 1964–81), 3.14.2.

14 *ST* 3.14.3 (translation slightly modified; cf. 3.31.7.2, where Thomas again states that Christ "assumed flesh untainted by sin, as was the flesh of man before sin [*ante peccatum*]"). Thomas immediately goes on to conclude that Christ "could, correspondingly, have taken on human nature without any disabilities." In the face of this clear distinction (reiterated in 3.14.3.1) between the assumption of human flesh on the one hand, and the assumption of its *defectus* on the other, Weinandy's claim (*In the Likeness of Sinful Flesh*, p. 51) that for Thomas "the sufferings and penalties of sin flowed directly from his freely assuming the humanity of Adam's race, and not from something he freely assumed and acquired in addition to his humanity" is not tenable.

15 Thus, "the body of Christ was in Adam as regards bodily substance [*corpulentam substantiam*] ... But it was not there seminally [*secundum seminalem rationem*], because Christ was not conceived from male seed. Thus he did not incur original sin." *ST* 3.31.1.3.

16 Heinrich Schmid, *The Doctrinal Theology of the Evangelical Lutheran Church*, 3rd edn. (Minneapolis, MN: Augsburg, 1899), p. 294. Some Lutheran Pietists were so intent on affirming the purity of Christ's human nature as distinct from that of postlapsarian Adamic humanity as to affirm a pre-existent humanity similar to Menno Simons' doctrine of pre-existent "heavenly flesh." See, e.g., Martin H. Jung, "Johanna Eleonora Petersen (1644–1724)," in *The Pietist Theologians*, ed. Carter Lindberg (Malden, MA: Blackwell, 2005), pp. 147–60.

17 M. Chemnitz, *De Duabus Naturis* (1570), 11; cited in Schmid, *Theology*, p. 299.

18 S. Maresius, *Collegium theologicum sive Systema breve universae Theologiae comprehensum octodecim disputationibus* (Geneva, 1662), IX.20; cited in Heinrich Heppe, *Reformed Dogmatics*, ed. Ernst Bizer (London: Allen and Unwin, 1950), p. 420. In contrast to Catholic theologians, the Reformed explicitly included ignorance among these "infirmities."

19 "Our affections proceed from corrupt flesh and forestall the judgment of reason and do not always obey reason. In Christ they did reside in sense appetition [as they do in other human beings]; but because he was without sin and always obeyed right reason, they were roused by right reason rather than by sense appetition." A. Polanus, *Syntagma Theologiae Christianae* (Hanover, 1624), 6.15, cited in Heppe, *Reformed Dogmatics*, p. 420. Cf. the *Leiden Synopsis* (Leiden, 1624): "It was not suitable for the Son of God to be united with a human nature liable to punishment because of sin [*peccato obnoxiam*]" (cited by Karl Barth, *Church Dogmatics* I/2, ed. G. W. Bromiley and T. F. Torrance [Edinburgh: T&T Clark, 1956], p. 153).

20 "... that He might perform the work of a mediator, and become a victim for our sins." J. A. Quenstedt, *Theologia Didactico-Polemica* (1685), 3.76; cited in Schmid, *Theology*, p. 300. Cf. J. H. Heidegger, *Medulla Theologiae Christianae* (Zürich, 1696), 17.16 (citing Heb. 2:17): "it behoved him not only to be a brother, but also to die and be made like all his brethren and tempted;" cited in Heppe, *Reformed Dogmatics*, p. 421.

21 The Reformed Scholastics argued that Adam's corruption was imputed to later generations of humanity because of the (logically) prior imputation of Adam's guilt, such that humans were corrupt because they were sinful rather than the other way round. See the helpful discussion in Oliver D. Crisp, "Did Christ Have a *Fallen* Human Nature?" in *Divinity and Humanity: The Incarnation Reconsidered* (Cambridge: Cambridge University Press, 2007), pp. 99–104; cf. Kapic, "The Son's Assumption," pp. 160–3.

22 "He was not a sinful man. But inwardly and outwardly His situation was that of a sinful man. He did nothing that Adam did. But he lived life in the form it must take on the basis of the assumption of Adam's act." Barth, *Church Dogmatics* I/2, p. 152. Barth acknowledged being anticipated in this claim by a range of nineteenth-century figures, including Edward Irving in Scotland and J. C. K. von Hoffman and H. F. Kohlbrügge in Germany.

23 Barth, *Church Dogmatics* II/1, p. 151; cf. p. 153: "God's Son not only assumed our nature but He entered the concrete form of our nature, under which we stand before God as men damned and lost." This aspect of Barth's Christology is closely bound up with his distinctive doctrine of election, according to which Christ's status as the Elect One whose election secures the salvation of all humanity is inseparable from his also being the Rejected One who bears God's curse. See especially Barth, *Church Dogmatics* II/2, pp. 346–7.

24 Hans Urs von Balthasar, *Mysterium Paschale* (Edinburgh: T&T Clark, 1990), p. 22.

25 Although, as already noted, Gregory of Nyssa's reflections do not fit easily within the categories of later debates, he did insist that Christ was not susceptible to any movements of the soul "opposed to virtue unencumbered by passion" precisely as a means of affirming that Christ's human nature was not in any way damaged or deficient. Gregory of Nyssa, *Against Eunomius* 6.3 (PG45:721C).

26 Orthodox theologians, for example, tend to view damage in terms of the acquisition of passions that hamper the exercise of reason and the will. To cite Gregory of Nyssa one last time, he describes the postlapsarian acquisition of passions in terms of a disease that affects humans' capacity to exercise choice (*proaireseōs ... nosos*). Gregory of Nyssa, *Against Eunomius* 6.3 (PG45:721D).

27 It is important to note at this juncture that even those who view Christ's human nature as unfallen can speak of *defectus* in that nature (see note 13 above). This Latin term, however, functions in such cases purely *negatively* to mean that Christ's human nature lacks perfections to which the Incarnate

Word would otherwise be entitled and, correspondingly, has certain susceptibilities (e.g., passibility, mortality) from which it would otherwise be exempt. It does not imply any deformation or defect (in the English sense of the word) in the nature as assumed and is, as such, compatible with the idea of Christ assuming an unfallen nature.

28  Alyssa Lyra Pitstick is therefore right to criticize Balthasar's tendency to interpret the principle that what is not *assumed* is not healed to mean that whatever is not *endured* is not redeemed. Christ heals human nature, not the various forces that afflict it. See Alyssa Lyra Pitstick, *Light in Darkness: Hans Urs von Balthasar and the Catholic Doctrine of Christ's Descent into Hell* (Grand Rapids, MI: William B. Eerdmans, 2007), pp. 96–7.

29  See Aquinas, *ST* 3.1.2 and *ST* 3.46.1–4.

30  It is tempting to cite so-called aphthartodocetists like the sixth-century bishop Julian of Halicarnassus as an exception, but even they did not question the reality of Christ's sufferings (to which a fully glorified human being would presumably not be susceptible). Insofar as they denied that Christ's human nature had any natural susceptibility to suffering, while also maintaining that he willingly subjected himself to it, their position is arguably not as discontinuous with standard defenses of Christ's "unfallen" human nature as it may first appear. One might also mention the Lutheran theologians of Tübingen in the seventeenth century, who argued from the doctrine of the communication of attributes that even during his earthly ministry Christ sat at the right hand of the Father according to his human nature, though they emphasized that Christ exercised the prerogatives of glory in a hidden way (hence the designation of this position as "*crypto*-kenoticism") and certainly had no wish to question the reality of Christ's passion.

31  What about the damned? They represent a theologically difficult category, and I have no space here to do justice to it. Under annihilationist schemes, of course (and Paul himself may well fall in this camp; n.b. the lack of any reference to the resurrection of unbelievers in 1 Cor. 15: 51–7 and 1 Thess. 4:13–17; cf. 2 Thess. 1:9), those who are not glorified simply cease to exist, so that there are no non-glorified human beings after the Last Judgment. For those who hold a doctrine of eternal punishment, the damned are viewed as human beings, yet insofar as they are not glorified their humanity is anomalous: if the saints in heaven cannot sin, the damned always sin – yet not in the same way that fallen human beings on earth do (viz., with the possibility of repentance). In this way they are human beings who have irrevocably failed to be human in the way that God intended. They are, so to speak, human inhumanly, just as demons are angelic beings who exist unangelically. As such (i.e., creatures created for glory who have become constitutionally incapable of being glorified), they fall outside the normal categories of salvation history. See in this context the description of the damned found in George Bernanos, *The Diary of a Country Priest* (New York: Macmillan, 1937), p. 177.

32  Paul's emphasis in 1 Thessalonians 4 on the equality of the faithful living and dead at Christ's return is theologically relevant here.
33  Cf. the claim in Heb. 5:8–9 that Christ "learned obedience through what he suffered." While learning may well be defended as characteristic of human nature in all stages of salvation history (especially if one should subscribe to Gregory of Nyssa's concept of *epektasis*), it seems doubtful that learning *through suffering* is characteristic of human nature in its glorified state.
34  Aquinas, *ST* 3.14.1 (translation slightly modified).
35  This same objection would apply to Crisp's suggestion ("Did Christ Have a *Fallen* Human Nature?," p. 116) that Christ may be said to assume the characteristics of fallen human nature without having a fallen human nature, in the same way that a person might be made to display "the symptoms of measles without ... having the virus." However such a person might appear to have measles, measles sufferers in the know would have to confess that she was not really one of them.
36  See the discussion in *Why God Became Man*, 2.10.
37  See Augustine, *Rebuke and Grace*, 33 (in *Answer to the Pelagians*, IV, ed. John E. Rotelle, O.S.A. [Hyde Park, NY: New City Press, 1997], p. 132). The textbook sequence according to which humanity was created able not to sin (*posse non peccare*), became unable not to sin (*non posse non peccare*) after the fall, and will in glory be unable to sin (*non posse peccare*) is certainly consistent with Augustine's thought, but is more clearly set out by Peter Lombard in *Sentences*, 2.25.5.
38  Maximus the Confessor, *Opuscula Theologica et Polemica* [hereafter *OTP*] 20 (PG91:236D); cf. *OTP* 7 (PG91:80C–D): "the human will [of Christ] is wholly deified [*diolou tetheoto*], in its agreement with the divine will itself, since it is eternally moved and shaped by it and in accordance with it" (translation from Andrew Louth, "Opuscule 7," in *Maximus the Confessor* (New York: Routledge, 1996), p. 186. See pp. 96–8 above.
39  In *Ambiguum* 10 Maximus avers that Christ's transfiguration on Mount Tabor was the result of an augmentation of the disciples' perceptive capacities rather than any objective change in his condition; but his point seems to be that here the disciples were miraculously enabled to see the uncreated light of the *divine* nature and not that Christ's human nature was already glorified.
40  As noted earlier, in affirming that Christ hungered willingly (*hekousiōs*), Maximus is not claiming that Jesus did not need to eat, but rather that in his hungering his will was immediately shaped by God's and for this reason pursued its natural functions with genuine freedom not marred by the possibility of mutability and sin. See *OTP* 7 (PG91:77A).
41  Maximus' denial that Christ possessed a gnomic will is perfectly consistent with this position, because the gnomic will is not a distinct psychic structure (i.e., a matter of *logos*), but simply the mode (*tropos*) in which non-deified wills operate (viz., through an extended psychological process characterized by deliberation and decision). In this same context, it is important to avoid

mischaracterizations of the will's deification either as the equivalent of omniscience or as some sort of trance-like state in which Jesus blindly follows divine directives. On the contrary, for Maximus the defining character of the deified human will is its *naturalness* (e.g., correspondence with both the finitude and freedom of human nature): "an active desire that is single and cognitive for whatever nature renders desirable." Maximus, *OTP* 1 (PG91:24C); see p. 100 above.

42  I borrow the terminological contrast between "whatness" and "whoness" from Serene Jones, "What's Wrong with Us?" in *Essentials of Christian Theology*, ed. William C. Placher (Louisville, KY: Westminster John Knox, 2003), p. 149.

43  As explained further in the following paragraphs, "Because we are fallen" or "Because we have damaged natures" are not possible responses, since to view sin as immediately *caused* by a damaged nature would make sin the responsibility of God, as the One who creates and sustains human nature. See also pp. 183–5 below.

44  Needless to say, none of this is to deny that environmental and genetic (i.e., "whatness") factors may play a powerful role in shaping desire and, correspondingly, sin; it is only to point out that none of these can finally be viewed as fully accounting for or explaining the behavior so long as the person experiences herself as an "I" (or "who").

45  In this respect, my understanding of Christ's sinlessness has certain similarities with Thomas's, though it does not depend on a commitment to Aristotelian biology. Christ's possession of a divine hypostasis is, as Thomas argues, the cause of his sinlessness, but this point is logically independent from the question of whether or not he has a human father, since (following the language of the current pope) Jesus' divinity "is not a biological but an ontological fact." Joseph Ratzinger, *Introduction to Christianity* (New York: Seabury Press, 1968), p. 208.

46  In this context, it is important to note that while I think that Maximus' analysis of the will provides a framework within which it is possible to affirm the fallenness of Christ's human nature, I do not think the latter view can be attributed to Maximus himself.

47  If it did not affect nature in its entirety, then there would be some aspect of humanity that did not require salvation, such that Christ's assumption of it – contrary to the witness of Heb. 2:17 – be superfluous.

48  In the language of later theology, Christ's human nature is *an*hypostatic (i.e., it has no human hypostasis), though it is *en*hypostatized by the Son.

49  Basil of Caesarea, Letter 261 ("To the Sozopolitans"), in *Basil: Letters and Select Works*, vol. 8 of *Nicene and Post-Nicene Fathers*, 2nd Series, ed. Philip Schaff and Henry Wace (Grand Rapids, MI: William B. Eerdmans, 1995 [1895]), p. 300.

50  Though he does not make systematic use of the person/nature distinction, Kapic ("The Son's Assumption," p. 164) does point out that advocates of Christ's assumption of a fallen nature emphasize "the Spirit's role in keeping

the *person* of Christ free from sin, though the human nature is itself 'sinful flesh'." The terminology is, however, imprecise, since the *person* of Christ is the divine Word and thus inherently free from sin; it would be more correct to speak of the Spirit keeping Christ's *human will* from sinning.

51 Anticipation of this later distinction, according to which only individual hypostases and not natures can be evil, is also visible at points in Augustine's writing: "It is not one who maintains that the nature of human beings is evil, but one who maintains that it is an evil, that is, it is not one who maintains that it is evil, but who maintains that it is something evil, who is forced to deny grace. For, when it is evil, it then needs grace the more. An evil man is, of course, an evil nature because a man is without doubt a nature ... How, then, is one who says this forced to deny grace since grace helps evil natures, that is, evil human beings, so that they cease to be evil? But we say one thing when we say: This human being is evil, and we say something else when we say, This human being is an evil. The former can be true; the latter cannot." Augustine, *UWJ*, 3.188.

52 It needs to be stressed here that this correlation between will and hypostasis does not mean their conflation. To invoke Maximus' terminology once again, the will is part of the structure (or *logos*) of human nature; by contrast, the hypostasis is not a structure at all, but simply the mode (or *tropos*) of the nature's existence in a particular instance (see note 41 above). In the case of humanity, the mode or "how" of the nature's existence is precisely as an agential "who." In other words, every hypostasis (viz., concrete example) of a human nature is a someone; and this someone (or "who") is the whole human being, body and soul – not just the will. For this reason, nothing could be further from the truth than to view the correlation between fallen will and sinful hypostasis as suggesting that the hypostasis is an object located "in" the will: the will's relationship to the hypostasis is not one of containment; rather (and as explained further below), the will is that dimension of human nature where sinfulness is made known.

53 Here Augustine's position is less clear-cut, for while he acknowledges that God makes nothing evil, he notes that this is only true "insofar as God makes them, not insofar as the lump of clay out of which he makes them is damaged and corrupted" (*UWJ*, 4.40). This way of putting it suggests an odd distance between God and the creature, as though the "lump of clay" with which God works were not itself the immediate product of God's creative activity. There is at least the savor of Manicheism about this language, as though the nature is itself – and not simply the defective willing of particular hypostases of that nature – were in some respect hateful to God.

54 Clement of Alexandria makes this point as follows: "Assuredly sin is an activity (*energeia*) not an essence (*ousia*): and therefore it is not the work of God." *Stromateis* 4.94.1; cited in Denise Buell, *Why This New Race: Ethnic Reasoning in Early Christianity* (New York: Columbia University Press, 2005), p. 123.

55 To be sure, our human nature in its present state is not what God ultimately intends for it, but this would be the case even if we had not fallen, since

(as Irenaeus argues in *Against Heresies*, 4.38) God formed human beings in a state of imperfection because it is natural for creatures, as temporal beings, to receive perfection over time.
56 The equivocation involved in talking about "natural" sin is well attested in the tradition. See, e.g., Calvin, *Institutes*, 2.1.10–11.
57 I use the term "implicate" as a (hopefully) neutral term that communicates the involvement of the self in sin without implying active complicity, perversity, or blameworthiness. In so doing, I am trying to show how sin can include even those whose sin cannot be helpfully described using categories of willfulness or perversity.
58 Augustine, *UWJ*, 5.42.

# Part III

# Reconstructing the Doctrine: Original Sin in Christian Practice

# 6

# Original Sin and Human Nature: Solidarity in Sin

If we recall the three "lapsarian questions" identified in Chapter 2 as the most pressing challenges to the contemporary plausibility of the Augustinian doctrine of original sin, the modern period has been particularly hard on the first of them. For while it is true that the idea of inherited sin has been subject to vehement criticism since Augustine's time, belief in a historical fall − that the first human beings had sinned and thus fundamentally changed the conditions of earthly existence − was widely accepted by Christians of all stripes well into the nineteenth century. Today there are still vehement defenders of the historical accuracy of Genesis 1–3, but the picture of the natural history of the human species in particular and the cosmos in general produced over the last two centuries by a convergence of data from geology, biology, paleontology, and genetics has strained the credibility of literal readings of the biblical creation stories past the breaking point. By Augustine's own hermeneutical criteria,[1] the tracing of all suffering to a primordial sin committed by the first human couple is no longer credible: the evidence that death, disease, and natural disasters of all sorts were a characteristic of life on earth eons before human beings appeared on the planet is overwhelming, and there is, correspondingly, no reason to believe that human existence was ever characterized by the absence of labor pains or an ability to acquire food without sweat. Nor are the principles of evolutionary biology consistent with the descent of all human beings from a single ancestral pair (the theory of human origins known as monogenesis).[2] Instead, the best available evidence suggests that modern humans emerged (in Africa rather than the Mesopotamian setting of Genesis 1–3) as a splinter population from pre-existing hominid groups within the last quarter of

---

*In Adam's Fall: A Meditation on the Christian Doctrine of Original Sin*, by Ian A. McFarland.
© 2010 Ian A. McFarland.

a million years. These data render contemporary attempts to defend a classical form of monogenesis unpersuasive.[3]

These developments pose serious problems for the doctrine of original sin, since simply abandoning questions of natural history altogether (e.g., by reinterpreting original sin with Kierkegaard, Niebuhr, or Tillich as a timeless feature of human ontology) risks undermining a central point of the Augustinian doctrine: namely, the importance of disjoining the origin of sin from the origin of human being as such. After all, Augustine's own increasing stress on the literal truth of the first chapters of Genesis over the course of his career was closely correlated with his insistence that all human beings were united in sin by virtue of their common descent from Adam. Even if later Christians were unable to agree about how all people came to share in Adam's sin, the idea of universal human sinfulness acquired a certain prima facie plausibility from the belief that everyone sprang from the same damaged stock. Within this framework, Augustine's doctrine of original sin dovetailed with already existing Christian use of Genesis 1–3 in the service of theodicy. But where the idea of evil entering the world through a single, identifiable transgression by the first human being has ceased to be defensible, the inevitability and universality of sin appear to be up for grabs. How can all human beings justifiably be convicted of sin from birth if it is no longer credible to assert that all human beings descend from a lone sinner at the dawn of history? Absent such a historical grounding, will not any doctrine of universal sinfulness necessarily impugn the goodness of the Creator?

## Original Sin and the Damaged Will

At the end of the previous chapter, I suggested that the distinction between nature and hypostasis provided a framework that made it possible to affirm both the inalienable goodness of human nature and the congenital sinfulness of every individual human being. Crucial to this claim was a particular understanding of the will. Building on the work of Augustine and Maximus, and with special reference to the implications of traditional Christological convictions regarding Christ's sinlessness, I argued that the will was an ontologically odd category. On the one hand, it is a constitutive feature of human nature; that is, to be human is (among other things) to have a will. Christians are therefore bound to confess that the will is ineradicably good. However much it may have been damaged by the fall, to say that the will is naturally or congenitally sinful is theologically illegitimate, because it would imply that God brings evil into being. Thus, in the same way that even a badly deformed leg is still good inasmuch as it is a leg, so a fallen will (however "fallen" may be defined) must be confessed as good insofar as it is a will. As argued in the last chapter, this point is useful in defending the contentious claim that Christ assumed a fallen nature: if the will remains ontologically good even when fallen, then Christ's sinlessness does not in itself speak against the idea that he had a fallen nature.

Yet the ontological oddity of the will among the various features of human nature does not allow us to stop here. If we could, then there would be no place for the doctrine of original sin: the claim that Christ's having a fallen will does not imply his sinfulness would seem to apply to the rest of postlapsarian humanity as well. This inference is blocked by the fact that the will, though part of human nature and, as such, inalienably good, is also the locus of personal agency; that is, to will is to be an "I" – a particular human hypostasis. Importantly, this does not mean that the will is the *source* of one's identity as a distinct hypostasis. Once again, Christological reflection makes this clear. Although Jesus has a human will, it is not the source or cause of his identity as the Second Person of the Trinity, which (at least according to the principles of Chalcedonian Christology) pre-exists the incarnation by which he has this human will. Instead, Christ's human will marks where and how he lives out this identity *humanly* – in much the same way that his (human) "spirit" is where he experiences strong emotions (see John 11:33).[4] Now, hypostasis does not pre-exist nature in any other human being. Correspondingly, our human natures are not for the rest of us a means by which we live out a pre-existent identity: we do not "assume" a human nature; we simply *are* particular instances of (fallen) human nature, with all its features. It follows that we do not have the same kind of "ontological surplus" with respect to our fallen human wills that Jesus – confessed as fully divine as well as fully human – has with respect to his.[5] Since our (human) wills are the locus of our agency, which has no reality separate from it, we cannot speak of the state of our will without implicating ourselves as responsible agents. Thus, for us – in stark contrast to Jesus – to *have* a fallen will is to *be* a sinner, because, unlike Jesus, who is divine as well as human, we have no pre-existing ontological leverage that allows us to turn our fallen wills to the good.[6] Inasmuch as our natures are fallen, we can do nothing but sin: the will may be naturally good, but our hypostatic instantiation of it is not.

In short, the ontological oddity of the will makes it possible to argue that for all human beings other than Christ,[7] a damaged (but still inalienably good) nature is invariably correlated with a hypostasis that is congenitally sinful (and thus estranged from God). Yet this is a purely formal point that leaves unaddressed the material question of *what kind of damage* to the will leads to this situation. As discussed in Chapter 3, Augustine answers this question in two different and not fully consistent ways. When speculating on humanity's condition before the fall, Augustine seems to view the damage sustained by the will in terms of a loss of control: in Paradise the will operated in accord with reason and was in command of all bodily movements; after the fall the will no longer had this level of control over the body. By contrast, when Augustine contrasts the condition of fallen humanity with the promised state of glory, he depicts the will's damaged state rather differently: as a kind of disorientation, in which the desires that motivate willing are focused on creatures rather than the Creator. In both cases, the damage sustained by the will as a consequence of the fall can manifest itself (in line with Paul's experience in Romans 7) as a matter of division, with the will torn between what it knows to be good and the evil it actually accomplishes. When grace heals the will, this division is overcome. But whereas in the first case this process seems to entail a restoration of self-*control*, in which the will regains sovereignty over bodily movements, in the second it is more the realization of self-*consistency*, in which my desires are so oriented that my willing corresponds with the truth of my nature as established by God.

I have already argued that evolutionary biology renders the interpretation of damage to the will as a loss of self-control implausible. There is no reason to suppose that human beings ever enjoyed the kind of control over bodily functions that Augustine seems to envision as Adam's original state, or that such control would be biologically advantageous.[8] Moreover, even on Augustine's own terms, envisioning the will as power or capacity to exercise control over the body would seem to undermine the role of (embodied) desire as that which motivates us to will the good no less than (in our unredeemed state) evil. In this respect, the "restless heart" that is so much at the heart of Augustine's understanding of the human condition seems oddly absent from his speculative forays on humanity's life in Eden.[9]

By comparison, natural history poses no such problems for interpreting the will's damaged state in terms of divided desire that can be healed by grace.[10] Furthermore, the correlation of damage with a distortion of desire is arguably more coherent with Augustine's own quite strong insistence on the non-competitive relationship between divine grace and human willing. Where damage is conceived as a loss of control, it is natural to imagine its healing in quasi-magical terms as the infusion of a power or capacity that had been lacking. It is hard to see how human beings might be said to participate in such a process; and, in any case, Augustine does not conceive the life of glory as a restoration to humanity's original state. Instead, he describes it in terms of desire that is wholly focused on God, so that the individual, led by a desire that is now rightly ordered, invariably wills rightly. Conceived in these terms, the healing of the will does not involve any special transformation of its inherent abilities. On the contrary, the structural features of willing remain unchanged throughout the transition from innocence through fallenness to glory: in all three cases the will follows desire. What changes is the *object* of desire: grace turns desire Godward and thereby allows human beings to will the good. In redemption and glory our willing – the same willing that in our unredeemed state invariably results in sin – brings us to the good, as a result of the fact that our desires have been transformed so as to make such willing possible and, indeed, natural.

It is in this respect that Maximus' doctrine of the will provides useful clarification and correction of Augustine's insights. His distinction between the natural and the gnomic wills provides a framework within which choice emerges as a contingent feature of human willing under conditions of ignorance rather than a constitutive feature of responsible agency. At bottom, willing is not tied up with the capacity for self-control associated with the rhetoric or experience of choice: even as God's freedom of will does not consist in any capacity to choose between options, but simply in the perfect correspondence between God's triune agency and God's loving nature, so human willing is free when it corresponds to its created end and not by its power to choose.

This line of argument suggests that the fallen will is "damaged" only in a very particular sense: namely, to the extent that the desires that naturally move it (viz., the desires that the human being experiences hypostatically as her own) are disordered – focused on temporal, created goods instead of the Creator who is their source and end. This state of affairs means that fallen human beings are unable to will the good, but this inability is not due to any loss of the will's intrinsic *capacities* (since it always follows desire), but rather in its *orientation* – parallel to the case of a person whose inability to see is due not to any change in the structure or functionality of the eye, the optic nerve, or the visual cortex, but to her sitting in the dark. Herein lies the essence of the "bondage" of the (fallen) will: since the will follows (and thus is bound to) desire, where desires are perverse, so is the will. From this perspective freeing the will does not involve its acquiring more power (whether through a "Pelagian" process of training or an "Augustinian" gift of grace), as though the will's bondage were analogous to its being in chains that might be broken with sufficient effort. It is more like being in quicksand, where greater effort only reinforces one's captivity, or (since the power of original sin is such that the sinner need not even be aware of her bondage) like following a will-o'-the-wisp that leads toward destruction rather than away from it.[11] In short, release from bondage does not entail giving the will more power, but rather putting the power it has to its proper use by changing the desires to which it is bound.[12]

This characterization of original sin raises the question of how it is that all human beings come to will defectively. Again, the claim that this defect is a universal, congenital condition means that it cannot be construed as a matter of choice, even leaving aside the point that one cannot be said to choose one's desires in sin any more than in redemption.[13] To be sure, we always sin willingly; but the reason we do so is because our distorted desires mean that our willing is always already infected by sin, so that – if the Augustinian position is correct – our sin is every bit as much a condition as a consequence of our willing. Now, if it is indeed the case that under a doctrine of original sin we sin *because* we are sinners, the conclusion seems unavoidable that our sinful state is finally God's responsibility as the one who made us that way. Needless to say, defenders of original sin will want to challenge that inference, but it is far from clear how they might do so.

## The Problem of the Origin of Original Sin

The standard Western Christian account of why human beings are afflicted by original sin is the story of the fall, interpreted through Augustinian categories. According to this view, the first human couple was created with wills capable of avoiding sin, but they were justly deprived of this gift when they transgressed God's command not to eat of the tree of the knowledge of good and evil. Moreover, this incapacity (along with various physical infirmities of the sort named by God in Gen. 3:16–19) has been inherited by all subsequent generations of humanity. God is, therefore, not responsible for original sin. The fault lies strictly with Adam and Eve, whose disobedience inflicted the damage on human nature that afflicts all their descendants.

Even if the historical accuracy of Genesis 2–3 is accepted, this explanation gets us only so far, since it is not at all clear that it is theologically coherent to speak of human beings inheriting a moral defect. A mother who regularly ingests an addictive substance during pregnancy may pass on a damaged nature (i.e., one marked by chemical dependence) to her child, but however one may judge the behavior of the mother, it does not seem reasonable to call the child a sinner. To be sure, Scripture speaks of God punishing "children for the iniquity of their parents, to the third and fourth generation" (Exod. 20:5, 34:7; Num. 14:18; Deut. 5:9), but since the very phrasing of this threat suggests diminishment over time, one might see this as simply a description of the natural consequences of a single act of punishment rather than its active renewal upon subsequent generations: in the same way that the children of a man who is thrown into prison and deprived of his possessions will suffer, so the punishment God inflicts on the sinful is so severe that its effects continue to handicap their descendants – without any necessary implication that these descendants themselves inherit their ancestor's guilt. Such an interpretation seems all the more likely given God's explicit denial that children are punished for the sins of their parents in passages like Ezek.18:1–20 (cf. Jer. 31:29–30). If so, there are evident problems with the idea that sinfulness is something we inherit.

Since Augustine himself connects infants' acquisition of original sin explicitly with the damaged desire (concupiscence) accompanying the sexual act by which they were conceived (to the extent that he thought it possible to explain Christ's freedom from original sin by reference to his miraculous conception[14]), it is customary to assume that Augustine had a "biological" understanding of its transmission. In fact, he was reluctant to speculate on how original sin passed from generation to generation. Hereditary models clearly held some attraction for him, given his desire to affirm that human beings were congenitally sinful and his corresponding rejection of the Pelagian claim that human beings acquired sin by imitation. At the same time, his metaphysical commitment to the spiritual rather than corporeal nature of the soul prevented him from adopting a straightforwardly traducianist theory, according to which the soul (with its sin) is passed on through the parents' genetic material. Thus, when it came to offering a concrete theory of how sin passes from parent to child, he confessed his ignorance.[15] Even when he invokes the example of Levi tithing Melchizedek from Abraham's loins (Heb. 7:9–10) in support of the principle that later generations share in the acts of their progenitors, he concedes that the idea of individuals pre-existing in their ancestors cannot be taken literally and suggests that here Scripture should instead be interpreted as referring to "[s]ome sort of invisible and intangible power ... located in the secrets of nature where the natural laws of propagation are concealed."[16] In short, while Augustine is firm in his insistence that sin is acquired "by generation" in order to secure the principle that human beings are congenitally sinful, he shows little enthusiasm for explicating the meaning of the phrase. Its force is largely privative: to exclude the Pelagian thesis that sin is acquired "by imitation."[17]

Subsequent reflection on the spread of original sin has worked with a range of metaphors and images. Two particularly well-defined and influential theories of original sin's transmission emerged within the Augustinianism of the Reformed tradition: the "realist" and "federalist" models. The former holds for a strongly ontological account of human unity: Adam's fall renders us all sinful, because we are all quite literally "in" Adam by virtue of our common descent from him as the first human being. By contrast, the federalist approach eschews reference to an ontological relationship of dependence in favor of a covenantal one ("federal" derives from *foedus*, the Latin word for covenant). Here our unity "in Adam" as sinners is more analogous to our unity "in Christ" as redeemed. It is not based on an ontological bond, but on the fact that God views us all "in Adam" in the same way that God views the elect "in Christ." We are distinct from Adam (as we are from Christ), but God treats Adam, the first human being, as a "public person" whose actions implicate his descendants, much as God treats Christ, the "second Adam," as a public person, whose actions count for those who have faith in him. In summary, while in realist accounts Adam is conceived as the head of a complex, temporally extended organism ("humankind"), in federalist accounts, Adam has more the status of the head of the public corporation ("Humanity, Inc."). In both accounts, however, human sinfulness is a function of our being "in" (or "under") Adam, though in the former this is a matter of the intrinsic, created structure of human nature, whereas in the latter it is a matter of separate divine determination.

Though it has antecedents going back to Augustine himself, perhaps the most consistent exposition of the realist position is given in the *Dogmatic Theology* of the nineteenth-century American theologian William Shedd. Operating out of a strong Augustinian understanding of the will as that which determines the character of all particular choices but which is not itself chosen, Shedd concludes that at birth the will of every human being has a definite inclination, which (since it is not chosen) must be inherited.[18] Developing this idea, he opts for an explicitly traducian account of the transmission of original sin in a way that Augustine was reluctant to do. According to Shedd, Adam was created with a will that was turned toward the good; his apostasy was a self-generated yet inexplicable perversion of his will's inclination, which is passed on to all his descendants as original sin.[19] Shedd contends that this transmission is consistent with divine justice, because in Adam human *nature* sinned, thereby implicating all who partake of that nature.[20] As he puts it, we are all guilty of Adam's sin in the same way that "the hand or eye acts and sins in the murderous or lustful act of the individual soul."[21] Insofar as the human nature is united in Adam, that nature is "responsible for all that is done by this unity."[22] Indeed, the unity is such that Adam's descendants share not only his corrupted state, but also his guilt for eating of the tree of knowledge of good and evil.

There are a couple of difficulties with this position. First, to attribute original sin to human nature as a whole seems to run counter to the basic Christian conviction that natures are always good in themselves, even if they are damaged by sin. Shedd attempts to meet this objection in line with much of the Augustinian tradition, by specifying that human nature can be called sinful only in a secondary sense, with reference to the "natural inclination" of fallen humanity, and not with respect to the created substance itself.[23] But if the transgression of original sin is an act of nature rather than person, it is hard to see how this distinction can be maintained. Recognizing that his realist ontology poses a special difficulty here, Shedd concedes that "the free agency of all mankind in Adam" is different from "the subsequent free agency of each individual."[24] Again, however, such a distinction seems problematic – especially given that Genesis does not depict the fall as a single, autonomous act by one primordial human being, but rather as a fairly complex exchange involving the serpent and two human agents.[25] The distinct (if equally culpable) transgressions of Adam and Eve render the emphasis on primal sin attributable to human nature as a whole problematic.[26]

Given that a central problem with the doctrine of original sin is the apparent injustice involved in God punishing countless later generations of human beings for their progenitor's transgression, the realist claim that agency can be ascribed to human nature as a whole is helpful in addressing problems of theodicy.[27] Realism protects God from any charge of arbitrariness by positing the tightest possible connection between Adam and his descendants: because as one nature they are also one agent, their collective condemnation requires no additional act of imputation on God's part to carry Adam's doom forward to subsequent generations. All are damned together, because they are fundamentally one entity. But the price of this defense of divine justice is the erasure of the distinction between person and nature in the case of Adam – a move that seems inconsistent with both Genesis (which depicts Adam as a particular person whose actions are distinct from those of Eve) and Paul (who views Adam as a type of that Christ for whom later theologians held the distinction between person and nature to be crucial). Ironically for a position that emphasizes so strongly the historicity of Adam, realism effectively mythologizes Adam by collapsing his personhood into his nature: he becomes humanity, not a human being.[28]

The anthropological costs of the realist position have made federalism more popular within the Reformed tradition.[29] Within federalism the distinction between person and nature in Adam is preserved: if Adam's sin is imputed to his descendants, it is not because it straightforwardly is theirs (i.e., by the kind of ontological identity that allowed Shedd to claim that "the posterity were *existent* and *present* in the progenitors by natural and substantial union"[30]), but because Adam represents them in such a way that his individual sin may be imputed to them. In the words of Francis Turretin (one of the first to express the point clearly), Adam was the head of humankind not only with respect to origin (i.e., physical and temporal priority), "but morally and in a representative sense."[31] Developed in this way, the federalist position seems at first glance to reflect much more closely with the Pauline parallel between Adam and Christ in Romans 5 than the realist alternative: in the same way that Christ's righteousness is imputed to humankind by virtue of God's decree alone (a point even realists are happy to concede), so is Adam's fault.[32] In both cases because God has made covenants with all humanity through these two particular individuals, their merits or demerits may justly be imputed to all human beings.[33]

At the same time, the idea of the imputation of original sin has always seemed to realists to raise serious questions regarding divine justice, especially given its apparent inconsistency with the principles of individual responsibility outlined in Ezekiel 18.[34] In this respect, the parallelism between Adam and Christ that arguably constitutes federalism's great strength over against realism also constitutes its most serious problem. That Christ's grace should redound to the benefit of all humanity seems reasonable enough: since Christ is fully divine as well as fully human, it makes sense that the form of human life lived by Christ should define human life for all. By contrast, to assign such a status to Adam, who (unless one subscribes to realism!) is ontologically no different from any other human being, cannot help but appear arbitrary. Herman Bavinck holds that it is justified by stressing that Adam and Christ are essentially similar:

> They have the human race not behind them but before them; they do not spring from it but give rise to it; they are not sustained by it but themselves sustain it; they are not the product of humankind, but are, each in his own way, the beginning and roots of it, the heads of all humanity.[35]

But the parallel simply does not hold up: that *Christ* sustains the human race is Christianity's core belief (and a linchpin of Chalcedonian Christology), but it is hard to see by what rationale *Adam* can be described as doing so. It is true that Adam might be said to "give rise" to and be "the beginning" of the human race insofar as he is the first human being; but there is no reason why Adam's being the *first* in a series should justify his *representing* the rest of the series in God's sight. Realists object to federalism on just these grounds, arguing that the federalist approach is able to secure human solidarity in sin only at the price of ascribing arbitrariness to God. No less problematic is the federalist penchant for characterizing Adam as a "head" of humanity alongside of Christ.[36] Paul never uses such language,[37] which makes Adam a counter-principle to Christ rather than himself the subject of Christ's redeeming work (indeed, according to tradition, the first of the dead to be liberated from hell) and thus a member with us of Christ's body.

Because both realist and federalist positions argue that all subsequent generations of human beings are somehow "in" Adam, they have a heavy stake in defending a monogenetic theory of human origins, if not necessarily the literal truth of Genesis 1–3. As already noted, such an account of human origins puts them at odds with contemporary evolutionary biology. This inconsistency with the best current scientific knowledge, however, is itself rooted in their common – and theologically problematic – commitment to an explanatory framework of cause and effect: Adam sinned (cause), and therefore all humanity is burdened with original sin (effect).[38] Within such an approach (whether developed along realist or federalist lines) the central question faced by defenders of the doctrine of original sin becomes how one person's sin can make other persons sinners; that is, not just incline, predispose, or influence them toward sin but actually *constitute* them as sinful. Both realist and federalist accounts answer this question by qualifying the extent to which Adam's descendants are (morally) "other" than he, arguing that they are all "in" him, whether by virtue of biology or divine decree, in a fashion that justifies the ascription of original sin to them. While some such qualification seems logically necessary, the problem with both lines of argument is that they are able to defend a universal human solidarity in sin only at the cost of positing a fundamental asymmetry between Adam and all other human beings, since it is only in the case of this one human being that a particular act of the will is able to cause damage to the human will in general that is transmitted uniformly (Christ, again, excepted) to all his posterity. If the fundamental equality of *all* human beings in sin, including Adam and Eve, is to be maintained, a different approach is needed.

## Reconceiving the Ontology of Original Sin

In searching for a plausible alternative, it is important to attend once again to the ontological oddity of the will. On the one hand, it is (in line with the insights of Maximus) a constitutive feature of human nature; on the other, it is that feature *of* human nature by virtue of which we experience ourselves as distinct *from* our natures as morally accountable agents. Thus, it is at once true that I will naturally and that in willing I mark myself off from my nature. It is natural for me, as an animal, to hunger and thirst. In this I am like my dog. But, unlike my dog, I am responsible for whether and what I eat and drink.[39] Correspondingly, the will at once appears as a point of commonality with other human beings and at the same time that which – even more than the physical limits of our bodies – divides us most clearly from them.

To the extent that the doctrine of original sin affirms a fundamental human solidarity in sin under God, both realist and federalist accounts of sin's transmission are right to want to qualify the degree to which we are all "other" than Adam; but they are unpersuasive insofar as they try to do so by focusing on Adam as the unique cause of original sin. At the same time, the typical modern alternative discussed in Chapter 2 – to view the fall as something that recurs contingently in each individual human being – will not do either, because it undermines human solidarity in sin by making each person's fall ultimately his or her own affair, however much it may be conditioned by a common ontology (for, e.g., Kierkegaard and Niebuhr) or shared environment (for, e.g., Schleiermacher and Karl Rahner). In short, while traditional approaches tend to obscure the degree to which original sin is *always* our own by conflating everyone with Adam, modern versions cut us loose from Adam and one another in a way that makes original sin *only* our own.[40]

One way to illuminate the character of human solidarity in sin without succumbing to either of these pitfalls is to contrast human beings with angels. For (at least according to the angelology of Thomas Aquinas, which I will be following here) the fact that angels are not – and, indeed, cannot – be burdened by original sin helps to bring into relief something of the distinctiveness of the human condition.[41] Both angels and human beings can sin, because, as creatures endowed with intellect, they both have wills. The force of this claim is as follows for Thomas: while all creatures naturally move toward the good, for angels and human beings this motion is bound up with their *knowing* and thus (willingly) *claiming* it as good rather than being passively drawn toward it by instinct.[42]

Moreover, it is because they have wills that angels, like human beings, have Christ as their head: both can be said to belong to the same body because they have a common end in the enjoyment of God's glory that is the proper end of their willing.[43]

For Thomas, however, these similarities between angels and human beings are matched by two striking differences. The first is that each angel is its own species, so that angels do not constitute a single race as human beings do. This difference between angels and human beings is itself a function of a still more fundamental contrast: the fact that angels do not have bodies. Because angels are for Thomas incorporeal (i.e., purely spiritual) beings, he concludes that they are, in the categories of Aristotelian metaphysics, pure form rather than a composite of matter and form, like us and other material creatures. Since for Thomas it is matter that differentiates the form (or species) "human being" into particular individuals like Mary and Paul, the fact that angels are pure form means that there is no possibility for individuation within an angelic species (or, to invoke more specifically theological terminology, for multiple hypostatizations of the same nature). Consequently, there is only one member (or hypostasis) in each angelic species, and every angel is a different species (or nature) from every other.[44]

Building on this framework, Thomas argues that it is possible to speak of Lucifer's sin as the cause of the sin of the other fallen angels only in the sense that (as Thomas reads the Bible) he persuaded them to rebel against God.[45] In this way, all the fallen angels other than Satan himself may be said to be guilty of sin by imitation. There is no other possibility: they cannot be sinful by generation, since angels do not reproduce and are thus not linked together by bonds of nature. Consequently, angels provide an example of creaturely glorification and damnation unrelated to the category of original sin. Like human beings, angels were created upright,[46] with wills free to turn to good or evil,[47] and required an additional gift of grace to achieve the final glory of the beatific vision.[48] Like human beings, some angels sinned; but their sin affected themselves alone. Thus, while the doctrine of original sin suggests that human beings fall and rise together, angels fall or rise by themselves.

This last observation points to the second significant difference between human beings and angels for Thomas: while the same human being who falls in Adam may rise with Christ, for angels falling and rising are mutually exclusive: those who fall will never rise, and those who, by confirming themselves in the good have risen to glory, can never fall. Fallen angels, unlike fallen human beings, cannot be redeemed. This feature of angels' existence also derives from their incorporeality. For Thomas, to have a body is not only to have the possibility of individuation, but also to be bound to time. As embodied creatures, for example, human beings can only acquire knowledge discursively, through the temporal process of reasoning, rather than with the immediate intuition of angels.[49] In this way, the body acts as something of a drag on the process of knowing, preventing us from grasping a truth all at once. This same "drag effect" is characteristic of human actions: because they are embodied, human beings cannot determine themselves once and for all in any particular act, and this is the ontological ground for the possibility of their repentance and redemption. That angels are unable to be redeemed is therefore not a mark of greater severity on God's part toward them than toward human beings, but simply a consequence of their makeup: as purely intellectual creatures, they do not have the kind of material "brake" on their actions that would allow them to repent.[50] Consequently, when they will they commit themselves completely and irrevocably to the object of their willing.[51] As soon as angels will, they turn either toward or away from God with a finality that commits them to one or the other course eternally.[52]

In short, when angels sin, they do so both fully and in isolation from one another: their willing is unimpeded and self-contained. Human sinning is more complicated. Because we are embodied, we cannot sin completely or irrevocably in our earthly lives, however perverse we may be.[53] Moreover, though our bodies differentiate us from each other as separate hypostases, they also point to our essential unity, since it is through our bodies that our nature is passed on from individual to individual, and it is through interacting bodily with one another that our individual identities are shaped.[54] These features of the human condition allow the claim of fallen humanity's oneness in Adam – and the correlative claim of universal sinfulness – to be seen in a different light. Now, if we follow traditional accounts of how sin spreads from Adam to the rest of us, the light does not appear to be favorable. On either a realist or a federalist account, our situation seems decidedly inferior to that of the angels, soteriologically speaking. On the one hand, we come to glory in the same way that they do: individually, by the reception of grace in faith. On the other hand, while angels also *fall* individually, human beings are damned *collectively*. Thus, while we humans rise individually by grace to become one in Christ, we fall through the nature by which we are one in Adam. If that's the case, it is seemingly better to be an angel.

But this is not the way Scripture sees it. It teaches that angels are nothing more than "spirits in the divine service, sent to serve for the sake of [us] ... who are to inherit salvation" (Heb. 1:14). God did not – and, if Thomas is right, could not – "come to help angels, but the descendants of Abraham" (Heb. 2:16). If human beings and angels alike are members of Christ's body, only the former are bone of his bones and flesh of his flesh (Eph. 5:32; cf. Gen. 2:23). Far from there being any ground for our being jealous of angels, it appears rather that our destiny is an object of wonder for them, an unfathomably gracious mystery into which they "long to look" (1 Pet. 1:12).

As part of this mystery, original sin is inseparable from the story of God's love for us. For though it points to something profoundly wrong with us, the emphasis is precisely on the *us*, on the fact that the failure is *ours*, something that we as human beings experience *together*. There is, correspondingly, something mistaken about taking original sin as an occasion for focus on *me* and *my* sin in isolation from the rest of the human family. This has nothing to do with seeking to mitigate my own sinfulness by appealing to the faults of others, let alone with trying to shift responsibility from myself to them.[55] Indeed, that move is simply another attempt to detach the "me" from the "us" in a way that fails to come to grips with the fact that my sinfulness is neither reducible to nor abstractable from everyone else's.[56] On the contrary, it is to recognize that my sinfulness is inseparable from everyone else's. Here it is crucial to remember that, as part of the wider mystery of salvation, original sin is not an empirically derived claim, but a matter of faith. To be sure, all of us – non-Christian no less than Christian – may have a vivid awareness of the pain we inflict on and endure from one another. We may even call it sin. But we know it as rooted in *original* sin only as we have been called by God to a new reality in Christ. As those who hear and respond to that call in this life, we remain sinners,[57] but we now are able – and for the first time – to recognize ourselves as the particular kind of sinners we are – human beings whose sin binds us together with all other human beings under God's judgment and in God's grace.

In line with the perspective, Jonathan Edwards preferred to speak of "the *coexistence* of the evil disposition" of sin *in* the hearts of Adam and Adam's descendants rather than of its "derivation" *to* their hearts.[58] He did so in order to challenge precisely the understanding of original sin as an effect transmitted down through the generations from a particular historical cause, like the force transmitted along a line of billiard balls knocking into each other on a pool table. Rather than a contagion that passes from parent to child, original sin is a feature of humankind in its fundamental unity from creation to eschaton. Nor is this unity to be conceived as a predetermined fact to which we – and God – are forced to adjust. It is instead a matter of vocation: we are one because God addresses us as one, thereby making it impossible for us to see one another except as those who have been called as one.[59] In short, our original sinfulness can only be experienced – and must therefore be interpreted – in terms of our unity before God. Viewed in this context, the vision of Isaiah in the heavenly court provides a model for Christian sin-talk: "Woe is me! I am lost, for I am a man of unclean lips, and I live among a people of unclean lips; yet my eyes have seen the King, the Lord of hosts" (Isa. 6:5). Each sentence in this passage is theologically significant. First, sin is an occasion for individual repentance, because it is a recognition of one's own lostness before God. But, second, one is never a sinner by oneself: as a *person* of unclean lips, one is always found among a *people* of unclean lips, a sinner among sinners in a way that reflects a fundamental human solidarity before God and, correlatively, provides a basis for genuine sympathy for and forbearance with one another.[60] And, finally, this sinfulness is recognized only in the presence of the God who immediately and without being asked declares, "... your guilt has departed and your sin is blotted out" (Isa. 6:7). One knows oneself as a sinner only as one knows that sin does not define either one's own humanity or the humanity of anyone else, however much it continues in practice to distort our relationships with God and each other.

   I do not claim that this Isaianic vision provides an answer to the question of how human beings come to be afflicted by original sin. On the contrary, I invoke it to suggest that such a question misses the point, because it trades on a misleading understanding of human being. The question presupposes that we are (first) agents who (then) receive a human nature, the various features of which we then integrate into our "selves." That is the picture suggested by an anthropology in which the will is conceived as the power by which we dispose (or find ourselves unable to dispose) of our nature – and thus as ontologically prior to our nature. It is a picture deeply engrained in the sensibilities of Western culture (especially, I suspect, among its more affluent members, among whom I count myself), but it is false. This is not to suggest that my "selfhood" or "personhood" is *reducible to* my nature (as though I became less of a person if my nature – my memory or will, say – were damaged); but it is to deny that it is in any respect *separable from* my nature. On the contrary, if the concept "nature" means anything at all, whatever attributes or qualities are taken to make up human nature are exhaustive of what "I" am. Thus, in the same way that Maximus insisted that Christ's two natures were not simply that *from* and *in* which he is, but also *what* he is, so "human" is not just some sort of ontological precondition for or substrate of our existence, but precisely what we are, without remainder.[61]

Where this is not recognized, the nature I share with others is finally not decisive for who I am, since "I" finally stand over against it. Similarly, where this is not recognized, the nature I share with other human beings does not establish real solidarity with them, because it (along with any damage that may afflict it) does not touch my real self – the "I" that hovers behind or above my nature like the proverbial ghost in the machine. If, however, we treat the will as part of human nature, then our understanding of ourselves and of our relationship to other people will be conceived on different terms. Chiefly, our wills will no longer appear as a point of fundamental discontinuity with other human beings, but – precisely as we recognize the truth of original sin – the point at which we find ourselves most clearly bound up with them.[62]

This point may be illustrated by contrasting two models of the damaged will. The first conceives it on analogy with a physical wound that I can isolate as a well-defined feature of my being with an assignable, external cause. Where this imagery prevails, original sin is fundamentally an individual affliction, however widespread it may be: others may have it, but that does not bear materially on my sin, except in the very restricted sense that it was caused by a common ancestor. In the second, original sin is conceived more along the lines of the kind of damage that afflicts the members of a radically co-dependent household. Here every individual's sin is intimately bound up with others' (in the sense that it can only be understood by reference to what everyone else is doing in the system), and yet the unity of the system is such as to preclude isolating any one member as the unique "cause" of anyone else's sin, let alone the oldest member of the family as the cause of *everyone* else's sin (even though that person will have been temporally the first sinner).[63] It will not do to make any one person the scapegoat: none is a sinner apart from the others – and none can be healed fully apart from the others.[64]

This analogy also illustrates another feature of original sin: that the solidarity it affirms does not mean an undifferentiated leveling of the sin of all those involved. We are all called from positions of equal need, but our unity is a function of our *inseparability* from those around us, not of our *interchangeability* with them. Original sin is universal, but it is not fungible – any more than the grace that is its cure. To understand myself as a sinner, I must understand my particular place as a person of unclean lips amid a people of unclean lips. The form that sin takes will differ from person to person, because everyone's lips are unclean in a different way. Isaiah's was not the same as King Uzziah's, nor is mine the same as yours.

Here again the ontological oddity of the will comes to the fore. On the one hand, our distorted desires, as the motive for all our willing, are not themselves something we will (indeed, with Paul we may find ourselves desiring against our will, whenever we find ourselves wishing our desires were different). From this perspective, we experience sin as a power that intrudes on us from without, shaping the mode of our willing. In this sense it is "original." But because those distorted desires are also ineluctably within us, sin's being "original" does not preclude its being *ours*. We can, of course, reason that we received our wills in this damaged state as part of our natures, and thus that we "inherited" them from our parents and grandparents and great-grandparents and so on, back up the human family tree. But because the will is the faculty in and through which I recognize my own agency, I can never coherently dissociate any defect in my willing from my agency. Consequently, "Adam" can only be regarded as the first in a series of sinners and not as the unique "cause" of subsequent human sin.[65] The language of causation is simply inadequate here: original sin is not a force that radiates forward or outward from a single point in a manner that would justify blaming our sinfulness on others.[66] "In Adam's fall / We sinned all" – not because we all somehow pre-exist *in* Adam (as in realism), or because God has predetermined that Adam will stand for the whole human race (as in federalism), but simply because we are all one *with* Adam, and thus that we share with him – and with each other – the same nature, marked by the damaged wills that turn us all invariably and catastrophically away from God.[67]

And yet though we turn from God, God does not turn from us. Indeed, our sinfulness is revealed only as God turns to us and, more specifically, only as God turns to us in mercy, confronting us as sinners with the grace of healing and reconciliation. Here, too, our unity in Adam is crucial. Because God addresses us as one with Adam, I do not need to worry whether the word of grace that came to Peter and Paul also applies to me: because my identity as a sinner is inseparable from theirs, when God appeals to them, God appeals to me also. Of course, this does not make it any less an appeal to *me* (any more than original sin I share with others is for that reason any less my own sin), but it is an appeal that I will hear as the grace it is only as I realize that it is addressed to me as a person of unclean lips among a people of unclean lips – and therefore only as I understand it as good news "for all the people" (Luke 2:10; cf. Acts 2:39).

Unlike angels, we are incapable of sinning either completely or in isolation from one another. In our alienation from God we are one (even as in our salvation we are called to be one), such that in our very wills – that aspect of our natures that at first blush seems to mark us off most clearly from one another – we find ourselves bound together with others as persons of unclean lips among a people of unclean lips. Our unity, however, is not undifferentiated in sin any more than it is in glory. We are all equally sinners, such that we can, with Paul, apply to ourselves the words of the Psalmist: "There is no one who is righteous, not even one" (Rom. 3:10; cf. Pss. 14:3, 53:3). But we are not all sinners in the same way, and the next chapter will begin to explore the concrete differences that mark our common participation in original sin.

## Notes

1 See especially Augustine, *The Literal Meaning of Genesis*, I.38–39, in Augustine, *On Genesis*, ed. John E. Rotelle, O.S.A. (Hyde Park, NY: New City Press, 2002), pp. 186–7.
2 While the science of genetics does establish that all living human beings share a common male and female ancestor (the so-called "Y-chromosomal Adam" and "mitochondrial Eve"), these two individuals appear to have been separated by something on the order of 2,500 generations, and neither can claim the distinction of having been the first modern human. See Peter A. Underhill, Peidong Shen, Alice A. Lin, et al., "Y Chromosome Sequence Variation and the History of Human Populations," in *Nature Genetics* 26:3 (November 2000), 358–61.
3 See the analysis of Henri Blocher who, with scant regard for the details of evolutionary theory, judges scientifically "plausible" the "hypothesis that the biblical Adam and Eve were the first parents of our race, some 40,000 years ago; and we may posit an initial period of fellowship with God in their lives before they apostacized" (*Original Sin: Illuminating the Riddle* [Grand Rapids, MI: William B. Eerdmans, 1997], p. 42). Less scientifically tendentious is Robert Jenson's proposal that Adam and Eve were "the first community of our biological ancestors who disobeyed God's command" (see his *The Works of God*, vol. 2 of *Systematic Theology* [New York: Oxford University Press, 1999], p. 150). A rather different approach, based on philosophical arguments developed at considerable remove from any attention to the details of evolutionary biology, is found in Karl Rahner's early essay, "Some Reflexions on Monogenism," in *God, Christ, Mary and Grace*, vol. 1 of *Theological Investigations* (New York: Seabury Press, 1974), pp. 229–96.
4 My choice of a non-material "organ" as a point of comparison is deliberate, as it avoids the linking of identity with any physiological process or body part. While I have no doubt that Jesus' experience of agency during his earthly ministry was (like that of any human being) inseparable from particular patterns of electro-chemical activity among the neurons in his brain, Christian belief in the resurrection (i.e., the transformation of the physical body into a spiritual one) – not to mention the importance of affirming the full humanity of people whose neurons for whatever reason fail to produce

the typical symptoms of conscious agency – precludes the equation of identity with any particular physical substrate.
5 The language of surplus should not be taken to imply that Jesus' (divine) hypostasis is to be conceived as some sort of occult substance that is separable from nature any more than our human hypostases can be so conceived. For Jesus no less than the rest of us, hypostasis is not a separate something over (let alone over against) nature. The "surplus" Jesus has with respect to his human nature is rather a function of the fact that his hypostasis is an eternal instantiation of – and thus subsists simultaneously in – his *divine* nature. As noted on p. 105 above, Maximus emphasizes this point by insisting that Christ exists not only from and in the two natures (phrasing which, taken in isolation, might suggest the hypostasis hovering mysteriously behind the natures), but also *as* the two natures (so Christ's hypostasis is in no way conceivable apart from his natures).
6 This is not to suggest that Jesus' impeccability is somehow self-generated (a model that would suggest the will were some sort of capacity or power). As a human being, his (human) will is led to desire the good by virtue of the gift of the Spirit, in the same way as is the case with every human being who wills the good. The point is simply that as the Second Person of the Trinity, he invariably receives the fullness of this gift (John 3:34) and acts upon it.
7 Catholics would, of course, also include Mary here.
8 See p. 72 above.
9 One might object here that there would be no occasion for the *cor inquietum* described in *Confessions* I.1 in the state of innocence, but insofar as Augustine understands the state of glory as qualitatively different from humanity's original state (since it is characterized by, e.g., an incapacity to sin and the transition from a physical to a spiritual body), even unfallen humanity would presumably have longed for the more profound intimacy with God that would come with translation from the earthly to the heavenly realm.
10 Philip Hefner argues that the tension between certain genetically hard-wired "selfish" behaviors and cultural demands for cooperation and altruism actually provides an explanation for the experience of the divided will in terms of evolutionary biology (see his book, *The Human Factor: Evolution, Culture, and Religion* [Minneapolis, MN: Fortress Press, 1993], ch. 8). The theological problem with this line of argument is that it makes original sin part of humanity's nature as created and thus not a result of any defect in willing.
11 The idea of the impotence of the will to free itself from sin should not be read in terms of a psychological description of the dynamics of temptation, as though the affirmation of original sin were an empirical statement about the ability of the will to engage in or refrain from a particular behavior (e.g., an alcoholic's ability to stay on the wagon). To confess the reality of original sin is not to claim that people cannot resist giving in to particular impulses (which they quite evidently can), but rather to reject the conceptual reduc-

tion of sin to the choice of evil over good. As will be explained in detail in the next chapter, this distinction is crucial if belief that all are sinners is to be kept from supporting the principle that all sin is blameworthy.

12  Thus Paul can describe being freed from sin as a matter of becoming "slaves of righteousness" (Rom. 6:18).

13  That is, while one always wills in accordance with one's desires, the content of desire is not itself a matter of willing. Once again, a person can do what she wants, but she can't want what she wants.

14  See, e.g., Augustine, *Unfinished Work in Answer to Julian* [hereafter *UWJ*], 1.66 (citing Ambrose, *De Noe*, 3 bis.7 and *Expositio euangelii secundum Lucam*, 2.56). Augustine was also inclined to view the Virgin Mary in a separate category, though not with the certainty of later Catholic dogma. See *Nature and Grace*, 42, in *Answer to the Pelagians*, I, ed. John E. Rotelle, O.S.A. (Hyde Park, NY: New City Press, 1997).

15  "In whatever manner and to whatever extent, all who have been born after [Adam] were that one, whether only in terms of body or in terms of both parts of the human being [viz., body and soul]. That is a point which I admit I do not know, and I am not ashamed, as you are, to admit that I do not know what I do not know." Augustine, *UWJ*, 2.178; cf. 4.104. See also 3.66: "But how do human beings know the sorts of bonds by which a nature is linked to the nature from which it was born?"

16  Augustine, *UWJ*, 6.22.

17  G. C. Berkouwer argues that in much subsequent Augustinian theology as well "generation" has functioned as a refusal to provide the kind of explanation of sin represented by the category of "imitation." See his *Sin* (Grand Rapids, MI: William B. Eerdmans, 1971), pp. 533–6.

18  William G. T. Shedd, *Dogmatic Theology*, 2nd edn. (New York: Charles Scribner's Sons, 1889), vol. 2, p. 141.

19  Shedd's distinction between the inclination of the will and the particular choices shaped by this inclination means that Adam's apostasy was not in itself a matter of choice, but a more ontologically fundamental act of self-determination that cannot be assigned a cause or reason, though its possibility can be accounted for by the fact that the initially good inclination of Adam's will, being created and therefore finite, was not immune to variation as God's is. See Shedd, *Dogmatic Theology*, vol. 2, pp. 135–6; cf. pp. 155–6, where Shedd (following Augustine) stresses that it "had to be *started* by Adam himself, as something entirely new and aboriginal," and that, as such, it was "intrinsically improbable ... unnatural and irrational."

20  "The evil desire and the evil act were the desiring and acting of the human nature in the first human pair." Shedd, *Dogmatic Theology*, vol. 2, p. 181; cf. p. 184, where original sin is ascribed to "the action of the common nature in Adam prior to any conception and birth."

21  Shedd, *Dogmatic Theology*, vol. 2, p. 191; cf. p. 188, where Shedd draws a parallel between the unity between Adam and his posterity on the one hand,

and the unity between Christ and believers on the other; but whereas he describes the latter as "spiritual and mystical," he characterizes the former as "substantial and physical."

22 Shedd, *Dogmatic Theology*, vol. 2, p. 192.
23 Shedd, *Dogmatic Theology*, vol. 2, p. 196.
24 Shedd, *Dogmatic Theology*, vol. 2, p. 186.
25 In this context, it is worth noting that while most Christian interpreters of Genesis 3 have assumed that Adam was absent while the serpent addressed Eve, the narrative neither states nor implies as much. As Phyllis Trible (drawing on earlier work by Katherine Sakenfeld and Jean Higgins) argues, the use of plural verb forms in Eve's dialogue with the serpent, as well as the specification that the man was "with" Eve in Gen. 3:6 suggest that Adam was present throughout. Phyllis Trible, *God and the Rhetoric of Sexuality* (Philadelphia, PA: Fortress Press, 1978), p. 113.
26 Of course, in stressing the singularity of Adam and his sin, Shedd is drawing on Paul rather than Genesis, and he is correspondingly eager to show that in Romans 5 Paul refers to a single, primordial sin as the origin of the human predicament. A detailed exegesis of this difficult passage is beyond the scope of this chapter, but Shedd's attempt to use it as evidence for a precise understanding of the mode of original sin's spread seems an over-reading of the first order. In Romans 5 Paul uses broad brushstrokes to communicate the astounding way in which the power of God revealed in Christ undoes the power of death unleashed by Adam, but he does not describe in detail how either power proliferates in history. And just as the obedience of Christ that Paul cites here as the source of justification is not reducible to a single event but refers to the whole of Christ's earthly ministry, it seems prudent to refrain from giving too much precision to the category of Adam's disobedience.
27 "This motive of God's justice is the dominant and decisive theme in realist theology." Berkouwer, *Sin*, p. 445.
28 Francis Turretin had earlier attempted to explain how one act of Adam can affect the rest of the human family in a way others do not by positing that Adam's status as *persona publica*, in virtue of which his actions could implicate the rest of humankind, was put aside after the fall (see his *Institutes of Elenctic Theology*, 3 vols., ed. James T. Dennison [Phillipsburg, NJ: P&R Publishing, 1992], IX.ix.11). While this approach is coherent from within the federalist framework within which Turretin was operating (since God is free to determine when Adam represents all humankind), it is hard to see how such an approach could work within realism – a point which Herman Bavinck invokes against the realist position (see his *Sin and Salvation in Christ*, vol. 3 of *Reformed Dogmatics*, ed. John Bolt [Grand Rapids, MI: William B. Eerdmans, 2006], p. 103).
29 Although Shedd argued that Augustine and all the early Reformers were realists (*Dogmatic Theology*, vol. 2, pp. 35–6), Bavinck counters that prior to the period of Reformed Scholasticism theologians' use of terms was

insufficiently precise to justify such a claim (*Reformed Dogmatics*, vol. 3, pp. 103–4). For a more detailed discussion of the difficulty in applying the designations "realist" and "federalist" to the confessions and theologies of the Reformation era, see Berkouwer, *Sin*, ch. 15.
30  Shedd, *Dogmatic Theology*, vol. 1, p. 38.
31  Turretin, *Institutes*, IX.ix.23.
32  Thus Bavinck (*Reformed Dogmatics*, vol. 3, p. 102) faults realism for inconsistency in viewing imputation as acceptable in reference to Christ's righteousness, but not in the case of Adam's sin.
33  So "both Adam and Christ were placed under an utterly special ordinance of God, precisely with a view to the special position they occupy in humankind" (Bavinck, *Reformed Dogmatics*, vol. 3, p. 105).
34  In a singularly unpersuasive attempt to rebut this charge, Bavinck suggests that Ezekiel 18 refers to the promise of the new covenant, in which baptism breaks the hold of original sin on the lives of believers (*Reformed Dogmatics*, vol. 3, pp. 104–5).
35  Bavinck, *Reformed Dogmatics*, vol. 3, p. 106.
36  This sort of characterization is a common move in federalist schemes. Blocher, for example, makes repeated references to Adam's "headship" (see *Original Sin*, pp. 51, 70, 97, 122, 130–132; cf. p. 80).
37  In fact, the designation of Christ as the "head" is a feature of the Deutero-Pauline epistles (Eph. 1:22, 4:15, 5:23; Col. 1:18, 2:10, 19) and is not found in the passages from Romans 5 and 1 Corinthians 15 where Paul draws parallels between Adam and Christ. To be sure, context suggests that Genesis 2–3 stands in the background of the notoriously difficult 1 Cor. 11:3, where Paul calls Christ "the head of every man" and "man the head of woman." But whatever "headship" one might ascribe to Adam on the basis of this passage is a matter of gender relations only (viz., his being the source of Eve; see vv. 8–9) and cannot be extended to his posterity as a whole; moreover, even this restricted sense of headship is heavily qualified in v. 11, where Paul affirms that all human beings stand in a relationship of mutual interdependence that makes them equals under God.
38  Shedd is typical in affirming that our sinfulness stands to Adam's "in the relation of effect to cause." Shedd, *Dogmatic Theology*, vol. 2, p. 192.
39  The question of our "responsibility" for autonomic functions (e.g., blinking, sweating, blood pressure, etc.) has been discussed on p. 72 above (cf. the reference to Cyril of Alexandria's claim that nothing in a rational nature is involuntary on p. 90). Here it may simply be noted that the conceptual difficulties are eased if the will is understood simply as the experience of the embodied self as an I rather than as a power by which the "I" exercises control over the body. It is also relevant here to remember again the category of unintentional sin in the OT (see pp. 6–8 above), according to which individual responsibility does not necessarily imply a power to have acted differently – though the lack of such power is crucial in assessing the level of one's responsibility.

40 In short, traditional accounts risk a "Manichaean" conflation of the fallen will with human nature, while modern accounts veer in the direction of a "Pelagian" individualism that sets the will over against nature.
41 It is worth stressing that because angels are being invoked only to serve as an ontological foil against which to illuminate certain features of human being, my anthropological conclusions do not depend on the truth of Thomas's angelology.
42 Thomas Aquinas, *Summa Theologiae* [hereafter *ST*], 61 vols. Blackfriars edn. (London: Eyre & Spottiswood, 1964–81), 1.59.1; cf. 1.59.3: "wherever intellect is found, there is free will."
43 Aquinas, *ST*, 3.8.4; cf. 1.62.1: "By the state of glory (*beatitudinis*) is meant that ultimate perfection of a nature endowed with reason or intellect: which is why it is naturally desired [by every such nature], since everything naturally desires its ultimate perfection" (translation slightly altered).
44 Aquinas, *ST*, 1.50.4; cf. 1.51.1. The Franciscans famously differed from Dominicans like Thomas on this point, arguing for multiple members of angelic species either by postulating the existence of an incorporeal matter that would provide the basis for individuation among angels (a position Aquinas specifically refutes in the cited article), or (in the work of Duns Scotus) by arguing for the category of an individuating difference at the level of form (*haecceitas*).
45 Satan is the cause of the other angels' sinning *quadam quasi exhortatione inducens*. See *ST*, 1.63.8.
46 Aquinas, *ST*, 1.62.3.
47 Note that though Thomas equates willing with choosing in 1.59.3.1, he acknowledges that angelic "choice" does not entail the process of deliberation that Maximus associated with *prohairesis*.
48 *ST*, 1. 1.62.2. Were such an additional gift of grace unnecessary, there would be no distinction between the natural goodness of angels and their supernatural end as intellectual creatures.
49 See, e.g., Aquinas, *ST*, 1.59.1.1.
50 See also *ST*, 1.63.83: "when an angel moves to an objective, whether good or bad, he moves with all that is in him; there is nothing to slow him down (*non habet aliquid retardans*)."
51 Aquinas, *ST*, 1.62.6.
52 Thomas takes some pains to note that the bad angels did not fall immediately *upon* their creation (*in primo instanti*), on the grounds that such teaching would implicate God in their sin, since "the activity that begins in a thing simultaneously with its existence has its origin in the cause from which it draws existence" (*ST*, 1.63.5). In the subsequent article, however, he does opine that the bad angels fell immediately *after* their creation (*post primum instans*). This point leads to further differences with human beings. Thus, while Christ is the head of all angels equally, since they are all united with him in the state of glory, he is the head of human beings in different degrees (*secundum diversos gradus*), depending on their particular location within the

53 Needless to say, Thomas holds that those who die in a state of mortal sin are irrevocably damned – but that belief derives precisely from the fact that death puts an end to the possibility of repentance; in short, with death they have moved beyond time, and have at that point willed with the completeness that for angels is simultaneous with their willing at all.

54 Thus, even if one holds to a creationist account of the soul's origin, God's creating the soul is contingent upon (even if temporally simultaneous with) the physical act of conception.

55 In this context, Bonhoeffer was quite right to see that it was impossible to link the guiltiness of the human race with particular culpable acts (viz., that of Adam, or, in liberal reinterpretations of original sin, those of human beings in general) with the guiltiness of the human race "without making one the reason for the other" and thus "excusing one by means of the other." *Sanctorum Communio: A Theological Study of the Sociology of the Church*, vol. 1 of *Dietrich Bonhoeffer Works*, ed. Joachim von Soosten and Clifford J. Green (Minneapolis, MN: Fortress Press, 1998), p. 115.

56 Berkouwer remarks that such a move underlies the complaint against God answered in Ezekiel 18: absent a vital sense of God's ongoing presence among and to the people as a whole, Ezekiel's contemporaries experienced divine judgment as the impersonal operation of karma. In rejecting the principle that the children suffer for the sins of the parents, Berkouwer argues, Ezekiel in no sense denies Israel's cross-generational solidarity as the people of God in favor of moral individualism; he simply denies that this solidarity is to be understood in terms of a relationship of mechanical cause and effect, as though the present generation were justified in viewing their suffering as nothing more than the consequence of their forebears' sin (see *Sin*, pp. 519–21).

57 "The reality of sin and the communio peccatorum remain even in God's church-community; Adam has really been replaced by Christ only eschatologically ... So long as sin remains, the whole of sinful humanity also remains in every human being." Bonhoeffer, *Sanctorum Communio*, p. 124.

58 Jonathan Edwards, *Original Sin*, vol. 3 of the *Works of Jonathan Edwards*, ed. Clyde A. Holbrook (New Haven, CT: Yale University Press, 1970), p. 391. For a review of the debates within Reformed circles over Edwards's understanding of the relationship between Adam and the rest of humankind, see Oliver D. Crisp, "On the Theological Pedigree of Jonathan Edwards's Doctrine of Imputation," *Scottish Journal of Theology* 56:3 (2003), 308–27.

59 Against any notion of ontological determinism, Edwards argues for any created substance, "there is no identity or oneness ... but what depends on the *arbitrary* [Edwards means "free" or "contingent," not "capricious"] constitution of the Creator; who by his wise sovereign establishment so unites these successive new effects, that he *treats them as one*, by communicating to them like properties, relations, and circumstances; and so, leads us to regard

168  Reconstructing the Doctrine

and treat them as one." Edwards, *Original Sin*, p. 405. For more on the correlation of original sin with the category of vocation, see Chapter 8 below.

60  Edwards draws precisely this conclusion: "This doctrine teaches us to think no worse of others, than of ourselves: it teaches us that we are *all*, as we are by nature, *companions* in a miserable helpless condition; which, under a revelation of the divine mercy, tends to promote mutual *compassion*." *Original Sin*, p. 424.

61  Here again recall Maximus' insistence that Christ's two natures are not simply that *from* and *in* which he is, but also *what* he is, pure and simple. See also Augustine's insistence (developed in his trinitarian theology) that person, though irreducible to substance, is inseparable from it in *The Trinity*, 7.6.11, ed. John E. Rotelle, O.S.A. (Hyde Park, NY: New City Press, 1991).

62  Though operating outside of an Augustinian theological context, Vladimir Lossky saw the tendency to use the will to distance oneself from others in this way as a mark of the fall. Instead of recognizing human nature as a unity, he suggested, the postlapsarian human being finds affirmation "in dividing – in parceling out – the unity of nature, each owning a portion … for himself, so that 'my' will contrasts 'myself' with all that is 'not I.'" Vladimir Lossky, *In the Image and Likeness of God*, ed. John T. Erickson and Thomas E. Bird (Crestwood, NY: St. Vladimir's Seminary Press, 1985), p. 107.

63  The analogy with original sin is strained when it comes to explain how children born into the family come to participate in its structures, but even here it is worth recalling the difficulty of characterizing any agent as simply passive in relation to its environment. Importantly, however, this affirmation of the irreducibility of agency is not the same as ascribing blame. See Chapter 7 below.

64  The degree to which the last clause of this sentence applies to the economy of salvation as well as family systems is, of course, contested. Christians have long held that some can be fully redeemed without all being redeemed, on the grounds that to maintain otherwise (i.e., to affirm that God has to save all human beings in order to save any) conflicts with fundamental Christian convictions regarding divine and human freedom: simply put, genuine reconciliation and love – the content of the Christian understanding of salvation – cannot be matters of necessity. At the same time, to affirm the unity of all people before God in sin and simultaneously to deny their unity in Christ seemingly requires the no less problematic conclusion that some human beings (viz., the damned) aren't finally human (i.e., bone of Christ's bone and flesh of his flesh) after all.

65  Once again, this point is important as a means of stressing that Adam is in no sense the "head" of humankind. Headship belongs to Christ alone, in whose body Adam is merely one member among others.

66  In this context, it is worth adding that the claim that all human beings (Christ excepted) are sinners with Adam does not mean that all are guilty of Adam's sin. That conclusion would violate God's decree that "only the person who

sins shall die" (Ezek. 18:4). Everyone is a sinner with Adam, but everyone's sin (and whatever measure of guilt accompanies it) remains her own. This point will prove crucial for the analysis of the existential and political dimensions of original sin given in Chapters 7 and 8 below.

67 A further advantage of refusing to speak of Adam as the unique cause of original sin is that it frees Christianity from commitment to the kind of monogenetic theory of human origins that contemporary evolutionary biology renders untenable.

# 7

# Original Sin and the Individual: Being a Sinner

Classical Protestant treatments of original sin included a distinction between the damage (Latin *vitium* or *macula*) and the liability (Latin *reatus*) that accrue to human beings by virtue of the fall.[1] With this framework in mind, the last chapter can be seen as an attempt to defend the contemporary plausibility of the category of *vitium* by exploring the notion of universal human participation in sin. The present chapter, by contrast, attempts to defend the idea of *reatus*. In other words, while the previous chapter discussed original sin in terms of its universal extension, this chapter turns to the intensive dimension of the doctrine by exploring what is implied by the claim that every human being (Christ excepted) is congenitally a sinner. One implication I will want to deny is that every person's sinfulness is identical to everyone else's because all are equally subject to original sin. Once again, the example of the co-dependent family serves as a useful analogy: though all are equally implicated in the destructive dynamics of the family system, not all are implicated in the same way. Likewise, we are all called from the same situation of estrangement to life in the one body of Christ; but just as each member is called *to* a different place in that body, so is each called *from* a different configuration of sin. A plausible doctrine of original sin needs to acknowledge that, in sin no less than glory, equality does not imply either identity or interchangeability.

Yet there are two serious objections that need to be faced in defending this claim. The first is perhaps the most longstanding and deep-seated worry about the Augustinian doctrine of original sin: that its model of the bondage of the will undermines human moral responsibility. According to this line of critique, because the belief that the will is bound to sin

---

*In Adam's Fall: A Meditation on the Christian Doctrine of Original Sin*, by Ian A. McFarland.
© 2010 Ian A. McFarland.

makes sin an ontological *condition* rather than a moral *consequence* of fallen human action, it follows that fallen human beings sin both always (i.e., their every act is a sin) and necessarily (i.e., they cannot not sin). If sin is so all-pervasive and unavoidable, the argument goes, then the idea of personal responsibility for sin becomes morally incoherent. It may remain the case that sin results in pain, alienation, and destruction, but it no longer makes any sense for anyone – including especially God – to hold the sinner responsible for it. Sin can only be a matter for personal repentance (as opposed to regret) if the sinner retains the possibility of not sinning, and this possibility is precluded by the Augustinian position.

The second objection also takes issue with the anthropological leveling implied by the doctrine of original sin, but from a different angle. Instead of deriving from a focus on the psychology of the sinner (viz., her inability to avoid sinning), it is based on consideration of the sin's concrete effects, charging that Augustinian hamartiology erodes the distinction between the perpetrators of sin and their victims. After all, if everyone is always a sinner, then there seems no ground for the kind of relative moral judgments that make it possible to distinguish between the sin of (for example) batterers and those they batter. Since according to the doctrine of original sin both groups are sinners – and, indeed, sin in everything they do – there seems no basis for arguing that the situation of the one is theologically more problematic than that of the other. Thus, if the first objection to the Augustinian position gives voice to the concern that the doctrine of original sin renders the idea of personal responsibility meaningless, the focus of the second is that the doctrine underwrites a policy of "blaming the victim" by assigning guilt in equal measure to violator and violated. In this way, the doctrine of original sin seems predisposed either to negate (the first objection) or pervert (the second objection) human moral judgment.

The question of the *reatus* of original sin thus introduces a set of problems arguably far more serious than those associated with the issue of original sin as *vitium*. The chief objections to the latter, as discussed in the previous chapter, were largely theoretical matters of historical and metaphysical coherence. By contrast, the objections connected with the former are more practical matters of consequence: the worry that when people believe themselves to be unavoidably sinful, they will either cease to feel responsible for evil when they should, or they will be driven to feel responsible when they shouldn't. Inasmuch as it is a central claim of this book that the doctrine of original sin helps to clarify and deepen rather than distort Christian understandings of human agency, both issues need to be addressed if the theological plausibility of an Augustinian perspective is to be preserved. We will begin with the second objection, seeking to clarify and defend Augustinian claims about original sin by looking at questions of accountability in relation to concrete instances of sinful behavior.

## The Scope of Sin

As already noted in Chapters 1 and 2, several contemporary theologians have sought to avoid some of the pitfalls associated with traditional forms of Christian sin-talk by making sin's public, concrete manifestations the touchstone of their hamartiologies. One approach not discussed earlier but particularly noteworthy in the present context is Andrew Sung Park's proposal that the Korean term *han* be deployed as a conceptual counterweight to the traditional Christian language of sin.[2] Park contends that the identification of sin as humanity's fundamental problem, with its corresponding emphasis on divine forgiveness as the solution to that problem, leads to a one-sided focus on the well-being of perpetrators of sin that is incapable of doing justice to the experience of those who suffer sin's effects. Introducing the concept of han, Park argues, helps to redress this imbalance, because han names the "abysmal experience of pain" produced by the violence of sin upon those who are its victims.[3] Park acknowledges that in practice sin and han are closely intertwined in individual and communal experience, since the frustration, bitterness, and resentment characteristic of han can itself lead to retaliatory violence against those who cause suffering. Nevertheless, sin and han fall in a definite order: han is the effect of which sin is the cause.[4] Furthermore, this sequence can be mapped on to the concrete socio-political hierarchies that give shape to human action on a large scale: "Sin is of the oppressor; han is of the oppressed."[5]

Despite Park's acknowledgment of the ways in which sin and han can be intertwined in the lives of concrete individuals, the force of his proposal rests on a clear distinction (one that, in principle, is present in every sinful act) between perpetrator and victim. Thus, although the mutually interactive dynamics of sin and han may produce an ongoing cycle of violence involving both groups, the respective roles of the sinner and the han-filled person in any such cycle are quite different: the former initiates and provokes; the latter suffers and reacts.[6] This schematization also leads Park to reject the claim that either sin or han is a universal condition, on the grounds that universal application of either term will dilute attention to the concrete differences between the situation of oppressor and oppressed. Instead, he emphasizes that the two categories refer to two different existential conditions and must be addressed in correspondingly different ways: while sin (as that which results in objective guilt) requires forgiveness, han (as that which generates shame) needs healing.[7]

Park's proposal is designed to be practical: the concept of sin cannot address the circumstances of oppressed or violated people, he argues, because it can only offer forgiveness; but those who have been sinned against do not need forgiveness, and to teach that they do simply compounds the injury done them by suggesting that they are somehow to blame for their condition. The doctrine of *original* sin makes things still worse because it both suggests that this blameworthiness is intrinsic to the victim's very being and simultaneously weakens (because it universalizes) the guilt of oppressors. Park therefore rejects original sin as inconsistent with the fundamental meaning of sin, which he defines as a deliberate act: "the volitional act of offense against God or others."[8] At the same time, he proposes that the kind of solidarity in misery to which the doctrine of original sin rightly points does accurately reflect certain salient characteristics of han. For example, he argues that the concept of han makes sense of the question of intergenerational transmission that has proved so problematic for the doctrine of original sin, since han, as the experience of pain caused by evil, correlates well with those dispositions to sinfulness that clearly can be passed down through the generations, whether by means of genetic inheritance (e.g., alcoholism) or through more complex modes of psychosocial transmission (e.g., a sense of personal inferiority or collective racial/ethic defilement).[9]

There can be no doubt that Park addresses theologically and pastorally important issues, not least in his insistence on the theological importance of distinguishing between committing a particular sin and suffering its effects. There can also be little question that Park is right to charge that traditional Christian treatments of sin in general and of original sin in particular have often served to exacerbate the pain of those who have been the victims of sin. At the same time, Park's own proposal depends on theological moves that are problematic in their own right. As a result, when he identifies the Augustinian doctrine of original sin as the place where traditional Christian teaching goes most awry by simultaneously exonerating the guilty and accusing the innocent, he fails to reckon with the ways in which that same doctrine both challenges his own central presuppositions and provides resources for addressing its own potential for abuse.

Fundamental to Park's hamartiology is his restriction of the scope of the term "sin." Although he acknowledges that sin can be directed against either God or other people, his analysis focuses almost exclusively on offenses against human beings. While such offenses are certainly sins, they do not come close to exhausting the range of the term in the broader Christian tradition, where the focus is generally on sin as resistance to God's will. From this more traditional perspective, the central characteristic of sin is that it disrupts and damages one's relationship to God, which cannot be reduced to (even though it cannot be separated from) one's relationships to other people. Thus, even though Jesus describes love of neighbor as "like" love of God, he nevertheless distinguishes them (Matt. 22:39). Similarly, Paul teaches that to be blameless in the sight of others (and even of oneself) is not to be blameless before God (1 Cor. 4:4; cf. Phil. 3:6) – and that it is when measured against this criterion, that no one is without sin (Rom. 3:23).

Park is, of course, well aware that he is breaking with the majority Christian tradition at this point. His aim in restricting the application of the term "sin" to willful acts of offense against others is to enhance the church's ability to deal pastorally with the material effects of sinful acts on human lives.[10] His contention is that by reducing the scope of the term "sin" to the relationships among people, the church will be more inclined to focus on the concrete realities of people's existence in attempting to rectify the effects of sin, and correspondingly less likely to use God-talk as an excuse for turning away from matters of human well-being in the here and now.[11]

While these goals are laudable, it is possible to make the case that Park's view of sin is itself guilty of a considerable degree of abstraction that impairs his ability to deal with the lived reality of human relationships that are the ostensible focus of his concern. Thus, central to Park's understanding of sin is the idea that sin is deliberate: "a willful act."[12] As Augustine recognized, the problem with this emphasis on volition is that it overstates the degree to which the sinner is in control of her actions. Part of the perplexity of sin is that while the sinner undoubtedly commits the sin and recognizes herself as responsible for it, the degree to which it is (to use Park's language) "volitional" or "willful" is much less easy to pin down. Even apart from any commitment to the doctrine of original sin, the complex mix of biological and environmental factors that contribute to human action make it difficult to state with any degree of certainty the extent to which a given human act – however devastating its effects – is rooted in the kind of self-possession that Park seems to require for an act to qualify as sin. The result is that far from bringing the desired moral clarity to the relationship of the wrongdoer and the one wronged, Park's definition risks making any such judgments more difficult.[13]

Beyond this failure to reckon sufficiently with the complexity of the oppressor's willing, Park's analysis is equally problematic when it comes to evaluating the will of the oppressed. A crucial component of Park's proposal for restricting the scope of sin is the clear distinction he draws between the oppressor as the active agent of sin and the oppressed as its passive victim. In setting up this framework, Park not only overestimates the degree to which the perpetrator of violence can be said to will her actions; he also underestimates the degree to which the will of the violated person is caught up in the dynamics of sin. Alistair McFadyen has made this point with particular force in his theological analysis of childhood sexual abuse as a framework for understanding the Augustinian doctrine of the bondage of the will. Drawing in particular on feminist studies of abuse, McFadyen observes that an integral part of the dynamic of abusive relationships is the abuser's co-opting of the child's will (e.g., by persuading her that no one will believe her if she reports the abuse, or by offering material inducements in exchange for acquiescence), enmeshing it with the will of the abuser so that the child "consents" to her abuse. The effectiveness of this process is such that to ignore the entanglement of the will of the abused in such situations by labeling them as purely victims of another's sin can actually exacerbate the deleterious effects of the abuse on the child's sense of self:

> Certainly, the abused need to be freed of inappropriate feelings of guilt, related to inaccurate senses of their power and agency in the situation … But a description of abuse which suggests that, because they are in no way the cause of abuse (being incapable of consenting), abused children exercised no agency or will renders them as powerless, passive objects, not subjects – of therapeutic processes as of abuse.[14]

As McFadyen is careful to note, the point of drawing attention to the role of the will of the abused in situations of abuse is not to make the abused child feel bad about herself (in this his conclusions are entirely consistent with Park's worry about the damaging effects of ill-considered talk about sin). On the contrary, his claim is that an Augustinian understanding of the bondage of the will may provide a conceptual framework that is therapeutically *more* effective than any alternative when it comes to helping heal the child's distorted sense of self.

In contrast to an Augustinian model, Park's strict dichotomization of perpetrators' sin and victims' han presupposes a highly punctiliar account of human relationships, in which sin is identified with very particular acts performed by discrete agents with the purpose of inflicting damage on a set of equally discrete patients. He is correspondingly unable to take stock of the ways in which particular actions are bound up with fundamental distortions of human agency that implicate the wills of both perpetrators and victims in radically different but nevertheless equally profound ways. Because human beings are irreducibly agents, their acts – whether as perpetrators or survivors of personal violation – always engage their wills, but they need not for that reason be willful. Indeed, what makes sin so catastrophic in an Augustinian perspective is the recognition that in sin (again, whether that sin is experienced from the perspective of the one who inflicts pain or the one who endures it) we so frequently will ways that run counter to what we want.[15]

As will be argued at length in the following section, all of this is not to posit any sort of moral equivalence between the abuser and the abused, the rapist and the raped, the torturer and the tortured. It is only to argue that the concrete dynamics of sin are too complicated to suffer reduction to a highly schematized opposition between fully responsible agents and utterly passive victims. A parallel might be drawn here with Michel Foucault's analysis of power in society. Against an oppositional framework that imagines power as a commodity that can be held and deployed unilaterally by one group over another, Foucault argues that power "circulates" throughout the social body so that individuals "are always in the position of simultaneously undergoing and exercising … power" and are never only "its inert or consenting target."[16] The manifestations and effects of power, of course, differ radically depending on where one is in the circulatory system, and in the same way that McFadyen's analysis of the will's bondage is not intended to blur the distinction between abuser and abused, Foucault's aim is not to deny that power gives rise to systems of domination in which particular groups are objectively disadvantaged; on the contrary, his goal is to bring the dynamics of domination into relief in a way that allows them to be challenged effectively. Likewise, an Augustinian model, by its suggesting a vision of sin as a power that implicates all persons (albeit in very different ways), would seem better positioned to address the complex and manifold character of human enmeshment in sin than a model based on a strict opposition between perpetrators and victims.[17]

## Sin and Agency

Even if this point is granted, however, it is hard to see how a model that views sin as humanity's common predicament before God can avoid the kind of leveling of the situation of violator and violated that Park and other contemporary critics have identified as a crucial problem with Augustinian hamartiology. Any theology that works from a belief in the universality of sin is seemingly going to lack the resources to make the kinds of relative determinations of responsibility necessary to redress the concrete damage that sin inflicts on individuals and communities. Indeed, such a theology is likely to make things worse (and thus itself become a further manifestation of sin), since proclaiming that all people stand in need of divine forgiveness of sin implies that victims of sin are in God's sight indistinguishable from those who have sinned against them.

The risk here is real, and it is correspondingly necessary to stress once again at the outset that the idea of a common human sinfulness – the core of the doctrine of original sin – no more requires that human beings be viewed as indistinguishable in God's sight than that the proclamation of a common salvation does. To say that all are equally sinners is not to imply that all are sinners in the same way, any more than the confession that all are members of the one body of Christ means that individuals' roles are interchangeable (see 1 Cor. 12:14–18). Nevertheless, the biblical witness provides no basis for the claim that these differences among people delegitimize the universal application of the term "sin." Jesus in the Sermon on the Mount presents an ethic that effectively convicts everyone of murder, adultery, and falsehood (Matt. 5:21–37) – a perspective consistent with Paul's affirmation that "all, both Jews and Greeks, are under the power of sin, as it is written: 'There is no one who is righteous, not even one'" (Rom. 3:10; cf. Pss. 14:3, 53:3).[18]

At the same time, it is also undeniably the case that Jesus' ministry has as its particular focus the well-being of those individuals and groups who suffer disproportionately from the effects of sin. After all, the same Sermon on the Mount that highlights the stringency of the law's demands begins by pronouncing God's particular favor toward the mournful, the meek, and the persecuted (Matt. 5:1–12).[19] And in Luke Jesus inaugurates his public ministry with a sermon in which he states that God had sent him specifically "to bring good news to the poor … to proclaim release to the captives and recovery of sight to the blind, to let the oppressed go free" (Luke 4:18; cf. Isa. 61:1). Indeed, it is precisely this association with the marginalized that leads to his being derided as a friend of sinners (Matt. 11:19 and par.; cf. Luke 15:1). Importantly, however, when asked to justify such behavior, he makes no attempt to deny that the people in question are in fact sinners. On the contrary, he justifies his actions precisely by appealing to their sinfulness: "Those who are well have no need of a physician, but those who are sick; I have come not to call the righteous but sinners to repentance" (Luke 5:30–2 and pars.).[20] In this way, he clearly categorizes the oppressed as sinners called to repentance and in need of forgiveness.

No less significant is the fact that the oppressed to whom Jesus ministers seemingly accept their identification as sinners (see, e.g., Luke 5:8, 7:36–50; John 5:14; cf. Matt. 15:26–7; Mark 9:17–24; John 8:1–11). If anything, it is just the acknowledgment of their sinful status that most clearly distinguishes the marginalized from the powerful in the Gospel narratives. The "righteous" who have "no need of a physician" fail to recognize their own need, and it is this failure that makes them incapable of hearing the gospel as good news for them:

> "What do you [chief priests and elders] think? A man had two sons; he went to the first and said, 'Son, go and work in the vineyard today.' He answered, 'I will not'; but later he changed his mind and went. The father went to the second and said the same; and he answered, 'I go, sir'; but he did not go. Which of the two did the will of his father?" They said, "The first." Jesus said to them, "Truly I tell you, the tax-collectors and the prostitutes are going into the kingdom of God ahead of you. For John [the Baptist] came to you in the way of righteousness and you did not believe him, but the tax collectors and prostitutes believed him; and even after you saw it, you did not change your minds and believe him." (Matt. 21:28–32)

In short, the oppressed recognize that their relationship with God is broken in a way that the righteous do not (cf. the parable of the Pharisee and the tax collector in Luke 18:9–14), and, insofar as they confess their need, they are able to receive the grace of forgiveness.

Yet here, too, there evidently remains more to be said. After all, in the passage from Matthew 21 it remains possible to identify genuine fault on the part of the repentant son; and if one turns to the particular groups Jesus mentions in interpreting that parable for his audience, one might well question whether tax collectors in particular, who functioned largely as professional extortionists shaking down the local population on behalf of the Roman Empire, can be classed among "the oppressed" (see Luke 19:1–9). Thus, even if it is conceded that no one is free from *actual* sins, it might be objected that the doctrine of *original* sin is problematic because it makes sin the defining feature of human identity and thereby fails to attend to the reality of those (especially – though by no means either exclusively or necessarily – women and children) who are by any objective measure more sinned against than sinner.

Of course, even very traditional hamartiologies generally acknowledge that original sin does not render everyone's actions equally destructive or vicious. Even among those whose sins are flagrant, it is possible to recognize that the sin of the torturer is of a different order than that of the philanderer. Yet the objection to Augustinianism is that such distinctions tend to be marginalized, because the doctrine of original sin undermines the possibility of quantifying sin. Within an Augustinian framework sin is creaturely resistance to God's will that results from defective willing on the part of the creature. Because sin is in this way inseparable from the very act of (fallen) willing, it cannot be prevented by the will. One may determine to some extent *how* one sins (since even the bound will is evidently not compelled to any particular action),[21] but not *whether* one sins. In this respect, sin is not a matter of more or less but of all or nothing: one sins *because* one is a sinner, and if one is a sinner, one's every action will be sin.[22]

Once again, however, the claim that every human being will invariably sin does not entail the claim that all sin in the same way. Nor are such differences in the character of human sinning exhausted by reference to various forms of active malfeasance (e.g., murder as opposed to adultery or lying).[23] When Jesus warns against *causing* someone to stumble (Matt. 18:6 and pars.; cf. Mal. 2:8), he implies that there is a category of sin that arises as a consequence of being actively sinned against. In other words, alongside the various forms of sin that result directly in the suffering of others, there is also sin that is *produced* by such suffering. The Gospel texts do not provide any explication of what Jesus has in mind, but the fact that the root of the word translated as "stumbling" used in these passages (*skandalizesthai*) connotes a trap or snare is suggestive of putting a person in a position where her freedom is impaired. Furthermore, since Jesus' explicit object of concern in these passages is the well-being of "these little ones *who believe in me*," it is natural to interpret this impairment as the result of some temptation or offense (both possible translations of *skandalon*) that undermines a person's capacity to believe. In other words, since trust requires confidence that the person trusted is well disposed toward you, one way to cause one of the "little ones" to stumble would be through words or actions that erode their sense of themselves as children of God and full members in God's covenant community.[24] This kind of worry about the well-being of the more vulnerable members of the community is evident in Paul's warning to the "strong" in the church at Corinth to "be careful that the power you have does not somehow become a stumbling-block to the weak" (1 Cor. 8:9),[25] as well as in his injunction to all members of the Roman church to "resolve instead never to put a stumbling-block or hindrance in the way of another" (Rom. 14:13). All these texts point to a kind of sin, occasioned by the sin of others, that would be likely to produce the sorts of characteristics that Park associates with those sinned against: resentment, passivity, and a sense of irreparable defilement.

If the sin of the oppressed is understood in this way, there is nothing implausible or unjust about seeing sin as a defining feature of their identity. To be sure, the unbelief that defines their sin is different in both origin and form than the sin of the oppressor, but given the variety of ways in which the term "sin" is applied in the Bible as a whole and the New Testament in particular, there is no reason not to call it sin.[26] Indeed, insofar as it describes the kind of broken relationship with God that is a common feature across the various sorts of acts that are called sin in Scripture, there is good reason to insist on naming it in just that way:

> Prophetic language that rightly names perpetrators [of oppression] is necessary but not sufficient; and it tends toward atheism whenever it calls traumatic distrust something other than sin, as though "God" were merely a background source of rightly-made moral judgments, and not a living presence calling all to a repentant turning across whatever sort of brokenness interferes with an ability to love and trust God above all else.[27]

The Gospel accounts suggest that a defining feature of Jesus' work among the marginalized was their reintegration into the community of God's people. This reintegration involved overcoming their own sin as well as revealing the sin of others (see, e.g., John 9:39–41). In particular, Jesus' practice of table fellowship seems to have been understood by friend and foe alike as a sign of reconciliation that modeled the breaking of sin's power to alienate those who had appeared to both themselves and others as beyond the possibility of reconciliation (Matt. 9:11 and pars.; Luke 15:2; cf. Luke 13:28–30).

Even at this point, however, lingering doubts remain about whether "sin" is the best term to describe the situation of those whose lack of faith is caused by having been sinned against. After all, the remedy for sin is forgiveness, and to claim that the "little ones" need to be forgiven seems to imply that they are at fault – an inference that Jesus' assertion that they have been *caused* (by someone else) to stumble seems explicitly designed to block. At one level, this concern can only be answered by pointing to the fact that the general application of the language of sin in the Gospels corresponds to an equally generalized understanding of the need for forgiveness: John preached repentance and forgiveness of sin to all without distinction (Mark 1:4 and par.), and Jesus instructs his disciples to do the same (Luke 24:47; cf. Acts 2:38, 5:31, 13:38; Eph. 1:7; Col. 1:14). At no point is there any suggestion that the situation of any person renders this message inapplicable to her.

Again, however, recognizing the universal application of the gospel of repentance and forgiveness takes away nothing from the equally striking fact that the Gospels depict Jesus' attitudes toward (marginalized) tax collectors and prostitutes on the one hand and (marginalizing) scribes and Pharisees on the other in very different terms. One way of accounting for this difference is to recognize a distinction between accountability and blame. Especially in the case of those who have been caused to stumble, to be guilty of sin is not necessarily to be counted worthy of blame; but neither is it to lose accountability for one's actions. In short, it is possible to be accountable and yet without blame. The difference is rooted in the nature of the two concepts. Blame is a *moral* category; a person becomes blameworthy because one is at fault for a particular act. By contrast, accountability is an *ontological* category: a person is accountable simply by virtue of being an agent.

Blame attaches to active forms of personal violation; one who commits such an act is blameworthy. To say this is not to deny that even what appear as the most intentionally vicious acts may be the product of complex psychological processes, but it is to recognize fault. To revert again to the example of childhood sexual abuse, empirical evidence strongly suggests that the experience of such abuse is a contributing factor to the behavior of adult abusers of children, but it remains crucial to a proper moral evaluation of the abusive relationship that the abuser – and only the abuser – is at fault for the abuse. The one abused is not.[28] It does not follow, however, that only the abuser is in the grip of sin. As already noted, one of the most devastating aspects of abuse is the way in which the abusive relationship implicates the will of the abused person. This process whereby the victim's sense of agency is distorted has two dimensions that are particularly important in the present context.[29] First (as noted above), it fosters a sense of guilt or blameworthiness for the abuse, by creating the impression in the victim that she willingly consented to it. This effect must be countered by stating as clearly and consistently as possible that the abused person bears no blame for the abuse. No less serious, however, is the legacy of her relationship with the abuser that undermines the victim's capacity to trust others – both God and human beings. Here – in sharp contrast to the abused person's mistaken sense of personal blameworthiness for the act(s) of abuse – the effect can only be countered by accentuating the individual's accountability, not for the abuse itself (that would be to return to the language of blame), but for her continued survival and healing. To receive Christ's forgiveness in this context is not to accept blame for some incident or set of incidents for which one is blameless,[30] but rather to confess that one's very self has been received and blessed by God notwithstanding one's own active resistance to God's love. It is to be given the capacity to trust God – and to know oneself liberated by that capacity – in spite of one's prior refusal to give God one's trust.

In short, at stake in the distinction between accountability and blame is the conviction that even one who cannot be *blamed* for not trusting God (for why should one who has been so profoundly betrayed by relationships open herself to another?) may nevertheless recognize an *accountability* before God that renders it meaningful to speak of both needing and receiving God's forgiveness. This recognition cannot be forced on anyone. To try to do so would only demonstrate a failure to appreciate that when sin is understood in terms of a fundamental disruption of a person's relationship with God, it can be recognized as sin only once it has been forgiven. It cannot be otherwise, since the content of the good news is precisely that God defines the essential character of that relationship quite apart from any merit or demerit on the part of human beings. Thus, all sinners – especially those who have been caused to sin – come to know that their wills have resisted God only as God shows us God's own will, which remains faithful to us in spite of our failure to be faithful to God.[31]

## From Actual Sin to Original Sin

Original sin refers to an inborn or congenital state that precedes and is the condition of all actual sin (i.e., all particular instances of human resistance to God's will). With this definition in mind, it should be clear that the two previous sections of this chapter have not dealt directly with the topic of original sin. Their purpose was rather to explore different examples of actual sin in order to argue that the coherence of the concept "sin" does not require its exclusive identification with clearly identifiable acts of willful offense against God or other people that are rightly matters of blame.[32] The kind of inability to trust God (or anyone else) characteristic of those who have been sinned against provides a plausible instance of an alternative form of sin. It is not a crime for which the sinned against are in any way to blame, but it can be (and, more to the point, has been) experienced by the oppressed as a sin for which they are accountable and in the face of which the gospel of forgiveness is heard as good news.[33] It is my contention that original sin is best understood along these lines, as a fundamental distortion of the will that is the ontological ground for the diverse, concrete acts of sin willed by oppressors and oppressed alike.

To return to the Scholastic categories introduced at the beginning of this chapter, arguing that one can be accountable for sin without being blamed for it provides a basis for defending the moral coherence of the claim that original sin is a matter of universal *reatus* (liability) as well as universal *vitium* (damage). That these two categories need to be distinguished follows from the principle that damage to nature (*vitium*) cannot in itself be called sin, since nature is always an immediate product of God's agency, and God's inalienable goodness means that every created nature (precisely *as* created) is inalienably good, however badly damaged it may be. Talk of sin presupposes some personal agency that resists – and is thus by definition other than – God's. Therefore, while *vitium* pertains to postlapsarian human nature, *reatus* is a function of the individual human hypostasis.

Once *vitium* and *reatus* are distinguished in this way, however, the question arises of how they are connected, given that nature and hypostasis are ontologically incommensurable. In line with the argument developed in Chapter 5 above, the link is found in the will, because it is at once part of nature (as argued by Maximus the Confessor against monothelitism) and that part of (postlapsarian) nature that is bound to sin (as Augustine maintained against the Pelagians). At one level, then, the will, as part of human nature, simply shares in the damage that afflicts the whole of human nature after the fall. Yet because the will is that part of my human nature in and through which I experience myself as an agent, damage to *it* invariably affects *me* – not simply constraining my capacities (as, say, damage to my foot or my reason might), but affecting my basic character – *who* as well as *what* I am as a human being. As created, the will is that feature of human nature by which human beings are freely (i.e., as self-conscious agents) empowered to desire God. When the will is damaged, therefore, its desire is no longer for God – and desire that is not oriented to God is by definition sinful.[34] As Augustine argued, such a change cannot be viewed in quantitative terms (as though it meant only that I were more likely to sin than would be the case otherwise), but entails a qualitative transformation of my status, so that I, as fallen, am also a sinner. My fallen nature (including my will, considered as a part of that nature) remains good, but my hypostasis – the mode by which I live out that nature as the particular person I am – is not.

In light of this proposal, it might seem to follow that original sin is simply a way of referring to the effects of the fall as it applies to the will in particular, since the fallenness of all the other components of human nature does not (and, indeed, cannot) produce sin apart from the will. But if (as argued in Chapter 5) Christ assumed a fallen nature and yet was free from all sin, this interpretation evidently cannot be accepted. To do so would be to conflate nature and hypostasis, as though the quality of the latter were determined by the characteristics of the former. Yet the whole point of the distinction between nature and hypostasis as applied to personal agents is that the latter is irreducible to the former: though there is never a hypostasis without a nature (since a hypostasis is simply a particular instantiation of a nature), accountability is a function of hypostasis in distinction from nature (since if acts are simply attributed to the nature, then it is no longer meaningful to speak of personal accountability). Consequently, though it is right to speak of human desires as distorted by virtue of a *vitium* inherent in postlapsarian human nature, this cannot be understood as a causal explanation of why fallen human beings are in fact sinners.[35] It simply describes the ontological form of human sin: as a fallen human being, I sin because I will what I desire, and my desires are distorted; nevertheless, this falls short of an explanation of *why* I desire as I do. Faced with that question, all I can say is that I am the kind of person (viz., a sinner) who desires that way. To the extent that I take the "I" in that response seriously, this answer is not an evasion of accountability, but its confession. The point of describing this situation as original *sin* is precisely to highlight this confession by acknowledging that at the most basic level all explanation of sin terminates in the sheer fact of my own hypostatic agency and cannot be devolved on to God or anyone else.

Of course, the most venerable and compelling objection to original sin strikes right at this point. If one is already a sinner prior to (and as condition of) any particular sinful deed, then it seems to make no sense to talk of accountability: a person cannot coherently be blamed for the conditions that govern her actions. And yet to view myself as accountable for my original sin is not the same as to affirm that I should be blamed for it (or, correspondingly, that I should feel guilty for it). Here again, it is necessary to remember that the ascription of blame (i.e., personal fault) is not a corollary to the acknowledgment of sin. Those who (following Jesus' language in the Gospels) have been *caused* to stumble are not rightly subject to blame, even though their stumbling qualifies as sin. Original sin can be conceived on analogy with this form of actual sin: in the same way that Christians want to claim that repentance and forgiveness are meaningful even for those who find their ability to love God vitiated by abusive relationships for which they are not at fault, so are they meaningful for the whole of fallen humanity insofar as postlapsarian human beings' ability to love God is congenitally impaired.[36] In both cases, the language of *blame* is out of place, because it presupposes a measure of deliberative autonomy (i.e., whether or not to participate in sin) that is simply absent; yet *accountability* remains, because the person who sins remains an agent – an "I" who as an I remains the ultimate ground of her actions – even in being caused to sin.

In this way, the doctrine of original sin insists on the absolute inalienability of each human being's hypostatic reality as a responsible agent before God. Yet the point of this insistence is not to burden people with a crushing and disabling sense of guilt for their inadequacy as congenital sinners. Here, once again, it is vital to remember that the doctrine of original sin is, existentially speaking, a consequence rather than the premise of the gospel: we know we are sinners only as God proclaims to us that our sin is forgiven. Rather than being a proper focus of our continued attention, therefore, original sin is and can be known by us only as a threat that has already been met and defeated by God.[37] And yet the doctrine remains crucial precisely because its defeat lies at the heart of the good news: God addresses me as a person who remains a person – a being not only loved by God (something that is also true of non-human creatures) but also by whom God desires to be loved – no matter how constrained or marred every objective ground of personhood in my nature may be. Original sin, properly understood, is the limit case of this claim. If it is viewed as an occasion for blame, it is misunderstood, because blame presupposes a measure of control over one's willing that is by definition excluded when speaking of congenital sin. But as a witness to human accountability (even where blame is out of the question), it affirms the integrity of one's agency, one's status as a person beloved by and called to love God, even where that freedom of the will that would appear to be – and by every objective measure is – the defining mark of that agency is utterly compromised. In summary, to proclaim that you have original sin that is forgiven by God (and to speak of original sin in any other way is to misapply the doctrine) is to say that God sees and claims you as a person called to live a life of love even where any personal merit for such a claim is absent.

It follows that an important function of the doctrine of original sin within the larger field of theological anthropology is to qualify the significance of the will in human self-understanding. As already noted, the will names the ontological context where one's sense of oneself as a hypostasis – as a distinct, self-conscious, specifically human agent – is localized. Insofar as to be an "I" is precisely to claim one's thoughts, feelings, and actions as *mine* (viz., as that which *I* thought, felt, or did), it would appear to demand the kind of freedom of the will for which Augustine's Pelagian opponents argued, such that the will, however wounded or weakened, remains fundamentally unconstrained in its willing. By insisting that the fallen will is, in fact, bound to sin (i.e., that postlapsarian human beings are unable not to sin), Augustine rejected the claim that there was any aspect or dimension of fallen human nature that provided an objective basis for God's approval, any leverage for our commending ourselves to God. Even the will – the center of the human sense of self – did not constitute such an ontological linchpin untouched by the fall, and, correspondingly, it could not be regarded as any more capable of guaranteeing one's identity before God than any other feature of human nature. Instead, the gospel tells us that we somehow remain agents – accountable before and beloved by God – in spite of our wills rather than because of them.

All this is not to deny that our willing is important for our relationship to God. It is simply to see its importance as one component within our full humanity, and one which, like every other such component, needs to be transformed by grace in order for us to love God as the specifically human agents we were created to be. Insofar as modern Western culture retains a strongly Pelagian cast to its anthropology, according to which we make ourselves the persons we are through our willing – by the (putatively autonomous) choices we make – this qualification of the will's place in theological anthropology is both sobering and empowering. It is sobering because it undercuts any sort of anthropological titanism that imagines that the "I" is sovereign even in its own house. It is empowering because this fact allows us to recognize that our status as human hypostases called and claimed by God is not dependent on (though it is, of course, also never realized in abstraction from) our natural capacities. If all are equally recipients of God's gracious affirmation of their status, then no objective inequality in their natural capacities (whether congenital or the result of environmental factors) can serve as a measure of that status.

This conclusion dovetails with a central feature of Maximus' anthropology as outlined in Chapter 4: because the will is a feature of human nature, it (along with all other such features) constitutes the ontological framework or matrix within which the hypostasis is made manifest, but it cannot be equated with the hypostasis or viewed as its source. Hypostasis is irreducible to nature, as the mode (*tropos*) in which the nature subsists. In this context, it is important to remember that the constitutive features of human nature (whatever these may be supposed to include) are by definition those features that all human beings have in common. As that dimension of human being that is irreducible to nature, hypostasis is an anomalous category: all human beings are hypostases, yet because the hypostasis refers precisely to the distinctiveness of each individual human being, it is misleading to speak of it as something common to all human beings. On the contrary, it refers to that which cannot be defined (e.g., in terms of its properties or capacities), but only named as an unrepeatable particular. Insofar as the doctrine of original sin, with its insistence on the accountability of even the congenitally sinful agent, points to a particularity of hypostasis that cannot be defined in terms of any human capacity, it functions to highlight rather than mask the distinctiveness of the individual.

It does not follow that original sin is somehow a necessary feature of human being – a "happy fault" (*felix culpa*) that should be construed as a benefit insofar as it magnifies our dependence on God's grace. Precisely because original sin is truly sin, there is nothing good or beneficial about it as such. The Christian confession that human beings, like all creatures, are created *ex nihilo* means that even if they were unfallen they would be no less dependent on God's grace for their flourishing. From this perspective, the doctrine of original sin does not add anything to theological anthropology. As that which resists God's will for the creature, sin is a surd, an intrusion upon creaturely flourishing rather than a factor that is in any sense integral to it. Indeed, the miracle is that this alien power is finally incapable of undercutting human being, so that however impotent (not to mention complicit) human beings appear in the face of its assault, it is not an insuperable obstacle to God. If the bondage of the will were such as to do what its critics fear it does – undermine human agency altogether – it would be just such an obstacle. Human creation would be destroyed, because the human person would be dissolved into an undifferentiated mass of fallen nature before which God's will for a loving relationship would be impotent, because there would be no one to respond to that love. That this is not the case, that even congenital sinners remain persons whom God recognizes and names as agents notwithstanding the corruption of their most "personal" creaturely capacities demonstrates that the greatest conceivable object to human glory is finally no obstacle to God. There is no good news in original sin; but it is part of the good news that by God's grace even original sin is incapable of having the final word on what it means to be human.

# Notes

1. The medieval Scholastics had used the language of *corruptio hereditaria* (inherited corruption) and *culpa hereditaria* (inherited guilt) to make this distinction, but the influence of federalist ideas led most Protestants to balk at the idea of *inherited* guilt. For a good summary of the details of Protestant orthodox terminology, see Oliver D. Crisp, *Divinity and Humanity: The Incarnation Reconsidered* (Cambridge: Cambridge University Press, 2007), pp. 96–106.
2. Andrew Sung Park, *The Wounded Heart of God: The Asian Concept of Han and the Christian Doctrine of Sin* (Nashville, TN: Abingdon Press, 1993).
3. Park, *Wounded Heart*, p. 15.
4. To be sure, "han sometimes causes individuals and communities to sin against the enemy" (Park, *Wounded Heart*, p. 74), but this sequence remains important as an indication of a fundamental asymmetry between sin and han, reflected at one point in his decision to characterize the retaliatory violence of the han-filled as "not sinless" rather than as positively sinful (*Wounded Heart*, p. 70).
5. Park, *Wounded Heart*, p. 69.
6. See Park, *Wounded Heart*, p. 76, where, against feminist attempts to broaden the concept of sin to include diffuseness and triviality, Park insists that a "character trait which has been developed by the infringement of outside forces cannot be called sin. It is instead han, the seat of the wound of victims."
7. Park, *Wounded Heart*, pp. 77, 81–5.
8. Park, *Wounded Heart*, p. 76.
9. "The idea of han may be a way to save and preserve the doctrine of original sin, whose principal intent is to describe the deep and connected dimension of the human predicament." Park, *Wounded Heart*, p. 81.
10. In this sense Park's motivation parallels Marjorie Suchocki's wish to attend to the effects of sin by defining it "primarily from the perspective of its relation to creation" as the "violation of the well-being of any aspect of creation." Marjorie Hewitt Suchocki, *The Fall to Violence: Original Sin in Relational Theology* (New York: Continuum, 1994), pp. 16, 48; cf. pp. 32, 66, and *passim*. See the discussion of Suchocki's work in Chapter 1 above.
11. Thus in the course of an extensive critique of the Reformers' doctrine of justification, Park supplements his charge that traditional theology focuses on the sinner instead of the one sinned against with the more general concern that "it focuses solely on our relationship with God, diminishing the significance of our relation with our neighbor." Park, *Wounded Heart*, p. 95.
12. Park, *Wounded Heart*, p. 79.
13. Without in any way seeking to make excuses for the behavior, the fact that child abusers are very often themselves former victims of abuse suggests that even in the case of the most serious, premeditated, and calculating sins,

*Original Sin and the Individual* 189

it can be difficult to assess the degree to which the act, though certainly willed, can be said to have been performed willfully.

14 Alistair McFadyen, *Bound to Sin: Abuse, Holocaust and the Christian Doctrine of Sin* (Cambridge: Cambridge University Press, 2000), p. 122. On the next page, McFadyen adds, "The significance of feminist discussions of childhood sexual abuse ... lies ... in the risky affirmation that the child's willing may be operative in abuse and that ... the denial of operant willing does not protect him from blame but confirms, repeats and further embeds abuse by continuing to narrate him as a passive object." For a thoroughgoing theological account of these dynamics from a feminist perspective, see Serene Jones, *Trauma and Grace: Theology in a Ruptured World* (Louisville, KY: Westminster John Knox, 2009).

15 See Chapter 3 above.

16 Michel Foucault, *Power/Knowledge: Selected Interviews and Other Writings 1972–1977*, ed. Colin Gordon (New York: Pantheon, 1980), p. 98.

17 "If we fail to comprehend the ways in which our willing (and so we as persons, as subjects) are opposed to God in sin, then we shall be unable ... to comprehend the way in which the dynamics of salvation address our situation; the way in which we are addressed by God in our sin and what we are called to through that address." McFadyen, *Bound to Sin*, p. 129.

18 One might also cite here the universalizing implications of Paul's (Gal. 5:3; cf. 3:10) and James's shared conviction that a violation of the law on any point undermines entirely one's status before God (Jas. 2:8–11).

19 The Matthean Beatitudes in Luke's Sermon on the Plain (Luke 6:20–3) are even more explicit in their proclamation of God's special favor toward the marginalized.

20 Note that in this passage Jesus applies to one and the same population the metaphors of illness/healing and sin/forgiveness that Park wants to divide between the oppressed and oppressors, respectively. As Miroslav Volf points out, Jesus' approach is counter-intuitive – and that is what makes it so revolutionary: "From the perspective of contemporary Western sensibilities, these two things together – divine love *and* human repentance – *addressed to the victims* represent the most surprising and, as political statements the most outrageous ... aspects of Jesus' message." *Exclusion and Embrace: A Theological Exploration of Identity, Otherness, and Reconciliation* (Nashville, TN: Abingdon Press, 1996), p. 113.

21 As Luther conceded in his debate with Erasmus over free will, even the fallen will remains able to turn to various external matters: I determine whether or not I go to church or refrain from cheating on my wife (i.e., I am free to keep from committing a crime); but I cannot determine to love God or my neighbor (i.e., I am not free to keep from committing sin). It is for this reason, Luther argues, that Paul denies that one is *justified* by works of the law, but not that it is possible to *perform* such works. See *Luther and Erasmus: Free Will and Salvation*, ed. E. Gordon Rupp and Philip S. Watson (Philadelphia, PA: Westminster Press, 1959), pp. 302–9; cf. p. 170, where

Luther (following Augustine) proposes "vertible choice" or "mutable choice" as preferable to "free choice" as a means of characterizing the kind of liberty (viz., with respect to external matters) that remains to the fallen will.

22  It is important to note here that this judgment does not preclude the possibility of making graded distinctions between particular sinful acts (e.g., recognition that murder is more serious than anger); it is, however, inconsistent with the claim that such distinctions reflect unambiguously the sort of differences in the sinner's relationship to God characteristic of the Catholic distinction between mortal and venial sins.

23  Traditional attempts to distinguish among different types of sin tend to operate in these terms. Thus, for example, in Aquinas's discussion of the question of the equality of sins in his treatise *On Evil* (ed. Brian Davies [New York: Oxford University Press, 2003]), he draws a distinction between the contempt for God characteristic of all sin and the particular act by which that contempt is shown. While with respect to the former all sin can be seen as equal (in light of God's infinite worth), with respect to the latter it is possible to speak of more or less contempt, depending both on the subjective disposition of the sinner (qu. 2, art. 9, ad 15), as well as of the sin's social consequences (qu. 2, art. 2, ad 8). Throughout, however, Aquinas conceives sin in terms of faulty willing within the context of the individual, with little regard for the ways in which broader social dynamics give rise to particular forms of sin.

24  Thus, one way in which Jesus responds to attacks on his regard for the marginalized is to emphasize their status as children of Abraham (Luke 13:16, 19:9; cf. 16:22).

25  My translation.

26  From this perspective, Park's insistence that a "character trait which has been developed by the infringement of outside forces cannot be called sin" (*Wounded Heart*, p.76; see note 6 above) appears as an arbitrary restriction on the semantic range of the term.

27  Amy Carr, "Enduring Radical Distrust: Sin and Redemption among the Sinned Against" (unpublished paper delivered at the annual meeting of the American Academy of Religion, 2007), p. 8.

28  Importantly, to make this point is not to encourage or justify the demonization of the abuser. It is, however, to affirm that in speaking to the abused person about the abuse, one can and must say with all possible clarity, "This was not your fault; the fault lies with the abuser." It probably also should be added that the view that the abuse was no one's fault is excluded *a limine*.

29  Two caveats need to be noted here. First, these two dimensions do not in any sense constitute an exhaustive account of the effects of childhood sexual abuse (or any other form of profound personal violation). Second (and correspondingly), it needs to be stressed that the process of caring for abuse victims is an extraordinarily complex task, the details of which will vary according to the situation of the particular individual being cared for. In short, the simplified schematization of the effects of abuse I offer here is

intended for analytical purposes only and not in any way as a blueprint for therapy.

30  In this context, note that the biblical witness to the universality of sin evidently does not preclude recognizing that certain persons are "blameless" (Hebrew *tām/tāmām*, Greek *amemptos*). See, e.g., Gen. 6:9; 2 Sam. 22:24; Job 1:1, 8; Luke 1:6; Phil. 3:6.

31  "... if we are faithless, [Jesus] remains faithful – for he cannot deny himself" (2 Tim. 2:13).

32  It is worth noting in this context how seldom in the Gospels Jesus' declarations of forgiveness are given in response to a particular, clearly identifiable transgression of the law. The only clear-cut case where Jesus' encounter with a sinner is explicitly correlated with a particular sinful act is the woman "caught in the very act of committing adultery" in John 8:1–11 – and here there is no declaration of forgiveness! Instead, Jesus suspends the accusation that would make forgiveness necessary (though he also counsels the woman not to sin again).

33  Of course, one may (following a standard Marxist critique of religion) interpret this experience as an example of "false consciousness" on the part of the oppressed, who have simply been bamboozled into interiorizing the value system of their oppressors. In some cases this is undoubtedly the case, but that it is not always so seems to be substantiated by the fact that in many cases this hearing of the gospel breeds neither passivity nor a sense of self-contempt, but empowerment and a commitment to the struggle for social transformation. See James H. Cone's reflections on this topic in *My Soul Looks Back* (Nashville, TN: Abingdon Press, 1982), especially chapters 1 and 5.

34  Needless to say, the point here is not that every human desire needs to have God as its *immediate* end. Human beings rightly have all sorts of entirely good desires for temporal goods (e.g., food, drink, sleep, companionship). But within an Augustinian framework such desires are only virtuous when ordered to God as their *final* end. It is this right ordering that original sin destroys.

35  For this reason my proposal for relating the *reatus* of the individual human being to the *vitium* of human nature must not be confused with the doctrine of "mediate imputation" associated with Josua Placaeus and the French Reformed school of Saumur in the seventeenth century. In order to address the problem of arbitrariness of federalist accounts of sin's transmission, Placaeus argued that Adam's *reatus* was imputed to his descendants not immediately (i.e., by the direct decree of God), but mediately, through humanity's inherited corruption (*vitium*). Placaeus was condemned at the Synod of Charenton (1644–5) for effectively denying imputation of Adam's *reatus* altogether, since he failed to account for why human beings should be afflicted with the *vitium* of the fall if they were not antecedently guilty of sin. In distinction from both Placaeus and his opponents, I am not arguing for any sort of divine imputation of *reatus*, but rather arguing that *reatus* is

an objective feature of the hypostases of fallen humanity (Christ excepted). Furthermore, over against Placaeus in particular I am not arguing that the fallenness of the will is the *cause* of human sin. The Synod of Charenton is quite right that such a position would undermine the basis for speaking of original *sin* at all, since nature would simply trump agency and undermine any basis for speaking of accountability. The nature–hypostasis distinction is useful in avoiding this problem, since the irreducibility of hypostasis to nature blocks the suggestion that the individual's *reatus* is caused by humanity's corrupt nature, and thereby provides an ontological framework within which it remains possible to preserve individual accountability for original sin. For an excellent summary of the debate surrounding the decrees of Charenton, see John Murray, *The Imputation of Adam's Sin* (Grand Rapids, MI: William B. Eerdmans, 1959), pp. 42–6.

36 I want to stress that I in no way mean to suggest that all human beings, as fallen, are equivalent to abused children or victims of analogous forms of profound personal violation. Childhood sexual abuse and its cognates, while tragically widespread, are particular forms of suffering that are in no sense whatsoever generalizable to humankind as a whole. The analogy with original sin is drawn *solely* with respect to ways in which personal agency is implicated in sin and not at all with respect to questions of pain and suffering experienced by the victims of these very concrete crimes. As with any analogy, it is important that whatever similarity exists includes an even greater dissimilarity.

37 While it would go beyond the scope of this chapter to address the question fully here, this emphasis on original sin's defeat points the way toward drawing a theologically significant link between the Augustinian doctrine and the practice of infant baptism. The latter is not needed in order to protect babies from the threat of hellfire, but the fact that those baptized as infants have no memory of the event helps to remind them and the church as a whole that their original sin has already been met and overcome quite apart from any merit or capacity on their part; that its power to define their life is irretrievably past and, as such, absolutely over and done with as a threat to their integrity as children of God.

# 8

# Original Sin and the Christian Life: Confronting Sin

What does it mean to be guilty of original sin – to sin "originally"? It has been a central feature of my argument that knowledge of original sin cannot be discovered from an examination of human behavior, since it is a claim about persons derived from the implications of the gospel preached *to* them rather than from any empirically identifiable features of the actions performed *by* them.[1] It follows that original sin is not a kind of act one commits: it refers to a status one always already *has*, not to anything one *does*. To be sure, a central implication of the doctrine is that human beings commit actual sins because they are afflicted by original sin, but the two remain qualitatively distinct. Original sin does not form part of a series with actual sins but is rather their ontological ground. To sin originally is therefore to be born a sinner – someone who necessarily commits actual sins. It is to have sin at the core of one's agency: to sin in being the particular person one is, as function of the way in which one hypostasizes one's human nature as a discrete agent before God. For this reason, the claim that original sin is universal needs to be supplemented by an insistence on its also being particular to every individual.

Out of a desire to draw attention to the particularity of each person's (original) sinfulness, I have sought over the course of the previous two chapters to draw attention to the diversity of the actual sins people commit. Not only is it the case (in line with the exacting moral standards of the Sermon on the Mount) that no one can claim a clean conscience before God, but there also remain significant differences in the way sin is manifest in different people, especially between those whose sin is a function of their being sinned against and those whose sin is the occasion for the sins of others. Because original sin is not reducible to actual sin,

---

*In Adam's Fall: A Meditation on the Christian Doctrine of Original Sin*, by Ian A. McFarland.
© 2010 Ian A. McFarland.

appreciating the diversity of the latter does not count as evidence for the former, but it does check the temptation to use the doctrine of original sin as an excuse for making Christian sin-talk hopelessly generic and abstract. If original sin is a function of the hypostasis (i.e, the particular mode or *tropos* in which each of us instantiates human nature), one would expect it be different in each individual, producing the greatest possible diversity of actual sins in a way that reflects the irreducible uniqueness of each human hypostasis.

And yet even if reflection on the variety of forms taken by actual sin may help to address some objections to the doctrine of original sin, the worry that the idea of original sin invariably diverts attention away from actual sin remains. After all, if everyone is a sinner (albeit in irreducibly different ways) and therefore stands in need of forgiveness, then focus on the particular form of actual sin of which individuals are guilty would seem to be beside the point. To be sure, on a practical level the need to secure the basic conditions for the possibility of human community will require that the most socially disruptive manifestations of sin be kept in check. There is therefore nothing inconsistent about affirming that all human acts are sins and recognizing that societies need to enact and enforce laws that address those forms of sin that threaten persons and property with arbitrary violence. At the same time, however, it seems that proponents of original sin will be inclined to view such developments as a purely political expedient largely exempt from theological evaluation. For although their convictions will lead them to concede that any given political order is sinful, their belief that any possible alternative will fall equally short of God's will would seem to render any efforts at improvement pointless. In this way, the doctrine of original sin seemingly predisposes one to expect little of politics beyond restraining those sins that constitute a direct and immediate threat to individual survival. Threats to human well-being that emerge from the political order itself (e.g., profound economic inequality) will not be denied, but neither do they seem likely to emerge as a focus of theological interest.

From the perspective of original sin's most trenchant contemporary critics, this tendency toward political quietism points to one of the most serious problems with the doctrine. If sin is original, if human beings are all perverse in a way that can only be addressed unilaterally by God's gift of grace, then there is no incentive to undertake the hard work necessary to address the manifold forms of actual sin in the world. Since everything people do is sin, there is little point in trying to identify or correct particular sins, beyond what is necessary to ensure the basic conditions for collective human survival. Indeed, to try to do more would seem to be problematic on two counts. Theologically, such action might seem to imply that sin is a problem that human beings can address on their own, apart from God. And politically, any attempt to challenge systemic manifestations of sin poses the risk of so undermining established political structures as to risk unleashing those especially destructive forms of sin that political structures are designed to keep in check.[2] Thus, even if the doctrine of original sin can be formulated in such a way as to avoid distorting the individual's sense of moral responsibility (as argued in the previous chapter), it is seemingly predisposed to lead to a political conservatism and passivity inconsistent with the ministry of Jesus, whose words and acts suggest that the gospel will be socially disruptive (see, e.g., Matt. 10:34–6 and par.; cf. Luke 4:18–19).

## From Original Sin to Actual Sin

To address this final challenge to the coherence of the doctrine of original sin, I will begin by reversing the analytical trajectory followed in the last chapter. There I examined particular forms of actual sin as a means of providing a conceptual framework within which to make sense of original sin, arguing that the radical mistrust characteristic of those who have been sinned against is an example of genuine sin that requires forgiveness and yet is not helpfully analyzed in terms of conventional moral categories of guilt or blame. These characteristics render such mistrust analogous to original sin, which, as a condition rather than a consequence of postlapsarian human willing, is also best understood in ontological rather than axiological terms. By moving in the opposite direction, I hope to show how original sin, though itself an ontological category, remains axiologically relevant, serving to enhance rather than encumber efforts to check people's participation in actual sin.

In pursuing this line of argument, moreover, I will continue to insist on the importance of maintaining a clear distinction between original sin as the antecedent condition of human willing and all of those particular instances of willing that constitute actual sin. This distinction has not always been observed within the Augustinian tradition, some of whose most able exponents (beginning with Augustine himself!) have defined original sin in terms of actual sin, as though it were a kind of proto-sin (pride, for example) underlying particular examples of actual sin.[3] Attempts to interpret original sin in this way, as itself a form of actual sin, naturally lead to the kind of inattention to the concrete effects of actual sin rightly castigated by critics of the doctrine both inside and outside the church.

After all, if the many external forms of actual sin are merely epiphenomenal manifestations of some common, internal flaw, then expending effort to try to understand the range of social, cultural, and historical circumstances in which they arise becomes theologically superfluous, since such knowledge can add nothing significant to our understanding of sin's origin and character. Moreover, the reduction of all actual sins to one basic type is likely to impede recognition of sins that do not readily conform to the picture of sin established by the dominant hamartiology.[4]

Now, to challenge the reduction of original sin to a particular form of actual sin is not to deny that the two are deeply connected. If they were not, then using the term "sin" for both would be pure equivocation. As argued in the second part of this book, the connection between them lies in the will, understood as that aspect of human nature by virtue of which my actions are grounded in my agency (viz., my experience of myself *as a self* – an "I" whose deeds I therefore claim as "mine"). In Augustinian perspective the fallenness of the will (an aspect of human *nature*) is correlated with that fundamental distortion of the self (i.e., the particular human *hypostasis*) by original sin that renders all postlapsarian human beings other than Christ congenital sinners.[5] As Augustine argued, this distortion centers on our desires: rather than desiring God above all things, we desire lesser goods; and it is because of this fundamental distortion of desire that we sin. In short, we commit *actual* sins because our desire has been corrupted by *original* sin, and our willing follows our desires (i.e., in the final analysis we always will what we desire, even when we wish our desires were other than they are).[6]

And yet though original sin is in this way the ontological ground of actual sins, it does not determine their form. Since original sin is distinct from all forms of actual sin, there is no possibility of defining it in terms of any particular type of act or attitude. Inasmuch as the doctrine of original sin implies that *every* human act and attitude is sinful, there is simply no basis for singling out any one particular subset of human behaviors (those that manifest some form of self-assertion, for example) as more indicative of humanity's congenital sinfulness than any other. Indeed, any such claims would directly undercut the doctrine of original sin by suggesting that some people (viz., those who displayed less of whatever behavior is judged to encapsulate the essence of sin) are less in need of redemption than others. Thus, in the same way that original sin cannot be derived from an examination of actual sin, so the knowledge of original sin allows no conclusions to be drawn about the form actual sin will take in any given instance.

It might seem that this line of reasoning simply brings us back to the problem of original sin's tendencies to ethical quietism: where all are equally sinful, it makes no sense to highlight any one person's sin over anyone else's, and attempts to address particular manifestations of sin seem correspondingly pointless. Yet further consideration suggests that the inability to identify original sin with any particular form of actual sin can actually work to promote ethical activism. After all, it is a crucial dimension of Christian piety that God's forgiveness of sin is inseparable from our repenting of it. This is not to say that forgiveness and repentance are a matter of economic exchange, as though God agreed to overlook our transgressions as a kind of payment for some feeling or expression of sorrow on our part. Repentance and forgiveness are two dimensions of a single event rather than a sequence describing a theological *quid pro quo*.[7] As two sides of a coin, however, they are inseparable: to receive forgiveness for a sin is impossible without knowing that sin for which one is being forgiven; and to know something one has done as a sin is to reject it as incompatible with one's identity as a child of God by repenting of it. From this perspective, to say that we sin in everything we do, but that God forgives our sin is theologically true, but existentially vacuous, because it leaves out the content of the sin for which forgiveness is offered. In order for God's forgiveness to be good news to us (i.e., something that actually meets us in and rescues us from our sin), we have to know *how* we sinned; and in knowing ourselves forgiven, we cannot help but seek to eradicate from our lives the sin that required such great mercy on God's part.[8]

An example may help to clarify this picture of the existential dynamics of sin and forgiveness. Suppose I help a blind person to cross a busy street. From an Augustinian position, that act was sinful, because, owing to the pervasive character of original sin, all my acts are sinful. As such, it requires forgiveness. But what exactly needs to be forgiven? To say that my deed was sinful is not necessarily to imply that I shouldn't have helped the person across the street. How then did I sin? One can imagine all sorts of possible ways. Perhaps I was condescending or arrogant in my attitude toward the person. Or maybe I was preoccupied with appearing virtuous in the eyes of some onlooker. Or my actions may have been motivated by fear that God would punish me if I failed to be of assistance. The possibilities are manifold. How then do I know where the problem lies? The answer is that I don't! Indeed, that's the real upshot of an Augustinian insistence on radical sinfulness: that sin is so much a part of who I am ("original" to my very being) that it is impossible for me to anticipate its particular form simply by virtue of a dogmatic knowledge of my sinfulness. And yet I can't hear the message that my sin is forgiven as good news for me unless I know wherein my sin lies. Otherwise, the message of forgiveness remains an abstraction that can gain no traction on my particular circumstances. Since my very sinfulness means that I lack the resources to gain this knowledge on my own, it follows that I come to know it only as I am told about it by someone else. How does that happen?

It is a classic feature of Christian tradition (based on passages like Rom. 3:20) that one way I come to know my sin is that God tells me of it through the law, which (in the words of Philipp Melanchthon) "always accuses."[9] Yet the knowledge of my sin that comes to me in this way is evidently general and imperfect, as suggested by Paul's observation that his lack of awareness of any transgression does not make him excused (1 Cor. 4:6). The possibilities of sin are simply too numerous for any finite code to be able to encompass them all and give us sure and concrete knowledge of how in fact our deeds fall short of God's glory. In the face both of sin's intractability and of the sinner's capacity for self-deception, some more immediate source of knowledge is necessary to identify the locus of sin in individual cases. Jesus' instructions to his disciples on how to manage their life together suggests that in practice this source is our neighbor – that we depend on each other to learn about our sins:

> "If another member of the church sins against you, go and point out the fault when the two of you are alone. If the member listens to you, you have regained that one. But if you are not listened to, take one or two others along with you, so that every word may be confirmed by the evidence of two or three witnesses. If the member refuses to listen to them, tell it to the church; and if the offender refuses to listen even to the church, let such a one be to you as a Gentile and a tax-collector." (Matt. 18:15–17)

In short, the one who is sinned against has an obligation to confront the sinner, and the sinner has an obligation to listen. The lesson seems clear: How do I know when I have sinned? When someone who is afflicted by my sin tells me so.

Feminist critiques of patriarchy in general and traditional Christian theologies in particular are a case in point. Though the biblical insistence on the fundamental equality of women and men in Christ (Gen. 3:28) arguably should have stimulated men to question women's subordination in church and society, those benefiting from a system of male privilege were able to make use of other passages (e.g., 1 Cor. 14:34–5; 1 Tim. 2:8–12, 15) as seemingly ready-made defenses of the patriarchal social order. That such arrangements are, in fact, not pleasing to God and should be confessed as sin became widely recognized only when women bore witness to their profoundly damaging effects. Further examples of the power of self-deception and self-interest to keep human beings willingly complicit in sin could be multiplied almost indefinitely, but each bears witness to this same principle: that sin is *acknowledged* only when and as it is *named* as a source of painful exclusion from the fullness of life that is God's will for all people (John 10:10).[10]

Needless to say, the claim that we come fully to know our sins only as those who feel its effects identify our actions as sinful does not mean that every naming of sin is accurate. After all, Augustinian doctrine maintains that the one who claims to be the victim of sin is herself a sinner and may therefore be mistaken in her assessment of a particular situation. In this context, one might see Jesus' instructions that accusations of sin, when rebuffed, need to be renewed in the presence of witnesses as an implicit recognition that an individual's identification of sin is open to contestation, which is to be resolved by widening the circle of conversation to include other parties. The point remains, however, that it is only by acknowledging the essential unknowability of one's own sin apart from the reality of its being challenged and confronted by those who feel its effects that meaningful engagement with that sin is possible. Joerg Rieger has given voice to this principle in his injunction that theological reflection begins by asking "what hurts" – seeking to find where it is that pain disfigures the human project.[11] In a more specifically hamartiological vein, Stephen Ray has proposed a set of protocols for responsible sin-talk that center on opening oneself up to the voices of those who suffer from sin, on the grounds that those who feel sin's impact are in a much better position to identify the dynamics of its operation than those insulated from its effects.[12] Thus, even as it is no accident that women remain in the forefront of naming the evils of sexism, so what attention to racism is present in mainstream theological discourse can be attributed to the interventions of persons of color; and the same pattern recurs with respect to questions of (for example) disability, sexual orientation, and ethnicity.

In summary, original sin produces actual sin, but its distinction from actual sin makes it impossible both for anyone to predict the form of actual sin it will produce in any given instance, and for the sinner in particular to have accurate knowledge of her own sin apart from dialogue with others. One can, of course, understand something of the genesis of particular forms of actual sin in retrospect. It is in this context that liberal and liberationist accounts of sin as a product of environmental (especially cultural and socio-economic) factors are helpful. Original sin dictates that the will turns away from God, but how it turns away depends on the desires that are present to it, and these are a function of environment. Thus, those whose social position places them in the ranks of those sinned against will not be in a position to commit as many of the sins as the more powerful who afflict them (so that, for example, in a patriarchal society men will be led to sin in ways that women are not, and vice versa). They will all *sin*, because their desiring is turned away from God; but they will sin *differently*, because their concrete situations present them with different objects of desire. The situation is analogous to a set of balls at the top of a hill: gravity will cause them all to roll downward, but their individual trajectories will vary depending on the topography they encounter along the way.[13]

## Original Sin as Unbelief

Having come this far, it is necessary to pause and consider a possible objection to this line of argument. I have maintained that the identification of original sin with a fundamental distortion of hypostasis that is prior to (though the enabling condition of) the commission of any actual sin precludes its identification with any form of actual sin. For example, it is not legitimate to see every actual sin as a manifestation of an "original sin" of pride. Indeed, attempts to understand original sin in such terms are pastorally dangerous in at least two respects. First, they tend to divert attention from the damage sin inflicts on others to the inner state of the sinner as the immediate focus of pastoral attention. Second, they tend to homogenize the situations of different sinners by virtue of this focus on a putatively common "root sin." In both ways, invoking original sin as a means of providing a universal diagnosis of actual sin impedes productive engagement with the latter: original sin becomes a motive for turning away from the concrete particularities of actual sin in exactly the way that critics of Augustinianism charge.

And yet it might seem that the line of argument I have been developing thus far does not in fact succeed in maintaining the strict line of demarcation between original and actual sin necessary to meet this line of criticism. After all, I have defined original sin as a turning of the will away from God as the ultimate object of human desire. It would therefore seem to follow that original sin *can* be identified with a particular form of actual sin: the sin of unbelief. In fact, this understanding of original sin is prominent in the Augustinian tradition. John Calvin, for example, argued that all actual sin originates in unfaithfulness (which he also identified as the primal sin of Adam),[14] and contemporary feminist theologian Serene Jones continues this trajectory when she defines unfaithfulness as the essence of sin.[15] Doesn't such language reintroduce the kind of conflation of original and actual sin that (I have argued) must be avoided if the doctrine of original sin is to prove theologically credible?

In order to return a negative answer to this question, it is necessary to distinguish the unbelief (or unfaithfulness) of original sin from a particular act of the will (i.e., an actual sin), and, correlatively, to show that such unbelief can be conceived as the prior condition of all such acts. As a first step, it is important to make it clear that the unbelief of original sin has nothing to do with a refusal to believe certain things *about* God or the world. In other words, where original sin is concerned, *un*belief must not be confused with *wrong* belief, which, as a particular movement of the will by which assent to a statement is given or withheld, is an actual sin. The congenital resistance to God that defines original sin is not a matter of doctrinal error, any more than the faith in God by which it is defeated is reducible to assent to a set of dogmatic propositions.

So far so good, except that the faith that justifies the sinner is, by common consent, a matter of trust in God's promise of forgiveness; and trust *is* unquestionably an act of the will, even if, in Augustinian perspective, the will is able to trust God only because God enables it to do so through the gift of grace. It would seem to follow that the resistance to God that this grace overcomes is equally an act of the will, but such an inference is not licit. Indeed, the very fact that grace is necessary to turn the will to God points to the illegitimacy of equating the unbelief that grace overcomes with an act of the will. To be sure, the will, unaided by grace, invariably turns away from God, with each concrete instance of willing constituting an actual sin; but this very inevitability indicates that the resistance to God that produces these sins is prior (and thus irreducible) to any particular act of willing. The overcoming of this resistance through grace is indeed an act – the act of faith – but that which is overcome is not in itself an act, but an ontological state that so determines action as to make grace the only possible antidote.

This way of distinguishing the unbelief of original sin from actual sin provides a framework within which it is possible to avoid the kind of ethical abstraction that tends to follow when original sin and actual sin are conflated. When original sin is equated with pride, for example, then it is natural enough to advocate humility as a general prophylactic aimed at minimizing its effects, with the result – rightly castigated by many modern critics of Augustinianism both inside and outside the church – that the poor are given the same advice as the rich who oppress them, thereby masking the sin of the latter (since their everyday participation in and furtherance of processes of social marginalization are viewed as unproblematic, so long as they are undertaken with a measure of personal reserve) while tending to misdiagnose the sins of the former (since any actions they undertake to challenge the status quo are interpreted as manifestations of pride). By contrast, where original sin is understood as unbelief, it makes no sense to prescribe belief as the appropriate response, since belief cannot be correlated with generalizable attitudes or forms of behavior in the way that humility can. For to believe (i.e., to trust in or be faithful to God) is to conform to God's will, and, as has been emphasized throughout this book, the fact that each person is called to her own particular and utterly unique place in the body of Christ means that the content of God's will for each person is resistant to framing in terms of universally applicable injunctions.[16]

This last point might seem overstated. For while one might grant that the particular shape of conformity to God's will varies from person to person, it does so only within definite limits. After all, even if belief does not have a fixed form, insofar as it is defined as conformity to God's will, any transgression of God's commandments would seem to constitute a clear violation of that will and, therefore, evidence of unbelief. In this way, the commandments would seem to provide a negative criterion of belief by virtue of their capacity to identify instances where God's will has been violated. Thus, although the fact that a person refrains from murder does not (according to the Sermon on the Mount) acquit her of having violated the Decalogue, surely the act of killing constitutes a clear violation of God's will (see, in addition to Exod. 20:13 and Deut. 5:17, Gen. 9:6). Yet the biblical picture is not so clear, given that God explicitly praises Abraham for his willingness to sacrifice Isaac (Gen. 22:15–18).[17] One might also cite Jacob's deception of Isaac (Gen. 27:6–33) and Hosea's taking "a wife of whoredom" (Hos. 1:2) as further instances of behavior that is evidently divinely approved (and in the case of Hosea, divinely enjoined) while sitting uneasily with the basic principles of God's law.[18] All these examples serve as a reminder that God's will is not bound to any list of commandments, and that true piety will recognize God's freedom in this regard. Thus, when cursed by Shimei during his ignominious flight from Absalom, David has the wisdom to observe, "If he is cursing because the Lord has said to him, 'Curse David,' who then shall say, 'Why have you done so?'... Let him alone, and let him curse; for the Lord has bidden him" (2 Sam. 16:10–11).[19]

The point of these observations is not to undercut the seriousness of God's law, or to suggest that it can simply be disregarded as irrelevant to human moral orientation. It is, however, to challenge their reliability of using the Ten Commandments (or any other list of moral injunctions) as an infallible index of any particular individual's standing before God. In short, in the same way that consciousness of our inherent sinfulness means that we can never view our own seemingly good deeds as evidence of belief, consciousness of God's freedom means that we cannot presume to interpret the seemingly sinful deeds of others as evidence of unbelief. This does not rule out practical efforts to proscribe or restrain sinful behavior (e.g., I may concede theologically the possibility that a thief is acting in accordance with God's will and yet judge politically that such a person should be restrained[20]), nor does it render pointless Christian preaching of the Commandments as genuinely reflecting God's will (in accordance with, e.g., Deut. 6:4–9; Matt. 5:19). It does, however, block any attempt to gauge the relative sinfulness of any individual by reference to the degree to which she appears to follow the Commandments, because it rejects any correlation of original sin with the kind of empirically identifiable faults that are named by the Commandments and subject to quantitative variation across individuals. Because original sin is the cause and condition of *all* postlapsarian human willing, any suggestion that there might be differences between individuals with respect to the level of their affliction by original sin is illegitimate. Differences in sin are significant only with respect to the concrete effects they have on the well-being of others, and not as an index of an individual's standing before God.

At the same time, *equality* in sinfulness does not imply *identity* in sinfulness. Here again it is important to remember (in line with the conclusions of Chapter 5) that original sin, precisely because it is genuinely sin, cannot be understood as a defect in nature that afflicts all persons in the same way. The distorted desires (and thus the sin) that characterize the fallen state lie with the hypostasis, in a lack of fit between the particular desires upon which the person willingly acts and God's will for that person. In other words, the source of that mismatch in willing is the agent herself, insofar as her distorted desires are irreducibly hers. The perversion of the hypostasis that constitutes original sin is one in which the hypostasis fails to desire (and therefore to will) in accordance with God's desire for it. Since God's desire for each hypostasis (viz., its proper place in the body of Christ) is unique, it follows that the original sin of each human being is correspondingly unique, issuing in actual sins that, while certainly capable of being compared and categorized with the sins of others, manifest each individual's own specific form of resistance to God. From this perspective, nothing could be further from the truth than to conceive original sin as some sort of general defect spread equally across the whole of humankind. Rather, in the same way that human beings' fundamental equality before God does not lie in some intrinsic characteristic, but in the extrinsic reality of God's call, so humanity's common defection from God does not lie in a common vice, but in each person's resistance to that call – a resistance that is equal to others' only in the fact of its being resistance, and not by reference to any of the actual sins through which that resistance is realized.

In this way, the specificity of the form of original sin to the individual is a corollary of its status as unbelief. Again, unbelief is nothing other than resistance to God's will (concretely, a failure to trust in and rely on God's will as one's ultimate good). But God's will for each individual is not reducible to any generalized list of commandments. This is not to say that the content of the divine will is in any way vague or uncertain; on the contrary, its resistance to being exhausted by any convenient list of rules derives from the fact that God's will has a particular shape for every moment of a person's existence, not only holding her in being but accompanying and directing her to her appointed end. It is therefore precisely the concrete specificity of God's will for each human hypostasis that renders any abstraction of the individual person's congenital resistance to that will in terms of some universalizable proto-sin illegitimate. Quite simply, what *counts* as resistance to God's will is irreducibly different for each person (e.g., one is called to marriage, another is not) and, indeed, varies from moment to moment within a person's life (e.g., one is called to marriage at 41, but not at 14).[21]

This understanding of original sin is further illuminated by Paul's claim that "whatever does not proceed from faith is sin" (Rom. 14:23). Paul makes this point in the context of arguing that a particular action (viz., eating meat) in itself neither commends us to nor alienates us from God: what matters is not the act, but the faith of the actor. This does not mean, however, that the subjective disposition of the actor is the operative criterion, as though one could justify a particular line of behavior simply by persuading oneself of its virtue.[22] Here as elsewhere in Scripture faith is defined by its *object*: what renders an action faithful is its correspondence to God's will. Thus, Paul's point in addressing the Romans is not that a particular behavior is indifferent, or even that its merits are to be assessed based on a personal estimation of its effects on the neighbor, but rather that its faithfulness is a matter of the individual's discernment of God's will for her. The doctrine of original sin provides a framework within which to apply this point regarding the need for discernment to the problem of faith more broadly. Because of original sin, we are unable to act from faith (and thus to know what it means to be faithful) on our own. Locked in unbelief, we are none of us able to avoid sin. The good news is that God has not left us in our sin. In Christ God has forgiven our sin and given us faith that frees us, however hesitantly and imperfectly, to know and do God's will. In sin we are deaf to God's call. By faith we are enabled to hear it.

## Vocation and the Defeat of Sin

While original sin is widely understood in both popular culture and traditional dogmatics as a common sin, the upshot of my argument is that such a characterization is true only in a very restricted sense. As unbelief, original sin is "common" to all human beings only in the way that having a personality is: as a feature of human nature that points precisely to each person's irreducible particularity. Thus, far from being some sort of shared defect – a kind of hamartiological lowest common denominator – that can be factored out when addressing the concrete details of a person's failure to follow God's will, original sin is that aspect of our being which pinpoints this failure most directly. In contrast to the personal specificity of original sin, the many actual sins (murder, adultery, theft, falsehood, and the like) that issue from it can in some respect be generalized across cases. Original sin resists any such generalization, because the unbelief at its heart is that of a specific hypostasis resisting God's specific, concrete, and utterly unique will for her in particular. In this way, original sin is at bottom a rejection of God's call, and it is defeated when and as that call is heeded. In other words, its defeat is the realization of one's *vocation*: God's calling to a particular form of life.

This correlation of the defeat of original sin with the living out of vocation is not meant to bypass the categories of justification (the forgiveness of sin) and sanctification (the sinner's transformation to holy living) that figure centrally in most Christian accounts of salvation. It does, however, suggest that the relationship among all these categories should be rethought, with vocation serving as the fundamental soteriological concept governing the interpretation of justification and sanctification. Because in most traditional accounts original sin is understood as a defect of *nature* shared indifferently by all human beings, justification all too easily comes to be understood as the generic forgiveness of an equally generic sinfulness, and sanctification as a no less general course of moral improvement for the forgiven sinner. In such a scheme vocation fades into the background, emerging only as a secondary modification of human life overlaid on these more foundational soteriological realities. By contrast, vocation becomes primary when original sin is understood as a distortion of the *hypostasis*: a person-specific resistance to God's call that is overcome only when and as that call is heard and obeyed. Within this perspective justification and sanctification name, respectively, the concrete acts of hearing and obedience through which, by grace, the believer is empowered to respond to God's call. In other words, they name the events by which God, in calling a person, forgives *her particular form* of resistance to God (justification) and marks out *her particular course* of future action (sanctification).

By virtue of this emphasis on the concrete and specific, viewing original sin as a failure of vocation rather than as a kind of background noise that has to be addressed before questions of vocation can be broached also has the potential to render treatments of justification less liable to overlook the costliness of grace and make discussions of sanctification less legalistic. In the effort to forestall any correlation of forgiveness of sin with human merit, classical Protestant emphases on justification by faith all too often had the unfortunate consequence of suggesting that the defeat of original sin was a process that did not involve the activity of the sinner herself in any significant way. Later Protestant insistence on justification by faith all too often reinforced this misunderstanding by abstracting the power of grace from even the formalities of baptism. The result, as Dietrich Bonhoeffer famously lamented, was "grace as bargain-basement goods, cut-rate forgiveness … doled out by careless hands without hesitation or limit."[23] Justification was thereby transformed from the constant accompaniment of Christian existence into its presupposition. This (characteristically Lutheran) misunderstanding of justification as a blank check that settles all accounts permanently in advance risked rendering everything that followed – all the particular decisions, acts, and commitments of a person's life – theologically superfluous, thereby evacuating vocation of its soteriological significance. Alternatively, a (more typically Reformed) stress on sanctification could lead to equally problematic conclusions. For example, the idea that certain forms of behavior might count as evidence of saving faith (the so-called "practical syllogism") could easily generate a narrow and rigid moralism, the practical effect of which was to equate the fulfillment of one's vocation with conformity to a limited set of well-established social roles. Under the former option original sin fails to be taken seriously as *sin* that continues to threaten a person; under the latter it fails to be understood as *original* and is confused with particular examples of actual sin.

Bonhoeffer understood that taking seriously the theology of the Reformers (especially Luther) ruled out from the start any construal of the relationship between justification and sanctification, faith and obedience, as a two-step process in which the latter followed the former. Instead, he insisted on their close interconnection, arguing that it was necessary to give equal attention to obedience as a condition of faith and to faith as a condition of obedience.[24] Implicit in this perspective on salvation is an understanding of the relationship between faith and obedience in which both alike were seen as a function of vocation. For Bonhoeffer the call of Jesus, exemplified in the summons to the disciples, is the point at which belief and obedience alike make their appearance. "Follow me!" is a summons that can be obeyed or disobeyed, but the fact of obedience is inseparable from faith in the one who calls. For how can a person follow without faith? And how can faith be present apart from the following?[25]

And yet while all are called to follow, what it means to follow is not the same for all. Paul's vocation was different from Peter's, and both are different from yours or mine. And because the content of the call is different for everyone, the concrete form that justification and sanctification take for each person is different as well. This certainly does not mean that everyone is justified by a different grace or answers to a different Lord, for all are members of the one body. Nevertheless, what it means concretely for Paul to be justified is as irreducibly particular as any of the finer points of his vocation, since justification is simply a way of speaking of the concrete fact of his having been called by God to life with God in spite of his sin.[26] It is for this reason – because justification is a function of vocation – that the faith by which this justification is received is inseparable from the obedience whereby one responds to God's call; for only in responding does one acknowledge that call – and the justification it implies – as genuinely to and for oneself. The form that sanctification takes will be similarly relative to each person's vocation and therefore remain a matter of discernment that is irreducible to (however much it may be informed by) already existing conventions of Christian piety.

The doctrine of original sin deepens Christian reflection on vocation by reminding us that resistance to God's will is (and, apart from grace, remains) our natural inclination. And precisely because it is our natural inclination, we are blind to its reality except insofar as it is called to our attention. This is not, of course, to say that we are altogether ignorant of our actions or incapable of seeing their effects, but it is to acknowledge our difficulty in identifying either as manifestations of sin. In this context, the "naturalness" of original sin is its most significant danger, because it vitiates our capacity to distinguish ourselves from our sin sufficiently to be able to see our actions as resistance to God's will. Of course, God's commandments remain a warning against particular sins, but, once again, original sin cannot be correlated with any of those sins in a way that would permit God's law to be used as an index of individual sinfulness. In addition to the radical teachings of the Sermon on the Mount, Jesus' words to the rich young man who had "kept all" the commandments "from [his] youth" (Mark 10:20) point to the fruitlessness of seeing any list of moral precepts as capable of insulating us from the power of sin. To suppose that such a list might do so only bears witness to the depth of sin's hold on us, by revealing both our failure to appreciate our own bondage, and our short-sightedness in imagining ourselves to be fundamentally autonomous beings who are able to chart their own moral course and need God only as a source of information regarding the relevant traffic regulations.

A proper theology of vocation challenges this vision of human autonomy. If human beings are truly creatures of God, then they can no more find fulfillment apart from God than a fish can flourish outside of water. And like water for a fish, God is for human beings not merely a supplemental part of the picture – a guide or auxiliary who supplies some (or even very many) of the pieces that give wholeness to human life. As the One in whom we live and move and have our being (Acts 17:28), God gives human life whatever substance, direction, and meaning it has at every point, and thus provides and sustains every human vocation in its entirety, from beginning to end. This identification of vocation with the whole of a person's life as conceived, enabled, and, ultimately, glorified by God means that in the same way original sin cannot be identified with a particular actual sin, so vocation cannot be identified with any particular role one plays: I am a father, a son, a brother, a husband, a citizen, a teacher; but none of these exhausts my vocation, even though all may and should manifest it – albeit with the same sort of partiality and imperfection that my actual sins manifest my original sin. My vocation is simply the whole of my life under God as one who has been called to be a member of Christ's body. As such, it is known to God from all eternity, but it will be known to me, fully and finally, only when it has been completed in glory. Before then both I and others come to know it only slowly and with a great admixture of error – though by grace glimpses of the whole may appear to encourage me along the way.

Yet there remains more to be said about the way in which this calling is lived out. Insofar as my vocation (however it may play out) is to be a member of Christ's body, it is intimately bound up not only with the God who calls, but also with all the other members of that body. Whatever my vocation may be, once its specifically Christological form is recognized, it follows that I can only live it out in coordination with all the other members whom God has called to places in the body different from yet directly impinging on my own.[27] In part this conclusion is simply a consequence of the fact that Jesus is no longer on earth to call any of us directly as the first disciples were called, so that God's call to each of us is invariably mediated through and discerned in conversation with other persons in the power of Jesus' Spirit. Yet for Jesus' first disciples no less than for us, an individual's flourishing is inseparable from the building up of the whole body – ultimately guaranteed and empowered by God but never experienced or understood apart from others. It follows that my vocation cannot be considered credible unless it displays some capacity to promote the flourishing of those around me.[28]

In its all-encompassing character original sin is the shadow of vocation and, as such, is the supreme impediment to my discerning both the will of God and the conditions of others' flourishing. Because it is a defect, a failure, an unfathomable intrusion upon the human beings God intended, it is only a shadow. It is not an equal partner, a parallel dark force that (as the Manichaeans thought) struggles with the light. It has no basis in our nature and therefore can only pervert it, as a mode of our nature's existence that drives it self-destructively to non-existence. As a shadow, it is readily dispersed by the light of God's call; indeed, it only clearly appears *as* a shadow by virtue of that light's shining. Yet in its perversity it remains deadly serious to the sinner and those around her. For if to have a vocation is to be called (in whatever unique, irreplaceable, and counterintuitive way) to build up the body of Christ, to sin is not simply to subvert one's own existence under God, but also to threaten the existence of all the body's members. The drive toward non-existence at the heart of sin ineluctably carries others along in its wake, so that if our salvation is ultimately linked with others in the body of Christ, our damnation implicates them no less – a point which resonates with Jesus' dire warning about the consequences of causing others to stumble.[29]

In the full extent of its perversion, our original sin, like the vocation it shadows, is known fully only to God, and to ourselves only piecemeal – as it is forgiven. And yet in the same way that our vocation comes into focus as we take on roles that contribute to the upbuilding of Christ's body in and through our engagement with other people inside and outside the church, so our sin comes into focus as we become aware of how our actions disrupt and damage that body through the pain and suffering of its members. Here again the commandments are a guide, but only a partial one. Ultimately, the intimate connection between vocation and original sin that arises from the latter's status as the refusal of vocation means that these two features of our existence are known in tandem, as our discernment of our callings, however imperfect and partial, brings into focus the ways in which we turn from them. In this way, every calling entails a commitment to work against sin, since to follow God's will is *eo ipso* to reject that which violates it. Thus, every calling, rightly discerned, cannot but include the commitment to confront those sins in which the individual comes to recognize herself as complicit. If we take this point seriously, we must look for guidance on how to combat sin from all quarters, but pre-eminently from those whom it harms and who thus are most familiar with the way it breaks down the body of Christ. Thus, we come to know both our sin and the calling that is the ground of its defeat through openness to the voices of others.

Having made this point, it must immediately be added that the utterly gracious character of vocation precludes the possibility that any actions we undertake can guarantee accurate knowledge of the shape of our calling or the character of our sin; but it does not follow that what we do is a matter of indifference. To the extent that the church takes seriously both the significance of individual callings and the power of sin to thwart their being heeded, its common life will include a range of concrete practices designed to facilitate attention to God's call. I have elsewhere termed such practices "protocols of discernment": patterns of behavior that an ongoing history of communal reflection and experience render relatively well defined, and yet which also retain a considerable degree of flexibility in execution.[30] Among these protocols are practices typically undertaken by the community as a whole, like the veneration of saints (who provide concrete examples of the wide range of Christian vocations) and service to the poor (whose social marginalization makes their perspective a vital point of reference for Christian identification of sin). Also included are more personally focused practices of spiritual direction and friendship (including, for example, marriage), which allow a more intimate context for conversation and critique based on a relationship of committed familiarity and mutual vulnerability. Foundational to all such practices, moreover, is the disciplined reading of Scripture, which provides the fundamental point of reference for knowing God's will for humanity as revealed in the person of Jesus Christ. An individual's participation in the broadest possible range of such protocols (and there is no set limit to their number or form) helps to bring the fullness of Christian experience to bear on the discernment of vocation.

Of course (and as has already been noted), there is nothing infallible about other people's perspectives, since they, too are afflicted by original sin. Even when the feedback we receive about the shape of our vocations comes by way of tried and tested ecclesiastical protocols, there is no guarantee that it will necessarily reflect God's will for us. Here, too, the doctrine of original sin is helpful in that it builds in a certain amount of skepticism with respect to others' opinions. Such skepticism is especially important in relation to the opinions of the powerful, whose position of privilege renders them less likely to be open to those new or unexpected manifestations of God's will that, by bringing new realities to the fore, invariably threaten the status quo. By the same logic, belief in original sin demands particular openness to the complaints of those on the underside of history, whose position on the margins of society is an index of their particular vulnerability to sin's effects.[31]

Thus, while such guidelines can never be taken as absolute, they highlight the degree to which Christian belief in sin's pervasiveness has very practical implications. Specifically, a church that confesses original sin will have as one of its primary tasks fostering an appreciation of the possibility that even the most longstanding practices, regarded as innocent or even virtuous by those engaged in them, may be manifestations of the grossest sin.[32] As already noted, the systematic marginalization of women from positions of public power in Western culture was long justified as the proper way of honoring women's distinctiveness. Similarly, Westerners defended the conquest and enslavement of non-European peoples as a means to spread the virtues of Western culture in general and the Christian faith in particular. Their sinful character was not revealed by virtue of the perpetrators' own capacities for introspection, but as those affected by such practices rejected their pretense to righteousness, thereby forcing those responsible for them to acknowledge them as sin. Similar processes are visible today in the rejection of heterosexism by gay and lesbian persons, who argue that the work of the Spirit in same-sex relationships is evident in the fruit they bear in the church – as is also the damage to individuals and the community caused by their exclusion from the church.[33]

Of course (and as all of these examples show), the process by which such sin is recognized and addressed is rarely quick, smooth, or unaccompanied by continued – and, quite often, increased – suffering on the part of those who are its victims. For communities as well as individuals, recognizing sin as sin, and thereby discerning the proper form of calling, is a process that is halting and uncertain. There is not even any guarantee that the direction of movement will always be in the right direction.[34] Certainly the biblical witness suggests that the power of sin will be no less pervasive and powerful at the end of history than in its midst, and that ultimately it will be divine action rather than the efforts of human beings that will bring its reign to an end (see, e.g., Rev. 19:11–21, 20:7–10; cf. 1 Cor. 15:23–6). Yet this point does nothing to dispense human beings from the work, however effective or ineffective it may appear, of pursuing God's call and (thereby) battling sin when and as sin's presence is disclosed to them.[35] Because for Christians the knowledge of sin is a reflex of the good news of God's victorious grace, it can never be something before which the individual bows her head in resignation, but must always be taken as an occasion for determined, steady, and forthright resistance.

## Conclusion

Why should Christians continue to talk about original sin? As should be clear from the foregoing, original sin as a dimension of Christian doctrine has nothing to do with promoting a spirit of pessimism regarding the human prospect, or of passivity before the enormity of evil in the world. On the contrary, such attitudes, under whatever confessional banner they may be put forth, are evidence of a profound failure to appreciate the significance of original sin, for they implicitly (or even explicitly) take sin as the primary reality of human being. For Christians, however, original sin should be understood as in every respect secondary: a shadow cast by human beings that is known in its absolute depravity and hopelessness (for it certainly does mark human beings as depraved and hopeless) only as it is dispelled by the light of the gospel. It has no proper place in human nature either as made by God or as destined by God for glory; and because it is the root of all actual sin, it is taken seriously by Christians only to the extent that they view it as something which has been excluded by God from the outset. It is therefore properly acknowledged when it is confronted as an object to be met with firm resistance and never with humble acquiescence.

Of course, because human beings are sinners, their knowledge of sin is never something acquired once and for all in this life. That Christ must always be preached to the lifelong Christian no less than to the neophyte reflects the fact that the shadow of original sin is never extinguished prior to glory. Indeed, the pervasiveness of human sin is such that its presence is all too easily overlooked, especially by those who (in perhaps the most insidious instance of sin) view their attendance on the good news of Jesus Christ as evidence that they have somehow acquired an advantage over or distance from sin that others lack. Taking seriously the gospel as news that is always supremely relevant to me at every point of my earthly pilgrimage demands the confession that sin's hold on my life is every bit as firm as its hold on the unbeliever – and that the grace by which its grip is broken claims the unbeliever no less than the greatest saint.

All this is not to imply that the point of the gospel is to remind us how sinful we are. The good news is not that we are sinners, but that we have been called by God (as *justified* sinners) to live a new life in Christ. The gospel does not serve the doctrine of original sin; original sin, if it has any place at all in Christian teaching, is legitimate only to the extent that it serves the gospel. This book is an attempt to show how, in the face of a range of plausible objections, the doctrine of original sin can render such service. Three points in particular have been noted.

First, original sin highlights *human solidarity under God*. In the face of the temptation to view some as nearer to God than others, or to establish hierarchies according to which the sin of some renders them less worthy of divine regard than others, the doctrine of original sin insists that no one has any greater claim on God than anyone else. On the contrary, all persons, however apparently corrupt and far from God they may appear, demand the Christian's compassion in the knowledge that all are the object of God's compassion, and that what is valued by God can never be an object of indifference or hatred to us.

Second, original sin forces us to rethink *the character of our integrity as moral agents*. Contrary to what we might wish to believe, we are not masters in our own house, because our power to shape who we are through our willing is illusory. To be sure, who we are is inseparable from what we will, but to determine what we will is not itself within the compass of our willing. The doctrine of original sin demands that we recognize that where our identities are most at stake – in what we love above all else – our wills have no power of their own to turn to God. And yet insofar as God's love for us does not depend upon (and is rather the cause of) our love for God, original sin also reminds us how much our identities are a gift, albeit a gift that we are called to work out and develop in loving response to the love that has called us into being. In this way, far from undermining our agency, the doctrine of original sin sets it in its proper light, as a love that is called into and sustained in being by a prior love, as a freedom realized through the grace that enables us to live out that love, and as a task that in its completion is always received and acknowledged as a gift.

Third, in the face of the myriad ways in which evil cloaks itself in goodness and triumphs through inertia and indifference, original sin provides *a spur to rouse us from moral complacency*. For if our lives are called by love into love, our response to that love is rendered impotent by original sin. Precisely because original sin is at bottom our failure to respond to (or even to acknowledge) God's call as that call confronts us at every point in our lives, sin threatens at every point in our lives in ways that cannot be anticipated by even the most thorough list of moral precepts. Indeed, so powerful is sin that any such list can itself be turned to its service. By keeping this reality before us, original sin alerts us to our inability to plumb our own depths, of our endless capacity for self-deception, and our consequent need to listen to others deliberately, patiently, and with humility in order both to gauge the depth of our sin and to engage together in the work of building up the body of Christ.

In all these ways (and quite in contrast to its reputation), original sin reminds us that God's word of grace is never generic, never to be understood as a principle that applies to all, willy-nilly, but always a word to and for a particular person, summoning *me*, summoning *you*, summoning those of whose existence we have no inkling away from the dead end of our fallenness into the new and glorious (if also rigorous and challenging) life of the children of God. In all this it remains imperative to distinguish in the sharpest possible way original sin from the gospel. It is not good news that we are sinners, and the realities of human solidarity, of the sheer giftedness of human existence, of our dependence on engagement with one another under God for our mutual flourishing are all matters of Christian anthropology that hold even apart from the fall and sin. And yet the content of the good news for us as fallen people is precisely that these truths continue to hold – and to work, by God's grace, to our benefit – in spite of our sin, that our inexplicable rejection of God's will for us can present no insuperable obstacle to the vindication of that will. To be sure, all this is good news that we need not have known, and that we must confess, in light of the incalculable suffering caused by human sin, it would have been better never to have known. But as we have in fact come to know it in Jesus Christ, we have a glimpse of a mystery that can only call forth wonder: God's capacity not merely to call life into being where life is absent, but to uphold life even where it has been rejected. The point of confessing this mystery is not to make us ashamed, for if Christ is not ashamed to call us brothers and sisters (Heb. 2:11), there is no place for shame on our part. It is simply to help us to be patient, honest, and vigilant as we live under God and with one another. The gospel allows no more from the doctrine of original sin, but it also requires no less.

## Notes

1. In the same way, an individual's status as a citizen of a country is not something that can be deduced with certainty on the basis of any behaviors she performs, but only by reference to an external affirmation of her status by some duly constituted authority.
2. This line of reasoning lay at the heart of Luther's inflexible opposition to all forms of popular revolt: "For insurrection lacks discernment; it generally harms the innocent more than the guilty ... It always results in more damage than improvement." Martin Luther, "A Sincere Admonition by Martin Luther to All Christians to Guard Against Insurrection and Rebellion," in *The Christian in Society II*, vol. 45 of *Luther's Works*, American edn., ed. Walther I. Brandt (Philadelphia, PA: Fortress Press, 1962), pp. 62–3.
3. A primary source for this tendency to conflate original and actual sin is the historical identification of original sin with the sin of Adam and Eve. After all, if the *original* sin of postlapsarian humanity is understood as identical with the *actual* sin committed by the first human beings, then the two are distinct only with respect to the mode by which individual accountability (*reatus*) is acquired (viz., directly in the case of actual sin, indirectly in the case of original sin), but not in terms of the fundamental character of the sin as an identifiable action in space and time for which the sinner is (therefore) liable. By contrast, if (as proposed in Chapter 6 above) original sin is decoupled from any causal link with the historical "first sin," this line of inference is broken.
4. This blindness to the sheer variety of sin has been a defining feature of the theological critiques of Augustinian hamartiologies made by feminist theologians, beginning with Valerie Saiving's groundbreaking article, "The Human Situation: A Feminine View" *Journal of Religion* 40 (April 1960), 100–12.
5. It is important to stress that this correlation does not amount to a relationship of cause and effect. As noted on pp. 183–4 above, if original sin were understood to be an effect of which the fall were a cause, it would be necessary either to argue that Christ had original sin or to deny that he had a fallen nature. Positing the fallenness of the will as the (efficient) *cause* of original sin entails the ontological reduction of hypostasis to nature, thereby making God (as the one who actively preserves and empowers human nature in its fallen state) responsible for sin. While there is never a hypostasis *apart from* a nature (since a hypostasis is always the hypostasis *of* a particular nature), the hypostasis can never be deduced from the nature. If it could be, then the incarnation (i.e., God's hypostatization of a non-divine nature) would be impossible.
6. Indeed, it is precisely because our desires are the ground of our willing that our actual sins may meaningfully be attributed to us in the first place: if the will were truly free in the sense that Augustine's Pelagian opponents wished

to claim, then it becomes unclear on what basis its acts (whether good or evil) are to be ascribed to us. For even if one were to maintain that it is because of the will that my mind turns in a particular way, and that my mouths, arms, or legs correspondingly move, it is not obvious that I should identify myself with this will, since its activity is, on this account, fundamentally undetermined by (and thus independent of) every other aspect of my humanity. By contrast, the Augustinian insistence that the will is enmeshed in the rest of human nature provides a much clearer line of accountability: my acts are mine because they are inseparable from the totality of the particular human being I am, rather than supervening upon my humanity by virtue of the activity of an ontologically autonomous will. See pp. 75–6 above.

7  See, e.g., John Murray, *Redemption Accomplished and Applied* (Grand Rapids, MI: William B. Eerdmans, 1955), p. 113: "The question has been discussed: which is prior, faith or repentance? It is an unnecessary question and the insistence that one is prior to the other is futile. There is no priority."

8  Needless to say, the fact that our efforts at eradication will be far from perfect does not render them any less existentially imperative (see Rom. 6:1–4). Insofar as to be forgiven is to receive the news that one is accepted in spite of the fact that one's deeds render one objectively unworthy of such acceptance, there is no other logically consistent reaction than to recoil in horror from the act(s) that make one so unworthy.

9  Philipp Melanchthon, *Apology of the Augsburg Confession*, Article IV, in *The Book of Concord: The Confessions of the Evangelical Lutheran Church*, ed. Theodore G. Tappert (Philadelphia: Muhlenberg, 1959), p. 112.

10  Cf., e.g., Cardinal Newman: "The iniquity ... of the slave trade ought to have been acknowledged by all men from the first; it was acknowledged by many, but it needed an organized agitation, with tracts and speeches innumerable, so to affect the imagination of men as to make their acknowledgement of that iniquitousness operative." John Henry Newman, *An Essay in Aid of a Grammar of Assent*, ed. I. T Kerr (Oxford: The Clarendon Press, 1985 [1870]), p. 56.

11  Joerg Rieger, *God and the Excluded: Visions and Blindspots in Contemporary Theology* (Minneapolis, MN: Fortress Press, 2001), p. 101. Rieger first introduces this idea in his earlier essay, "Developing a Common Interest Theology from the Underside," in *Liberating the Future: God, Mammon, and Theology*, ed. Joerg Rieger (Minneapolis, MN: Fortress, 1998), pp. 124–41.

12  "Privilege should be given to the testimony of those persons who bear the brunt of social sin in a given context. That is to say, we must explicitly recognize that materially excluded or culturally disdained persons and communities are in a far better position to describe how social sin is working ... than persons who are culturally empowered. By methodologically giving this privilege to the testimony of oppressed persons and communities, we significantly enhance the value of our sin-talk." Stephen G. Ray, Jr., *Do No*

*Harm: Social Sin and Christian Responsibility* (Minneapolis, MN: Fortress Press, 2003), p. 134.

13  All this is not to deny that sins like anger, lust, and falsehood are available to everyone and correspondingly widespread (although even here there is considerable room for variation, so that, e.g., anger can manifest itself in aggressive shouting or sullen withdrawal). It is, however, to recognize that the particularities of environment make certain concrete forms of sin available to some and not to others. For example, a person who is not entrusted with the care of others' money cannot embezzle.

14  John Calvin, *Institutes of the Christian Religion*, II.i.4, ed. John T. McNeill (Philadelphia, PA: Westminster Press, 1960), p. 245. Calvin explicitly commends the identification of Adam's sin with unfaithfulness as preferable to Augustine's characterization of pride as the beginning of all evils. For Calvin pride follows unfaithfulness. Cf. Martin Luther, *The Freedom of a Christian*, in *Career of the Reformer I*, vol. 31 of *Luther's Works*, American edn., ed. Harold J. Grimm (Philadelphia: Fortress Press, 1957), p. 350: "... what greater rebellion against God ... is there than not believing [God's] promise? ... Therefore God has rightly included all things, not under anger or lust, but under unbelief ..."

15  Serene Jones, "What's Wrong With Us?" in *Essentials of Christian Theology*, ed. William C. Placker (Louisville, KY: Westminster John Knox, 2003), p. 149. Jones offers an extended reflection on the relationship between her views on sin and those of Calvin in her book, *Feminist Theory and Christian Theology: Cartographies of Grace* (Minneapolis, MN: Fortress Press, 2000), pp. 97–124.

16  This insight lies at the heart of Augustine's famous prayer, "Grant what you command, and command what you will" (*Confessions*, 10.29 [Oxford: Oxford University Press, 1999]), which outraged Pelagius for its (deliberate!) failure to specify the content of God's commands. See Augustine's account in *The Gift of Perseverance*, 53, in *Answer to the Pelagians*, IV, ed. John E. Rotelle (Hyde Park, NY: New City Press, 1997).

17  The fact that God ultimately intervened to prevent Abraham killing his son is beside the point, since (certainly from the perspective of the Sermon on the Mount) Abraham's intention to follow through on God's initial command would constitute a clear violation of the divine prohibition against murder.

18  Jacob's very name (*Yaʻaqob*) is etymologically related to the Hebrew word for deviousness (*aqob*), and Jesus himself alludes to the patriarch's reputation for sharp practice (characteristic of his relationship with his uncle Laban as well as his brother Esau) in John 1:47. The precise significance of "wife of whoredom" (*'essheth zᵉnunim*) in Hos. 1:2 is debated, but it clearly suggests that Hosea's choice of a spouse would not have conformed to his contemporaries' notions of marital propriety.

19  David's eventual victory over Absalom evidently led him to conclude that Shimei was not speaking at God's command and therefore was worthy of

punishment (1 Kings 2:8–9; cf. 2 Sam. 19:16–23), but this later development is not in any way inconsistent with his earlier response to Shimei's cursing, given at a point where God's judgment was still in doubt. Thus, Luther cites Job as an example of someone who seems to blaspheme and yet is ultimately vindicated by God (see Margin Luther, *Lectures on Romans*, 9:19, vol. 25 of *Luther's Works*, American edn., ed. Hilton C. Oswald [St. Louis, MO: Concordia, 1972], p. 391). Bonhoeffer approvingly summarizes Luther's position as affirming that there are times when "God would rather hear the curses of the godless than the hallelujahs of the pious." Dietrich Bonhoeffer, *Ethics*, vol. 6 of *Dietrich Bonhoeffer Works*, ed. Clifford J. Green (Minneapolis, MN: Fortress, 2005), p. 124.

20   Indeed, this distinction is integral to modern theories of civil disobedience as developed and practiced, e.g., by Gandhi and King: the one who breaks the law for the sake of conscience must be willing to undergo the specified civil penalty.

21   This point exposes the profound error of "What would Jesus do?" theology. Jesus, as a particular hypostasis, has his own calling that is not the same as Peter's or Mary's or mine. When faced with a problem of moral discernment, the proper strategy is therefore not to ask what *Jesus* would do (most simply, because what Jesus *would* do, he has *already done*), but rather to seek to know what God would have *me* – a person quite distinct from Jesus – do. In any particular instance, the example of Jesus (as well as of the saints) may certainly prove illuminating as instantiating forms of behavior in accordance with God's will, even as the Commandments highlight behaviors that are opposed to it. In no case, however, can such models, whether positive or negative, be viewed as absolute. So Paul teaches that as much as we should support one another in the pilgrimage of faith, in the final analysis, "All must test their own work; then that work, rather than their neighbor's work, will become a cause for pride. For all must carry their own loads" (Gal. 6:4–5).

22   If that were the case, then there would seem to be nothing objectionable in Eve's taking of the fruit, or Saul's sparing of the king of the Amalekites, since in both cases the agents seem to have been persuaded in their own minds that their action was reasonable (see Gen. 2:6 and 1 Sam. 15:20–1).

23   Dietrich Bonhoeffer, *Discipleship*, vol. 4 of *Dietrich Bonhoeffer Works*, ed. Clifford J. Green (Minneapolis, MN: Fortress Press, 2003), p. 43.

24   "The concept of a situation in which faith is possible is only a description of the reality contained in the following two statements, both of which are equally true: *only the believers obey*, and *only the obedient believe*." Bonhoeffer, *Discipleship*, p. 63.

25   See Bonhoeffer, *Discipleship*, pp. 57–8; cf. pp. 46, 62.

26   In this context, it is worth pointing out that the traditional association of baptism with naming preserves something of the connection between justification and vocation: to be forgiven one's sin (and most especially one's original sin) is to be called *as* the particular person one is in order *to be* the

particular person God intends. "Become who you are" is a perfectly apt way of putting it, since for human beings (unlike angels) identity is a function of life in time.

27  In addition to Paul's references to the interdependence of the members of the body of Christ in Romans and 1 Corinthians, one might also cite in support of this claim the principle that even the most blessed of the saints is not to be made perfect apart from the rest of God's people (Heb. 11:40).

28  In this context, it is worth recalling Dorotheus of Gaza's image of the spoked wheel as the model of the kingdom: closer proximity to God at the center is inseparable from closer proximity to the other spokes, not because others are God, but because they, like oneself, have their source and end in God.

29  This is not to say that we are ever the efficient cause either of others' salvation or of their damnation, but only to note that we are part of the fulfillment of God's will for others, whether in glory or its rejection.

30  Ian A. McFarland, *The Divine Image: Envisioning the Invisible God* (Minneapolis, MN: Fortress Press, 2005), pp. 62–4, 152–67, and *passim*.

31  See note 12 above.

32  As Charles Mathewes puts it, an Augustinian perspective "forbids us from imputing too pure motives to ourselves. All our actions have the taint of an illegitimate (because self-aggrandizing) self-interest ... The language of sin and love strongly encourages us always to see ourselves as flawed, imperfect, perpetually open to correction and inevitably in need of improvement." Charles Mathewes, *A Theology of Public Life* (Cambridge: Cambridge University Press, 2007), p. 284.

33  See, e.g., Eugene F. Rogers, Jr., *Sexuality and the Christian Body: Their Way Into the Triune God* (Oxford: Blackwell, 1999).

34  The speed and efficiency with which the German National Socialist state was able to isolate and exterminate one of Europe's most highly assimilated Jewish populations stands as a sobering warning against any illusions of inevitable historical progress in human efforts to confront sin.

35  Cf. Ezek. 2:4–7: "I am sending you to them, and you shall say to them, 'Thus says the Lord God.' Whether they hear or refuse to hear (for they are a rebellious house), they shall know that there has been a prophet among them. And you, O mortal, do not be afraid of them, and do not be afraid of their words, though briers and thorns surround you and you live among scorpions; do not be afraid of their words, and do not be dismayed at their looks, for they are a rebellious house. You shall speak my words to them, whether they hear or refuse to hear."

# References

Abelard, Peter. *Ethics or the Book Called "Know Thyself."* In *A Scholastic Miscellany: Anselm to Ockham*, ed. Eugene R. Fairweather, trans. Gerald E. Moffat. Philadelphia, PA: Westminster, 1956, pp. 288–97.

Anselm of Canterbury. *Why God Became Man*. In *A Scholastic Miscellany: Anselm to Ockham*, ed. Eugene R. Fairweather. Philadelphia: Westminster, 1956, pp. 100–83.

Aquinas, Thomas. *On Evil*, ed. Brian Davies. New York: Oxford University Press, 2003.

Aquinas, Thomas. *Summa Theologiae*, 61 vols., Blackfriars edn. London: Eyre & Spottiswood, 1964–81.

Augustine of Hippo. *Answer to the Two Letters of the Pelagians*. In *Answer to the Pelagians, II*, ed. John E. Rotelle, O.S.A., trans. Roland J. Teske, S.J. Hyde Park, NY: New City Press, 1997, pp. 97–219.

Augustine of Hippo. *The City of God against the Pagans*, ed. R. W. Dyson. Cambridge: Cambridge University Press, 1998.

Augustine of Hippo. *Confessions*, trans. Henry Chadwick. Oxford: Oxford University Press, 1991.

Augustine of Hippo. *The Deeds of Pelagius*. In *Answer to the Pelagians, I*, ed. John E. Rotelle, O.S.A., trans. Roland J. Teske, S.J. Hyde Park, NY: New City Press, 1997, pp. 307–70.

Augustine of Hippo. *The Gift of Perseverance*. In *Answer to the Pelagians, IV*, ed. John E. Rotelle, O.S.A., trans. Roland J. Teske, S.J. Hyde Park, NY: New City Press, 1997, pp. 191–239.

Augustine of Hippo. *Grace and Free Choice*. In *Answer to the Pelagians, IV*, ed. John E. Rotelle, O.S.A., trans. Roland J. Teske, S.J. Hyde Park, NY: New City Press, 1997, pp. 71–107.

---

*In Adam's Fall: A Meditation on the Christian Doctrine of Original Sin*, by Ian A. McFarland.
© 2010 Ian A. McFarland.

Augustine of Hippo. *The Grace of Christ and Original Sin*. In *Answer to the Pelagians, I*, ed. John E. Rotelle, O.S.A. trans. Roland J. Teske, S.J. Hyde Park, NY: New City Press, 1997, pp. 371–448.

Augustine of Hippo. *The Literal Meaning of Genesis*. In *On Genesis*, ed. John E. Rotelle, O.S.A., trans. Edmund Hill, O.P. Hyde Park, NY: New City Press, 2002, pp. 155–506.

Augustine of Hippo. *Marriage and Desire*. In *Answer to the Pelagians, II*, ed. John E. Rotelle, O.S.A., trans. Roland J. Teske, S.J. Hyde Park, NY: New City Press, 1997, pp. 11–96.

Augustine of Hippo. *Nature and Grace*. In *Answer to the Pelagians, I*, ed. John E. Rotelle, O.S.A., trans. Roland J. Teske, S.J. Hyde Park, NY: New City Press, 1997, pp. 196–265.

Augustine of Hippo. *The Perfection of Human Righteousness*. In *Answer to the Pelagians, I*, ed. John E. Rotelle, O.S.A., trans. Roland J. Teske, S.J. Hyde Park, NY: New City Press, 1997, pp. 266–305.

Augustine of Hippo. *The Punishment and Forgiveness of Sins and the Baptism of Little Ones*. In *Answer to the Pelagians, I*, ed. John E. Rotelle, O.S.A., trans. Roland J. Teske, S.J. Hyde Park, NY: New City Press, 1997, pp. 19–132.

Augustine of Hippo. *Rebuke and Grace*. In *Answer to the Pelagians, IV*, ed. John E. Rotelle, O.S.A., trans. Roland J. Teske, S.J. Hyde Park, NY: New City Press, 1997, pp. 109–48.

Augustine of Hippo. *The Spirit and the Letter*. In *Answer to the Pelagians, I*, ed. John E. Rotelle, O.S.A., trans. Roland J. Teske, S.J. Hyde Park, NY: New City Press, 1997, pp. 133–94.

Augustine of Hippo. *The Trinity*, ed. John E. Rotelle, O.S.A., trans. Edmund Hill, O.P. Hyde Park, NY: New City Press, 1991.

Augustine of Hippo. *Unfinished Work in Answer to Julian*. In *Answer to the Pelagians, III*, ed. John E. Rotelle, O.S.A., trans. Roland J. Teske, S.J. Hyde Park, NY: New City Press, 1999.

Babcock, William. "Augustine on Sin and Moral Agency." In *Journal of Religious Ethics* 16 (1988), 28–55.

Balthasar, Hans Urs von. *Cosmic Liturgy: The Universe According to Maximus the Confessor*, trans. Brian E. Daley, S.J. San Francisco: Ignatius Press, 2003.

Balthasar, Hans Urs von. *Mysterium Paschale*, trans. Aidan Nichols. Edinburgh: T&T Clark, 1990.

Barth, Karl. *Church Dogmatics I/2*, ed. G. W. Bromiley and T. F. Torrance. Edinburgh: T&T Clark, 1956.

Basil of Caesarea. Letter 261 ("To the Sozopolitans"). In *Basil: Letters and Select Works*. Vol. 8 of *Nicene and Post-Nicene Fathers*, 2nd Series, ed. Philip Schaff and Henry Wace, trans. Bloomfield Jackson. Peabody, MA: Hendrickson, 1995 [1895], pp. 299–301.

Bathrellos, Demetrios. *The Byzantine Christ: Person, Nature, and Will in the Christology of Maximus the Confessor*. Oxford: Oxford University Press, 2005.

Bavinck, Herman. *Sin and Salvation in Christ*. Vol. 3 of *Reformed Dogmatics*, ed. John Bolt, trans. John Vriend. Grand Rapids, MI: William B. Eerdmans, 2006.

Bennett, William J. *The Broken Hearth: Reversing the Moral Collapse of the American Family*. New York: Broadway, 2003.

Berkouwer, G. C. *Sin*, trans. Philip C. Holtrop. Grand Rapids, MI: William B. Eerdmans, 1971.

Bernanos, George. *The Diary of a Country Priest*. New York: Macmillan, 1937.

Berthold, George C. "Did Maximus the Confessor Know Augustine?" *Studia Patristica* 17 (1982), 14–17.

Biddle, Mark E. *Missing the Mark: Sin and Its Consequences in Biblical Theology*. Nashville, TN: Abingdon Press, 2005.

Blocher, Henri. *Original Sin: Illuminating the Riddle*. Grand Rapids, MI: William B. Eerdmans, 1997.

Bloom, Alan. *The Closing of the American Mind: Education and the Crisis of Reason*. New York: Simon & Schuster, 1987.

Bonhoeffer, Dietrich. *Discipleship*. Vol. 4 of *Dietrich Bonhoeffer Works*, ed. Clifford J. Green, trans. Barbara Green and Reinhard Krauss. Minneapolis, MN: Fortress Press, 2003.

Bonhoeffer, Dietrich. *Ethics*. Vol. 6 of *Dietrich Bonhoeffer Works*, ed. Clifford J. Green, trans. Reinhard Krauss, Charles C. West, and Douglas W. Stott. Minneapolis, MN: Fortress Press, 2005.

Bonhoeffer, Dietrich. *Letters and Papers from Prison*, ed. Eberhard Bethge, trans. Reginald Fuller, Frank Clark, et al. New York: Macmillan, 1972.

Bonhoeffer, Dietrich. *Sanctorum Communio: A Theological Study of the Sociology of the Church*. Vol. 1 of *Dietrich Bonhoeffer Works*, ed. Joachim von Soosten and Clifford J. Green, trans. Reinhard Krauss and Nancy Lukens. Minneapolis, MN: Fortress Press, 1998.

*The Book of Concord: The Confessions of the Evangelical Lutheran Church*, ed. and trans. Theodore G. Tappert. Philadelphia, PA: Muhlenberg, 1959.

Buell, Denise. *Why This New Race: Ethnic Reasoning in Early Christianity*. New York: Columbia University Press, 2005.

Burns, J. Patout. *The Development of Augustine's Doctrine of Operative Grace*. Paris: Études augustiniennes, 1980.

Calvin, John. *Institutes of the Christian Religion*. 2 vols., ed. John T. McNeill, trans. Ford Lewis Battles. Philadelphia, PA: Westminster Press, 1960.

*The Canons and Decrees of the Council of Trent*, ed. and trans. H. J. Schroeder, O.P. Rockford, IL: TAN Books, 1978 [1941].

Carcione, Filippo. "Enérgheia, Thélema e Theokínetos nella lettera di Sergio, patriarca di Costantinopoli, a papa Onorio Primo," *Orientalia Christiana Periodica* 51:2 (1985), 263–76.

Carr, Amy. "Enduring Radical Distrust: Sin and Redemption among the Sinned Against." Unpublished paper delivered at the annual meeting of the American Academy of Religion, 2007.

Cary, Phillip. *Inner Grace: Augustine in the Traditions of Plato and Paul*. New York: Oxford University Press, 2008.
*The Catechism of the Catholic Church*, 2nd edn. New York: Doubleday, 1997.
Catholic International Theological Commission. "The Hope of Salvation for Infants Who Die Without Being Baptized." <http://www.vatican.va/roman_curia/congregations/cfaith/cti_documents/rc_con_cfaith_doc_20070419_un-baptised-infants_en.html>.
Cone, James H. *My Soul Looks Back*. Nashville, TN: Abingdon Press, 1982.
Cooper, Adam G. *The Body in St. Maximus the Confessor: Holy Flesh, Wholly Deified*. Oxford: Oxford University Press, 2005.
Crisp, Oliver D. *Divinity and Humanity: The Incarnation Reconsidered*. Cambridge: Cambridge University Press, 2007.
Crisp, Oliver D. "On the Theological Pedigree of Jonathan Edwards's Doctrine of Imputation," *Scottish Journal of Theology* 56:3 (2003), 308–27.
Cyril of Alexandria. *Apologeticus contra Theodoretum pro duodecim Capitibus*. In *Patrologia Graeca*, vol. 76: 386–452, ed. J. Migne. Paris, 1859.
Cyprian of Carthage. Letter 58 ("To Fidus"). In *Fathers of the Third Century: Hippolytus, Cyprian, Caius, Novatian*. Vol. 5 of *Ante-Nicene Fathers*, ed. Alexander Roberts and James Donaldson. Edinburgh: T&T Clark, nd.
Doucet, Marcel. "La volonté humaine du Christ, spécialement en Son agonie. Maxime le Confesseur, interprète de l'Écriture," *Science et Esprit* 37:2 (1985), 123–59.
Edwards, Jonathan. *Original Sin*. Vol. 3 of the *Works of Jonathan Edwards*, ed. Clyde A. Holbrook. New Haven, CT: Yale University Press, 1970.
Faber, Eva-Maria. "Grace." In *Encyclopedia of Christian Theology*, ed. Jean-Yves Lacoste. New York: Routledge, 2005 [1999].
Farley, Wendy. *Tragic Vision and Divine Compassion: A Contemporary Theodicy*. Louisville, KY: Westminster/John Knox, 1990.
Farrell, Joseph. P. *Free Choice in St. Maximus the Confessor*. South Canaan, PA: St. Tikhon's Seminary Press, 1989.
Farrer, Austin. *The Freedom of the Will*. New York: Charles Scribner's Sons, 1958.
Foucault, Michel. *Power/Knowledge: Selected Interviews and Other Writings 1972–1977*, ed. and trans. Colin Gordon. New York: Pantheon, 1980.
Garlington, Don B. *Faith, Obedience, and Perseverance: Aspects of Paul's Letter to the Romans*. Tübingen: Mohr-Siebeck, 1994.
Gestrich, Christof. *The Return of Splendor to the World: The Christian Doctrine of Sin and Forgiveness*, trans. Donald Bloesch. Grand Rapids, MI: William B. Eerdmans, 1997 [1989].
Gregory of Nazianzus. Epistle 101 ("To Cledonius Against Apollinaris"). In *Christology of the Later Fathers*, ed. Edward R. Hardy. Philadelphia, PA: Westminster Press, 1954, pp. 215–24.
Gregory of Nyssa. "Address on Religious Instruction." In *Christology of the Later Fathers*, ed. Edward R. Hardy. Philadelphia, PA: Westminster Press, 1954, pp. 268–325.

Gregory of Nyssa. *Against Eunomius*. In *Dogmatic Treatises, etc.* Vol. 5 of *Nicene and Post-Nicene Fathers*, 2nd Series, ed. Philip Schaff and Henry Wace, trans. William Moore and Henry Austin Wilson. Peabody, MA: Hendrickson, 1995 [1893], pp. 33–248.

Gregory of Nyssa. *The Life of Moses*. New York: Paulist Press, 1978.

Gregory of Nyssa. *On the Making of Man*, in *Dogmatic Treatises, etc.* Vol. 5 of *Nicene and Post-Nicene Fathers*, 2nd Series, ed. Philip Schaff and Henry Wace, trans. William Moore and Henry Austin Wilson. Peabody, MA: Hendrickson, 1995 [1893], pp. 387–427.

Gross, J. *Geshichte des Erbsündendogmas. Ein Beitrag zur Geschichte des Problems vom Ursprung des Übels*. 4 vols. München: Ernst Reinhardt, 1960–72.

Harnack, Adolf *History of Dogma*. 7 vols. 3rd. edn., ed. A. B. Bruce, trans. Neil Buchanan, James Millar, E. B. Speirs, et al. London: Williams & Norgate, 1896–9.

Hefner, Philip. *The Human Factor: Evolution, Culture, and Religion*. Minneapolis, MN: Fortress Press, 1993.

Heinzer, Felix. *Gottes Sohn als Mensch: Die Struktur des Menschseins Christi bei Maximus Confessor*. Freiburg: Universitätsverlag Freiburg Schweiz, 1980.

Heppe, Heinrich. *Reformed Dogmatics*, ed. Ernst Bizer, trans. G. T. Thomson. London: George Allen & Unwin, 1950.

Honorius I, Epistle 4 ("*Ad Sergium Constantinopolitanum Episcopum*"), in *Scriptorum Ecclesiasticorum qui in VI Saeculi Prima Parte Floruerunt*. Vol. 80 of *Patrologiae Cursus Completus, Series Latina*, ed. J.-P. Migne. Paris, 1863, coll. 470–4.

Irenaeus of Lyons. *Against Heresies*. In *The Apostolic Fathers with Justin Martyr and Irenaeus*. Vol. 1 of *Ante-Nicene Fathers*. American edn., ed. the Rev. Alexander Roberts and James Donaldson. Grand Rapids, MI: William B. Eerdmans, nd.

Jacobs, Alan. *Original Sin: A Cultural History*. New York: HarperOne, 2008.

Jenson, Robert W. *The Works of God*. Vol. 2 of *Systematic Theology*. New York: Oxford University Press, 1999.

Jones, Serene. *Feminist Theory and Christian Theology: Cartographies of Grace*. Minneapolis, MN: Fortress Press, 2000.

Jones, Serene. *Trauma and Grace: Theology in a Ruptured World*. Louisville, KY: Westminster John Knox, 2009.

Jones, Serene. "What's Wrong with Us?" In *Essentials of Christian Theology*, ed. William C. Placher. Louisville, KY: Westminster John Knox, 2003, pp. 141–58.

Julian of Norwich. *Showings*, trans. Edmud Colledge, O.S.A. and James Walsh, S.J. New York: Paulist Press, 1978.

Jung, Martin H. "Johanna Eleonora Petersen (1644–1724)." In *The Pietist Theologians*, ed. Carter Lindberg. Malden, MA: Blackwell, 2005, pp. 147–60.

Kapic, Kelly M. "The Son's Assumption of a Human Nature: A Call for Clarity," *International Journal of Systematic Theology* 3:2 (July 2001), 154–66.

Käsemann, Ernst. *Commentary on Romans*, trans. Geoffrey W. Bromiley. Grand Rapids, MI: William B. Eerdmans, 1980.

Kelly, J. N. D. *Early Christian Doctrines*. Revised edn. San Francisco, CA: Harper & Row, 1978.

Kierkegaard, Søren. *The Concept of Anxiety: A Simple Psychologically Orienting Deliberation on the Dogmatic Issue of Hereditary Sin*, ed. and trans. Reidar Thomte. Princeton, NJ: Princeton University Press, 1980.

Kraftchick, Steven J. *Jude/2 Peter*. Nashville, TN: Abingdon Press, 2002.

Larchet, Jean-Claude. *La dvinisation de l'homme selon saint Maxime le Confesseur*. Paris: Les Éditions du Cerf, 1996.

Lossky, Vladimir. *In the Image and Likeness of God*, ed. John T. Erickson and Thomas E. Bird. Crestwood, NY: St. Vladimir's Seminary Press, 1985.

Louth, Andrew. *Maximus the Confessor*. New York: Routledge, 1996.

*Luther and Erasmus: Free Will and Salvation*, ed. and trans. E. Gordon Rupp and Philip S. Watson. Philadelphia, PA: Westminster Press, 1959.

Luther, Martin. *The Freedom of a Christian*. In *Career of the Reformer I*. Vol. 31 of *Luther's Works*. American edn., ed. Harold J. Grimm, trans. W. A. Lambert. Philadelphia: Fortress Press, 1957, pp. 333–77.

Luther, Martin. *Lectures on Romans*. Vol. 25 of *Luther's Works*. American edn., ed. Hilton C. Oswald. St. Louis, MO: Concordia Publishing House, 1972.

Luther, Martin. "A Sincere Admonition by Martin Luther to All Christians to Guard Against Insurrection and Rebellion." In *The Christian in Society II*. Vol. 45 of *Luther's Works*. American edn., ed. Walther I. Brandt, trans. W. A. Lambert. Philadelphia, PA: Fortress Press, 1962, pp. 51–74.

Madden, John. "The Authenticity of Early Definitions of Will (*Thelesis*)." In *Maximus Confessor. Actes du Symposium sur Maxime le Confesseur Fribourg, 2–5 septembere 1980*, ed. Felix Heinzer and Christoph Schönborn. Fribourg: Éditions Universitaires, 1982, pp. 61–79.

*Magistri Petri Lombardi parisiensis episcope sententiarum in iv libros distinctae*. 3rd edn., ed. Ignatius Brady, O.F.M. et al. Grottaferrata: Collegium Sanctae Bonaventurae, 1971.

Markschies, C. *Gnosis: An Introduction*. Edinburgh: T&T Clark, 2003.

Mathewes, Charles T. *Evil and the Augustinian Tradition*. Cambridge: Cambridge University Press, 2001.

Mathewes, Charles T. *A Theology of Public Life*. Cambridge: Cambridge University Press, 2007.

Maximus the Confessor. *Amiguorum Liber*. In *Maximi Confessoris Opera Omnia*. Vol. 91 of *Patrologiae Cursus Completus, Series Graeca*, ed. J.-P. Migne. Paris, 1863, coll. 1031–1417.

Maximus the Confessor. *Disputatio cum Pyrrho*. In *Maximi Confessoris Opera Omnia*. Vol. 91 of *Patrologiae Cursus Completus, Series Graeca*, ed. J.-P. Migne. Paris, 1863, coll. 287–360.

Maximus the Confessor. *Maximus Confessor: Selected Writings*, ed. and trans. George C. Berthold. New York: Paulist Press, 1985.

Maximus the Confessor. *On the Cosmic Mystery of Jesus Christ: Selected Writings from Saint Maximus the Confessor*, ed. and trans. Paul M. Blowers and Robert Louis Wilken. Crestwood, NY: St. Vladimir's Seminary Press, 2003.

Maximus the Confessor. *Opuscula Theologica et Polemica*. In *Maximi Confessoris Opera Omnia*. Vol. 91 of *Patrologiae Cursus Completus, Series Graeca*, ed. J.-P. Migne. Paris, 1863, coll. 9–214.

Maximus the Confessor. *Quaestiones ad Thalassium I (Quaestiones I–LV, una cum latina interpretatione Ioannis Scotti Eriugenae)*, ed. C. Laga and C. Steel. Vol. 7 of the *Corpus Christianorum Series Graeca*. Turnhout: Brepols, 1980.

Maximus the Confessor. *Quaestiones ad Thalassium II (Quaestiones LVI–LXV, una cum latina interpretatione Ioannis Scotti Eriugenae)*, ed. C. Laga and C. Steel. Vol. 22 of the *Corpus Christianorum Series Graeca*. Turnhout: Brepols, 1990.

McFadyen, Alistair I. *Bound to Sin: Abuse, Holocaust and the Christian Doctrine of Sin*. Cambridge: Cambridge University Press, 2000.

McFarland, Ian A. *Difference and Identity: A Theological Anthropology*. Cleveland, OH: Pilgrim Press, 2001.

McFarland, Ian A. *The Divine Image: Envisioning the Invisible God*. Minneapolis, MN: Fortress Press, 2005.

McFarland, Ian A. "The Fall and Sin." In *The Oxford Handbook of Systematic Theology*, ed. John B. Webster, Kathryn Tanner, and Iain Torrance. Oxford: Oxford University Press, 2007, pp. 140–59.

Melanchthon, Philipp. *Apology of the Augsburg Confession*, Article IV. In *The Book of Concord: The Confessions of the Evangelical Lutheran Church*, ed. Theodore G. Tappert. Philadelphia: Muhlenberg, 1959.

Menninger, Karl. *Whatever Became of Sin?* London: Hodder & Stoughton, 1973.

Murray, John. *The Imputation of Adam's Sin*. Grand Rapids, MI: William B. Eerdmans, 1959.

Murray, John. *Redemption Accomplished and Applied*. Grand Rapids, MI: William B. Eerdmans, 1955.

Newman, John Henry. *An Essay in Aid of a Grammar of Assent*, ed. I. T Kerr. Oxford: The Clarendon Press, 1985 [1870].

Niebuhr, Reinhold. *Human Nature*. Vol. 1 of *The Nature and Destiny of Man: A Christian Interpretation*. Louisville, KY: Westminster John Knox, 1996 [1941].

Niebuhr, Reinhold. *Man's Nature and His Communities: Essays on the Dynamics and Enigmas of Man's Personal and Social Existence*. New York: Charles Scribner's Sons, 1965.

Origen of Alexandria. *De Principiis*. In *Fathers of the Third Century: Tertullian, Part Fourth; Minucius Felix; Commodian; Origen, Parts First and Second*. Vol. 4 of *Ante-Nicene Fathers*. American edn., ed. the Rev. Alexander Roberts and James Donaldson. Grand Rapids, MI: William B. Eerdmans, nd.

Pagels, Elaine. *Adam, Eve, and the Serpent*. New York: Vintage, 1988.
Park, Andrew Sung. *The Wounded Heart of God: The Asian Concept of Han and the Christian Doctrine of Sin*. Nashville, TN: Abingdon Press, 1993.
Pascal, Blaise. *Pensées*, trans. W. F. Trotter. London: J. M. Dent & Sons, 1958.
Peters, Ted. *Sin: Radical Evil in Soul and Society*. Grand Rapids, MI: William B. Eerdmans, 1994.
Pitstick, Alyssa Lyra. *Light in Darkness: Hans Urs von Balthasar and the Catholic Doctrine of Christ's Descent into Hell*. Grand Rapids, MI: William B. Eerdmans, 2007.
Plantinga, Cornelius, Jr. *Not the Way It's Supposed to Be: A Breviary of Sin*. Grand Rapids, MI: William B. Eerdmans, 1995.
Rahner, Karl. *Foundations of the Christian Faith: An Introduction to the Idea of Christianity*. New York: Crossroad, 1990.
Rahner, Karl. "Some Reflexions on Monogenism." In *God, Christ, Mary and Grace*. Vol. 1 of *Theological Investigations*. New York: Seabury Press, 1974, pp. 229–96.
Ratzinger, Joseph. *Introduction to Christianity*. New York: Seabury Press, 1968.
Ray, Stephen G., Jr. *Do No Harm: Social Sin and Christian Responsibility*. Minneapolis, MN: Fortress Press, 2003.
Ricoeur, Paul. *The Symbolism of Evil*. Boston, MA: Beacon Press, 1967.
Rieger, Joerg. "Developing a Common Interest Theology from the Underside." In *Liberating the Future: God, Mammon, and Theology*, ed. Joerg Rieger. Minneapolis, MN: Fortress Press, 1998, pp. 124–41.
Rieger, Joerg. *God and the Excluded: Visions and Blindspots in Contemporary Theology*. Minneapolis, MN: Fortress Press, 2001.
Rogers, Eugene F., Jr. *Sexuality and the Christian Body: Their Way Into the Triune God*. Oxford: Blackwell, 1999.
Saiving, Valerie. "The Human Situation: A Feminine View," *Journal of Religion* 40 (April 1960), 100–12.
Schleiermacher, Friedrich. *The Christian Faith*. 2nd edn., ed. H. R. Mackintosh and J. S. Stewart. Edinburgh: T&T Clark, 1928 [1830].
Schmid, Heinrich. *The Doctrinal Theology of the Evangelical Lutheran Church*. 3rd edn., trans. Charles A. Hay and Henry E. Jacobs. Minneapolis, MN: Augsburg Publishing House, 1899.
Schoonenberg, Piet. *Man and Sin: A Theological View*. Notre Dame, IN: University of Notre Dame Press, 1965.
Schwager, Raymund. *Der wunderbare Tausch: zur Geschichte und Deutung der Erlösungslehre*. München: Kösel, 1986.
Shedd, William G. T. *Dogmatic Theology*, 2 vols. 2nd edn. New York: Charles Scribner's Sons, 1889.
Sherwood, Polycarp. *An Annotated Date-List of the Works of Maximus the Confessor*. Studia Anselmiana, fasc. XXX. Rome: Herder, 1952.

Stone, Michael Edward. *Fourth Ezra: A Commentary on the Book of Fourth Ezra*. Minneapolis, MN: Fortress Press, 1990.

Suchocki, Marjorie Hewitt. *The Fall to Violence: Original Sin in Relational Theology*. New York: Continuum, 1994.

Tennant, F. R. *The Sources of the Doctrines of the Fall and Original Sin*. Cambridge: Cambridge University Press, 1903.

Tertullian. *On Baptism*. In *Latin Christianity: Its Founder, Tertullian*. Vol. 3 of *Ante-Nicene Fathers*. American edn., ed. the Rev. Alexander Roberts and James Donaldson. Grand Rapids, MI: William B. Eerdmans, nd.

Tertullian. *On the Resurrection of the Flesh*. In *Latin Christianity: Its Founder, Tertullian*. Vol. 3 of *Ante-Nicene Fathers*. American edn., ed. the Rev. Alexander Roberts and James Donaldson. Grand Rapids, MI: William B. Eerdmans, nd.

Tertullian. *A Treatise on the Soul*. In *Latin Christianity: Its Founder, Tertullian*. Vol. 3 of *Ante-Nicene Fathers*. American edn., ed. the Rev. Alexander Roberts and James Donaldson. Grand Rapids, MI: William B. Eerdmans, nd.

Theophilus of Antioch. *To Autolycus*. In *Fathers of the Second Century*. Vol. 2 of *Ante-Nicene Fathers*. American edn., ed. the Rev. Alexander Roberts and James Donaldson. Grand Rapids, MI: William B. Eerdmans, nd.

Thunberg, Lars. *Microcosm and Mediator: The Theological Anthropology of Maximus the Confessor*. 2nd edn. Chicago, IL: Open Court, 1995.

Tilley, Terrence W. *The Evils of Theodicy*. Eugene, OR: Wipf and Stock, 2000.

Tillich, Paul. *Systematic Theology*. 3 vols. Chicago, IL: University of Chicago Press, 1951–63.

Torrance, T. F. *The Trinitarian Faith*. Edinburgh: T&T Clark, 1995.

Trible, Phyllis. *God and the Rhetoric of Sexuality*. Philadelphia, PA: Fortress Press, 1978.

Turretin, Francis. *Institutes of Elenctic Theology*. 3 vols., ed. James T. Dennison, trans. George Musgrave Giger. Phillipsburg, NJ: P&R Publishing, 1992.

Underhill, Peter A., Peidong Shen, Alice A. Lin, et al., "Y Chromosome Sequence Variation and the History of Human Populations," *Nature Genetics* 26:3 (November 2000), 358–61.

Verghese, Paul. "The Monothelite Controversy – A Historical Survey," *The Greek Orthodox Theological Review* 13:2 (Fall 1968), 196–211.

Volf, Miroslav. *Exclusion and Embrace: A Theological Exploration of Identity, Otherness, and Reconciliation*. Nashville, TN: Abingdon Press, 1996.

Ware, Timothy. *The Orthodox Church*. Harmondsworth: Penguin, 1963.

Weil, Simone. *Waiting for God*. New York: Harper Colophon, 1973 [1951].

Weinandy, Thomas. *In the Likeness of Sinful Flesh: An Essay on the Humanity of Christ*. Edinburgh: T&T Clark, 1993.

Wetzel, James. *Augustine and the Limits of Virtue*. Cambridge: Cambridge University Press, 1999.

Wiley, Tatha. *Original Sin: Origins, Developments, Contemporary Meanings*. New York: Paulist Press, 2002.
Williams, M. A. *Rethinking "Gnosticism": An Argument for Dismantling a Dubious Category*. Princeton, NJ: Princeton University Press, 1996.
Williams, N. P. *The Ideas of the Fall and of Original Sin: A Historical and Critical Study*. London: Longman, Green and Co., 1927.

# Index

Abelard, Peter 23
accountability 172, 181–2, 184–5, 187, 192, 215–16
actual sin 19–22, 34–5, 38–9, 41, 43–4, 48, 68, 130, 178, 182, 184, 193–7, 199–201, 203–6, 208, 212, 215
Adam
  as cause of sin 153–4, 159, 169
  and Christ 152–3
  disobedience 31, 34, 37, 71, 83, 148, 164
  as first sinner ix–x, 4, 159–60
  guilt of 10, 130, 135, 149, 151
  as head 150, 152–3, 165, 168
  historicity of 144, 152
  life "in" 150–1, 153
  prelapsarian condition 74, 125
  as representative 150, 152–3
  sin of 8, 29–31, 52, 61, 120, 151, 191, 215
  Y-chromosomal 161
  *see also* Eve
agency 8–9, 11, 17–18, 20, 24, 39, 48, 63, 65, 69–70, 72–3, 76–7, 82–3, 85–7, 94, 97, 107, 110–11, 127, 129–31, 145, 147, 151, 160–2, 168, 171, 175–6, 181, 183–5, 187, 192–3, 196, 213
angels 51, 154–7, 160, 166–7, 219
Anselm of Canterbury 37, 120–1, 123–5, 133
anthropology
  biblical 11
  consumerist 5
  theological ix–xii, 92, 158, 185–7, 214
  *see also* Augustine of Hippo; Maximus the Confessor
aphthartodocetists 136
Aquinas, Thomas 37, 54–5, 121, 123–6, 134, 138, 154–5, 157, 166–7, 190
Augustine of Hippo
  anthropology of 65, 69–70, 74, 107, 120, 146, 162
  and biblical interpretation 52, 143–4
  Christology 133
  doctrine of original sin 29, 32–6, 46, 49, 52, 61–2, 66, 87, 89, 108, 117–18, 120, 132, 144, 149–50, 163, 196, 217

---

*In Adam's Fall: A Meditation on the Christian Doctrine of Original Sin,* by Ian A. McFarland.
© 2010 Ian A. McFarland.

## Index

and evil  139
and the fall  71–5, 78, 84, 107, 117, 120, 137, 146, 183
and glorified humanity  114–15
*Marriage and Desire*  67–70
and Maximus the Confessor  88–90, 92, 100–1, 105, 107–8, 117, 147
on Paul  67–69, 82–3
*The Punishment and Forgiveness of Sins and the Baptism of Little Ones*  62
*Rebuke and Grace*  74
on sexual desire  71–2, 83–4, 149
on the status of infants  32–3, 38–9, 51, 56, 62, 65–6, 71, 75, 79, 82, 107, 149
Trinitarian theology  168
and the will  62–5, 67–87, 89–90, 107, 109, 117, 131, 146–7, 174, 186, 215
*see also* concupiscence; theodicy

Balthasar, Hans Urs von  122
baptism  3, 38–9, 49, 51, 53, 55–6, 61–2, 66–8, 81–2, 165, 192, 206, 218
Barth, Karl  122, 135
Basil of Caesarea  128
Bavinck, Herman  28, 54, 56, 152, 164–5
beatific vision  155; *see also* deification
Bellarmine, Robert  54
Berkouwer, G. C.  24, 163–5, 167
Berthold, G.  108
blame  xii, 18, 47, 57, 128–30, 140, 163, 168, 173, 181–5, 189, 195
Blocher, Henri  161, 165
body
 of Christ  x, 114, 134, 153, 155, 157, 168, 170, 177, 202–3, 207–10, 214, 219

human  7, 31, 67–8, 71–2, 85, 88, 97, 106, 125–7, 129, 134, 139, 146, 156, 161–3, 165
social  176
Bonhoeffer, Dietrich  4–5, 13, 21–2, 26, 47, 167, 206–7, 218

Cain  8
calling *see* vocation
Calvin, John  56, 119, 132, 140, 201, 217
Carr, Amy  190
Cary, Philip  52, 79–82
Catholicism
 *Catechism of the Catholic Church*  37–8, 53–5
 Council of Trent  37, 54–5
Chalcedon *see* Christology
Chemnitz, M.  134
Chesterton, G. K.  24
choice  xii, 5–9, 11, 15, 17–8, 23–4, 27, 44, 65, 72–4, 76–81, 84–7, 94–7, 99–101, 103–4, 107, 109, 111, 113–4, 135, 147–8, 150, 163, 166, 186, 190
Christ *see* Jesus Christ
Christology
 of Chalcedon  90–1, 119, 145, 153
 dyothelite  92–4, 97–100, 105, 108, 111
 *see also* anthropology; crypto-kenoticism; election
church  ix–x, 4–5, 10, 29, 36, 46, 167, 174, 179, 192, 198, 210–11; *see also* body
civil disobedience  218
Clement of Alexandria  139
co-dependence  159, 170
commandments  8, 80, 85, 202–4, 208, 210, 218; *see also* law
concupiscence  54–5, 65–8, 70–1, 73, 77–8, 81–4, 149
Cone, James H.  191

# 232 Index

conscience  13, 23, 44, 193, 218
covenant  150, 152, 165, 179
creation
  as beginning  74, 78, 108, 157, 166
  doctrine of  105
  from nothing  19, 50, 129, 187
  goodness of  28, 34, 44, 46–7, 51, 108, 117, 132
  in Scripture  143
  sin against  16, 26, 188
Crisp, Oliver  135, 137, 167, 188
crypto-kenoticism  136
Cyprian of Carthage  61, 79
Cyril of Alexandria  89–90, 109, 165

damnation  3, 35, 38, 46, 56, 66–7, 75, 82, 135–6, 151, 155–6, 167–8, 219
de Lubac, Henri  54
death
  fear of  89, 95, 98–9, 126
  of Jesus Christ  123–4
  as natural  31, 134, 143
  as punishment  24, 37, 46, 61, 88, 122, 128, 164
  and repentance  167
deification  92, 99, 100–6, 110, 113, 115–16, 125–6, 138; *see also* beatific vision; glory
deliberation  93, 95–101, 105, 114–15, 137
desire
  distortion of  83, 146, 148, 159–60, 184, 203
  market-driven  4
  natural  109, 166
  and sin  8, 27, 163
  and willing  64–78, 80–6, 94–5, 100, 107, 115, 126–7, 138, 146–8, 160, 162–3, 183, 196, 203, 215
  *see also* concupiscence; God
Dorotheus of Gaza  219

Edwards, Jonathan  157, 167–8
election  39, 135
Eve  161, 218; *see also* Adam
evil
  acquiescence to  14, 17, 27
  as act  7, 10–12, 20, 46, 216
  and choice  27, 33, 44, 78, 90, 95, 163
  and desire  81, 146, 163
  experience of  12, 17–19, 68, 212
  and faith  114
  and nature  108, 118, 129, 131, 139
  origin of  13, 30–1, 49–51, 143–4, 217
  and original sin  38, 55–6, 82, 157
  radical  4, 17
  resistance to  5, 13, 17
  tragic dimensions of  17
  tree of the knowledge of  29, 148, 151
  and the will  64–5, 77, 155
  *see also* concupiscence; creation; han; theodicy
evolution  14, 17, 72, 143–4, 146, 153, 161–2

faith  x–xi, 11, 21, 27, 29, 33, 42, 49, 62, 75–6, 80–1, 83, 86, 114, 150, 156–7, 167, 180, 201, 204–7, 211, 216, 218; *see also* Adam; unbelief
fall  xii, 27–36, 40–6, 48, 50–1, 54–5, 58, 66, 71–5, 78, 80, 83–6, 88–9, 94–6, 107–8, 112, 115, 117–27, 133, 137, 143–8, 150–1, 154–6, 160, 164, 166, 168, 170, 183–4, 186, 191, 214–15; *see also* theodicy
Farley, Wendy  16–18, 27–8
federalism  150, 152–4, 156, 160, 164–5, 188, 191

feminism
    and hamartiology  188, 201, 215
    and sexual abuse  189
    and theology  198
forgiveness  10, 15–16, 21, 25–8, 61,
    70, 172–3, 178, 180–3, 185,
    189, 191, 194–5, 197–8, 201,
    205–6, 216; *see also* gospel; grace
Foucault, Michel  176
free will *see* will
freedom
    and autonomy  4, 11, 26
    and choice  xii, 5–6, 15, 27, 33,
        73–4, 78, 80, 94, 99, 103, 107,
        111
    and finitude  43
    of God  116, 147, 168, 202–3
    and grace  213
    and human nature  x, 21, 23, 28,
        31–2, 47–8, 62–3, 88, 92, 132,
        138
    of indifference  xii, 72
    and responsibility  15
    and self-transcendence  43–5, 57–8
    of the will  xi, 38, 55, 73, 75–6,
        85–6, 99, 106, 114, 137, 185–6
    *see also* original sin

Garlington, Don  24
Gestrich, Christoph  25
glory  25, 28, 33, 38, 80, 82, 84, 90,
    92, 100–7, 110, 113–14, 118,
    124, 126, 136–7, 146–7, 155–6,
    161–2, 166, 170, 187, 198, 208,
    212, 219
gnomic will *see* will
Gnosticism  30–1
God
    Creator  30–1, 50–1, 76, 92, 99,
        108, 138, 144, 146–7, 167
    image of  52, 114
    mercy of  10, 65, 131, 160, 168,
        197

object of human desire  66, 76,
    100, 115, 147, 183, 186, 191,
    196, 200
transcendence of  37
will of  xi, 7, 13, 35, 37, 64,
    66, 92–3, 95, 98, 100, 102,
    105, 108, 112, 119–20, 125–7,
    131, 174, 179, 182, 187, 194,
    199, 202–5, 207–11, 214,
    217–19
*see also* Trinity; will
gospel  4–5, 21, 26, 33, 42, 48, 62,
    65, 97, 110, 178–81, 183–4,
    186, 191, 193, 195, 212–14;
    *see also* forgiveness; grace; Social
    Gospel
grace
    "cheap"  27, 206
    and forgiveness  178
    gift  213
    and glorification  99, 103, 155–6,
        166
    and the Holy Spirit  115
    human dependence on  33, 47,
        62–3, 66, 68–9, 72–3, 86, 107,
        113, 118, 120, 130, 139, 187,
        194
    and Jesus Christ  100, 112, 126
    and justification  206
    and knowledge of God  36
    and nature  73, 76–8
    and original justice  54
    and original sin  33, 213
    particularity  114, 159–60, 207,
        214
    prelapsarian  73–4, 86
    and salvation  33–5
    and the will  65–6, 69, 75, 80–2,
        85, 100–2, 104, 106, 146–7,
        186, 201
    *see also* forgiveness; gospel; vocation
Gregory of Nazianzus  118
Gregory of Nyssa  120

guilt
  angelic  155
  collective  17, 167
  and complicity  18
  congenital  31–5, 81–2
  individual  13, 15, 26–8, 38, 42–3, 56–7, 68, 158, 168–9, 171, 173, 175, 181, 185, 191, 215
  inherited  45, 188
  and original sin  9, 21, 34–5, 40, 52, 57, 65–7, 130, 151, 184, 193–5
  see also Adam; federalism; realism

hamartiology  3, 11–12, 25, 47, 130, 132, 171, 173, 177, 196, 215
han  172–3, 175, 188
Harnack, Adolf von  91, 109
Hefner, Philip  162
Holy Spirit  49, 56, 73, 81, 83, 85, 114–15, 138–9, 162, 209, 211
Honorius I, Pope  91–2, 108–10, 133
human nature
  constitutive features  187
  damage to  31, 33–5, 37–8, 40–1, 44, 73, 123–5, 127–9, 131, 145, 148–9, 168, 183–4, 191
  deification  99–100, 138
  goodness of  144
  and grace  65
  and incarnation  129
  of Jesus Christ  xi, 96–8, 105, 112–13, 118–25, 127–31, 133–9, 162
  open-endedness  126–7
  and original justice  54
  and original sin  151, 163, 212
  and personality  205
  and the will  xi–xii, 64, 67, 69–70, 76, 94, 96–7, 101–4, 106, 108, 126–8, 130, 138–9, 144–5, 154, 159, 166, 183–4, 186, 196, 216
  see also Adam; hypostasis; total depravity; will
hypostasis
  of angels  155
  of Jesus Christ  93–4, 97, 111, 121, 125, 127–9, 138, 145, 162, 218
  and nature  93, 101, 106, 116, 119, 128–30, 145, 162, 183–4, 186–7, 192, 215
  and *reatus*  183
  and sin  127–30, 139, 194, 200, 203–6
  *tropos*  96, 105, 139
  and will  101, 112, 127–9, 139, 144–5, 186, 196
hypostatic union  129

incarnation  74, 94, 119–21, 129, 133, 145, 215
Irenaeus of Lyons  31, 51, 53, 89, 132, 140

Jenson, Robert  161
Jesus Christ
  fear of death  89, 98, 126
  in Gethsemane  92, 99, 101–2, 112–13
  and gnomic will  93, 96, 98–9, 112, 137
  as head  114, 152–3, 155, 165–6, 168
  humanity  97, 118–32
  and natural will  93–5, 98, 101
  obedience of  98–100, 126, 137, 164
  as revelation  210, 214
  as Savior  x, 4, 32, 35–6, 45–6, 48, 62, 66, 79, 119
  as second Adam  150

Second Person of the Trinity
  96, 121, 123, 125, 127–8, 145,
  162
 sinlessness of 96, 118, 120–3, 125,
  127–32, 138, 144–5
 and sinners 177–8
 table fellowship 180
 teaching 178–9, 198–9, 209
 testing of 118, 124
 two wills 93
 *see also* body; Christology; grace;
  hypostasis; monoenergism;
  monothelitis; Trinity
Jones, Serene 138, 189, 201, 217
Julian of Eclanum 69, 75–7, 80
Julian of Halicarnassus 136
Julian of Norwich 133
justification 30, 55, 164, 188, 205–7,
  218
Justin Martyr 30

Kant, Immanuel 4
kenosis *see* crypto-kenoticism
Kierkegaard, Søren 43–4, 154

"lapsarian questions" 32–3, 143
law
 of God 5, 7, 10, 24, 56, 67,
  69–70, 78, 83, 85, 177, 189,
  191, 198, 202–3, 208
 human 194, 218
 natural 63, 89, 100, 149
 of sin 9, 67, 69
 *see also* commandments; Sermon on
  the Mount
*Lawrence of Arabia* 75
Leontius of Byzantium 105
liberal theology 39, 167, 199–200
limbo 38, 55
Lossky, Vladimir 168
love 185–6, 213–14
 commandment 8, 174
 divine 10, 65, 73, 80, 85, 103,
  129–32, 157, 182, 185–7, 189,
  213–14
 human x, xii, 71–2, 74, 76, 80–1,
  84, 102–4, 106, 180, 185–6,
  189, 213–14, 219
 and reconciliation 168
Luther, Martin 189–90, 207, 215,
  217–18

Maresius, S. 134
Mary, Virgin 162–3
Mathewes, Charles 85–6, 219
Maximus the Confessor
 anthropology of 94, 102, 107,
  115, 131, 186
 and Augustine 88–90, 92, 100–1,
  105, 107–8, 117, 147
 and choice 94–7, 99–101, 103–4,
  107, 109, 111, 166
 Christology 89, 91–100, 105–6,
  117, 125–6, 133, 137–8, 158,
  162, 168
 and deification 92, 99, 100–6,
  110, 113, 115–16
 *Disputation with Pyrrhus* 97
 and the fall 88–9, 94–6, 107–8,
  112, 115, 117
 and monothelitism 90–4, 98, 102,
  108, 110, 112, 115, 117
 and original sin 88–9
 and the will 93–101, 103–4,
  111–15, 117, 137–9, 147,
  154
McFadyen, Alistair 23, 86, 175–6,
  189
Melanchthon, Philipp 198, 216
Menninger, Karl 25
mistrust *see* trust
monoenergism 91–2
monogenesis 143–4, 153
monothelitism 90–4, 98, 102,
  108–10, 112, 117, 133
Murray, John 192, 216

natural will *see* will
nature *see* human nature; hypostasis
New Testament   7, 10, 23, 30, 180
Newman, John Henry   216
Niebuhr, Reinhold   22, 24, 27, 43–5, 57–8, 144, 154

obedience   88, 98–100, 102, 106, 126, 137, 164, 206–7
Old Testament   6–7, 10, 50, 52, 61
Origen of Alexandria   49, 51
original justice   37, 54
original sin
  and anxiety   43, 57
  Augustinian doctrine of   xii, 38, 52, 117, 143–4, 170, 173, 175, 192, 199, 215
  congenital   x–xi, 3, 20, 32–5, 39–41, 45–7, 62, 66, 71, 88–9, 108, 117, 120, 130–1, 148–50, 182, 185–7, 196, 201, 204
  corporate   42
  defect   x, 38, 40, 148, 203–5, 209
  disposition   38, 41, 127, 157, 173
  distortion   37, 183, 200, 206
  development of doctrine   29–35
  Eastern Orthodox views   32, 34, 53, 88–9, 135
  existential inevitability   42–5
  and experience   19–20
  and faith   157
  and the gospel   33, 48, 193
  and guilt   33, 40, 130
  inheritance   xii, 53, 56, 61, 87, 121, 143, 148–50, 160, 173, 191
  as lack   36–9
  mediate imputation   191–2
  moral critique of   170–1, 179
  natural   130, 151, 207
  ontological   xii, 32, 40, 42, 48, 130–1, 171, 183–4, 193, 195–6, 201

  origin of   148–53
  originating   41, 52
  political critique of   194–5
  *reatus*   170–1, 183, 191, 215
  scientific critique of   143–4, 153
  social context   39–42
  solidarity in   35, 154, 213
  transmission of   10, 14, 31, 34, 58, 87, 130–1, 148–50, 154, 173, 191
  *vitium*   170–1, 183–4, 191
  *see also* actual sin; blame; concupiscence; damnation; evil; fall; federalism; guilt; han; human nature; pride; realism; sin; solidarity; unbelief

Park, Andrew Sung   172–7, 180, 188–90
Pascal, Blaise   21, 28
patriarchy   198
Paul, St.
  and Adam   30–1, 151–3, 164–5
  and body of Christ   219
  and Christ   82, 120, 122, 152–3, 165
  eschatology   136–7
  and the law   7, 83, 189
  and sin   7, 9–11, 24, 47, 49, 67–70, 72, 86, 146, 160–1, 163, 174, 177, 198, 204
  and the "strong"   179
  and vocation   218
Pelagius   56, 61, 80, 85–6, 114, 120, 217
Peter Lombard   137
Pitstick, Alyssa Lyra   136
Placaeus, Josua   191–2
Plantinga, Cornelius, Jr.   12, 14–15, 25–6, 28
Polanus, A.   134
practical syllogism   206
pride   195, 200–2, 217–18

process metaphysics   26–7
protocols of discernment   210–11

quietism   194, 197

Rahner, Karl   56, 154, 161
Ray, Stephen G., Jr.   12, 25, 199, 216
realism   150–4, 156, 160, 164–5
repentance   16, 136, 156, 158, 167, 178, 180–1, 185, 189, 197, 216
resurrection   84, 126, 128, 136, 161
Rieger, Joerg   199, 216
righteousness, original *see* original justice
Rogers, Eugene F., Jr.   219

saints   70, 86, 100, 103, 113–15, 136, 210, 218–19
Saiving, Valerie   215
salvation
  economy of   33, 35, 38, 42, 46, 56, 62–3, 92, 123, 135, 156–7, 160, 167–8, 177, 205, 209
  human need of   24, 32, 35–6, 39–40, 42, 48, 63, 138, 156
salvation history   136–7
sanctification   205–7
Schleiermacher, Friedrich   39–42, 154
Sermon on the Mount   177, 193, 202, 208, 217; *see also* law
sexual abuse   175, 181, 188–90, 192
Shedd, William   52, 109, 150–2, 163–5
Simons, Menno   134
sin
  acknowledgement of   199
  as act   9–10, 35, 66
  and agency   9
  and angels   154–6
  and bodies   155–6
  bondage   27, 35, 58, 208
  as choice   15, 17–18, 20
  as deviation   119
  as external power   8–9, 11
  and finitude   17, 43, 47
  and hypostasis   127–30, 139
  involuntary   76, 86
  knowledge of   21, 36, 39–40, 157–8
  lawlessness   7
  "participation model"   14–16, 19, 36
  rebellion   6, 14, 16, 31, 217
  "responsibility model"   12–14, 19, 36
  and the sinned against   130, 177–80, 182, 188, 193, 195, 198
  social   16, 25, 36, 39–42, 190, 194, 196, 216
  "tragic model"   16–19, 36
  unintentional   6–8, 11, 23, 165
  universality of   9–11, 17, 22, 34–6, 78, 131, 144, 148, 153, 156, 159, 170, 172, 177, 183, 187, 192, 200
  *see also* actual sin; blame; concupiscence; creation; evil; forgiveness; guilt; original sin; Paul; repentance; violence
Social Gospel   56
solidarity
  of Christ with human beings   93, 118–19, 122, 131
  of human beings before God   158, 213–14
  of human beings in sin   4, 35–6, 153–4, 159, 173
  of Israel   167
Spirit *see* Holy Spirit
Suchocki, Marjorie Hewitt   14–17, 26–8, 188
suffering   xii, 17–18, 27–8, 32–3, 46–8, 53, 58, 88, 99, 122, 124, 126, 134, 136–7, 167, 172–3, 179, 192, 209–11, 214

Tatian 30
temptation 42–3, 115, 124, 162, 179
Tennant, F. R. 49
Tertullian 31, 49, 51, 66, 81
theodicy 30–2, 34, 38–9, 45–6, 48, 53, 144, 151
Theophilus of Antioch 30–1, 50–1
total depravity x, 44–5, 56
Trinity x, 19, 90; *see also* God; Jesus Christ
*tropos* 96, 99–101, 103, 105, 112–14, 137, 139, 187, 194
trust 179–82, 102, 195, 201–2, 204
Turretin, Francis 152, 164–5

unbelief 80, 180, 200–5, 217

victims 15, 18, 21, 171–3, 175–6, 181, 188, 192, 211; *see also* sin
violence 13–16, 26–7, 172, 175, 188, 194
virtue 17, 53, 103, 135, 204
vocation 157–8, 205–11, 218
Volf, Miroslav 189

Walaeus, Antonius 56
Weil, Simone 18, 28
Weinandy, Thomas 133–4
Wetzel, James 79–80, 83, 86, 101, 114
will
  and Augustine 62–5, 67–87, 89–90, 107, 109, 117, 131, 146–7, 174, 186, 215
  bondage of 35–6, 76, 147–8, 170, 175–6, 187
  and choice 76, 78, 89–90, 107, 113–14
  and control 7, 63, 65, 67, 71–3, 75–6, 78, 83–5, 107, 126, 146–7, 165, 174, 185
  damaged 144–8, 158
  divided 69, 75, 162
  fallen 127–30, 145, 147, 186, 189–90
  gnomic 93, 95–101, 103–4, 111–15, 137
  as locus of personal agency 145
  as mode of personal agency 63–4, 102
  moved by God 65, 73, 81, 100, 106–7
  natural 93–6, 98, 101, 103, 111, 114–15
  ontological oddity of xii, 126, 128, 144–5, 154, 159–60
  Pelagian views 63, 65, 67, 70, 72–6, 78, 85–7, 107, 109, 126, 147, 149–50, 166, 183, 186, 215–16
  prelapsarian 72–4, 77–8, 84, 89–90, 107, 125
  and self–determination xi–xii, 63, 79–80, 102, 105, 109, 112
  *see also* deification; desire; evil; freedom; grace; human nature; original sin; sin
Williams, N. P. 30, 49–53